Advance Praise for *Humani*

The global co-operative movement could provide a genuine alternative to the ravages of predatory finance capitalism — if only it started acting like a movement! This book makes the case, connecting the dots among far-flung sites of co-operation and resistance, tracing the outlines of a humane alternative to the deadly business of business as usual.

— Avi Lewis, filmmaker, *The Take*

The historical and contemporary yearning and struggle to incarnate economic democracy is theoretically and practically depicted in this lucid work. The author engages the reader in concrete experiences from across the globe, and one cannot help but come away more informed and inspired by the diverse challenges that people have overcome by organizing their economic affairs through co-operatives. Researchers, activists, practitioners, policy makers and students across a wide range of disciplines, especially economics and business, need the tonic and the analysis present in this welcome volume. Democracy is being advanced in exciting ways and we need to get on with the job of scaling up its role where we live and work across the globe.

— Michael Lewis, Executive Director,
Canadian Centre for Community Renewal
Lead Investigator, British Columbia-Alberta
Social Economy Research Alliance

The culmination of fifteen years of research, both at the theoretical and the empirical level, this book brilliantly speaks in favour of co-operatives, today a much-neglected economic institution. Moving from the consideration that market institutions induce desirable *and* undesirable social traits in people, the author defends the thesis that society can no longer exonerate itself from the duty of considering the effects of different economic systems on human character. Whence the title of the book. *Humanizing the Economy* discusses in a critical way both the possibilities and the challenges that the movement for economic democracy is facing in the age of globalization and the third industrial revolution. Restakis's well written, jargon-free book should be read by anyone seriously interested in the future of our market systems.

— Stefano Zamagni, Prof. of Economics,
University of Bologna and Johns Hopkins University,
Bologna Center for Civil Economy

In the hyper-charged conflict between the global economy and global justice, John Restakis makes the case that ordinary people can take direct economic action to meet their own needs. He mixes history, ideas, and present-day struggles in an account that is personal, passionate, and informed.

— Brett Fairbairn, Provost,
Professor of History,
University of Saskatchewan

Humanizing
the Economy

CO-OPERATIVES
in the AGE *of* CAPITAL

John Restakis

NEW SOCIETY PUBLISHERS

Cover design by Diane McIntosh.
© iStock Dar Yang Yan (globe) / Gary Godby (text frame)
Jesus Conde (hands) / Peter Zelei (background)

Printed in Canada. First printing September 2010.

New Society Publishers acknowledges the support of the Government of Canada
through the Book Publishing Industry Development Program (BPIDP)
for our publishing activities.

Paperback ISBN: 978-0-86571-651-3
eISBN: 978-1-55092-461-9

Inquiries regarding requests to reprint all or part of *Humanizing the Economy*
should be addressed to New Society Publishers at the address below.

To order directly from the publishers, please call toll-free
(North America) 1-800-567-6772, or order online at www.newsociety.com

Any other inquiries can be directed by mail to:
New Society Publishers
P.O. Box 189, Gabriola Island, BC V0R 1X0, Canada
(250) 247-9737

New Society Publishers' mission is to publish books that contribute in fundamental ways to building an
ecologically sustainable and just society, and to do so with the least possible impact on the environment,
in a manner that models this vision. We are committed to doing this not just through education, but
through action. Our printed, bound books are printed on Forest Stewardship Council-certified acid-
free paper that is **100% post-consumer recycled** (100% old growth forest-free), processed chlorine
free, and printed with vegetable-based, low-VOC inks, with covers produced using FSC-certified
stock. New Society also works to reduce its carbon footprint, and purchases carbon offsets based on an
annual audit to ensure a carbon neutral footprint. For further information, or to browse our full list of
books and purchase securely, visit our website at: www.newsociety.com

Library and Archives Canada Cataloguing in Publication

Restakis, John
        Humanizing the economy : co-operatives in the age of capital / John Restakis.

Includes index.
ISBN 978-0-86571-651-3

        1. Cooperative societies. I. Title.

HD2963.R47 2010   334   C2010-905267-6

NEW SOCIETY PUBLISHERS
www.newsociety.com

Mixed Sources
Cert no. SW-COC-001271
© 1996 FSC
FSC

Contents

Acknowledgments

Inevitably, a book like this comes about because of the contributions, intended and unintended, of a score of people beyond the author. This book is a project that has been over a decade in gestation. Over this time, countless individuals have left their mark on my passage through a period of professional work that marks the culmination of a lifetime in activism and advocacy. It is impossible to name them all, but there are a number without whom this book would not have been possible.

My long time collaborator and friend, Bob Williams, shared with me a passion for the exquisite delights of Bologna and the inexhaustible lessons of that unique region which we both endeavored to bring to the frontlines of the work for economic reform that we were both engaged in, in our own ways, in British Columbia. Bob was, with me, the co-founder of the Bologna Summer Program for Co-operative Studies at the University of Bologna, where much of the material for this book was first explored. Vancity, the queen of credit unions in Canada, provided shelter and sustenance for this work.

Among my formative influences very early after my entry into the co-op movement was Robin Murray. He is that rare breed of economist who has immersed himself in the struggles and aspirations of everyday people and although he doesn't know it, it was he who guided my steps to the co-operative economy of Emilia Romagna. He was the first to read the manuscript of this work, and I am grateful for his comments. I am also grateful for the guidance and insight provided me by Brett Fairbairn at the University of Saskatchewan. Brett is among Canada's most eminent co-op historians and his comments on the early rise of the co-op movement in England were of immense value to me. My close friends Rick Wilks and Karen Kuzmochka read the manuscript, pronounced it persuasive but a bit dense, and advised me to write another book.

This book would not have been possible without the financial support of a number of organizations. I am thankful for the research funds made available to me by the BC/Alberta Social Economy Research Alliance (BALTA) and the faith put in this project by Mike Lewis and the infinite patience shown by Stuart Wulff, the indomitable guardian of BALTA's countless research strands. I have also been supported in this work by Dr. Ian MacPherson and the BC Institute for Co-operative Studies which he founded at the University of Victoria, and by its new formation as the Centre for Co-operative and Community-Based Economy under the leadership of Ana Maria Peredo. My greatest debt of gratitude is due to Stefano Zamagni of the University of Bologna, and to his equally gifted wife and colleague at the University of Bologna, Vera Negri Zamagni. Between these two gifted teachers and thinkers, I have found the means to frame my understanding of co-operative economic theory and practice and to place it in the workings of real places and institutions. And to Stefano in particular, words hardly convey my appreciation for his generosity of intellect, his capacity for sheer, selfless giving and his granting me, and countless others engaged in social change work, a vocabulary for describing what we do and why we do it. He is my mentor and he, too, doesn't know it. I wish also to express my thanks to the people who have made possible the work I do, day in and day out, at the BC Co-operative Association — my Board of Directors. Throughout the years, I have never felt from them a moment's hesitation or lack of faith in the countless schemes I have come up with to further the co-op idea in British Columbia. They made it all possible and without their support, I would never have been able to take the year-long sabbatical during which this book was researched and written.

Finally, I must pay tribute to those anonymous individuals who took the time to speak to me, to share their stories and give substance to the ideas I have tried to express in this work. Nothing would have been possible without them. Their quiet and courageous labor, their perseverance in the face of insuperable odds, remain a constant and humbling inspiration. Theirs is the work that keeps the flame of co-operation burning bright. This book is dedicated to them, and most of all to those fierce spirits in the brothels of Sonagachi who took a total stranger into their trust.

Introduction

As dawn broke on the morning of November 30, 1999, several hundred people appeared in the quiet streets near the Seattle Convention Center and began to take control of key intersections. Soon, marchers converging on the area from across the city joined them. With protesters locking up the intersections and swelling numbers of marchers blocking access to the convention center, downtown Seattle became a mass of chanting, surging humanity. Police were soon overwhelmed and the numbers of protesters soared. By noon, the size of the protest had exceeded 50,000 people and coverage of the event was spanning the globe.

Earlier in the week, while delegates were still arriving in Seattle for the World Trade Organization (WTO) Ministerial Conference, tensions between developing nations and the wealthy economies of the United States and Europe were already reaching a boiling point. Previous rounds of talks in Melbourne in 1997 and with the WTO's predecessor organization, the General Agreement on Trade and Tariffs (GATT), had yielded little progress on a host of issues. Poor countries were buckling under the burdens of high foreign debts, protectionist trade barriers and the movement of capital that was capable of making or breaking national economies. The atmosphere was further aggravated by fears that the United States was prepared to discard previous international agreements on jobs and cultural and social issues to advance the narrow interests of big business. Frustration and an electric sense of unease were in the air. The street protests that commenced on that grey winter morning lit a fuse to a powder keg.

For the next three days, protesters fought a pitched battle with police as WTO organizers and delegates struggled to resume talks while the sounds of fighting, breaking glass and sirens could be heard on the streets below. In the end, over 600 people were arrested. But for the first time, an international meeting of the WTO was prevented from concluding its business and the organization was indelibly tainted with the perception that it was elitist, undemocratic and isolated from the plight of the world's poor. With round-the-clock media coverage, the term "anti-globalization" finally broke through to the American mainstream.

The heart of the struggle in Seattle and in subsequent meetings of international organizations like the World Bank and the International Monetary Fund (IMF) has been the place of democracy within economies. In Quebec City, in Genoa, and in cities the world over global justice became the rallying cry for festering anger and frustration at the growing inequities and injustices that seem to come hand in hand with the advancement of a new global economic order. In June 2010, at the meetings of the G20 and G8 in Toronto and Huntsville, the security measures surpassed $1 billion in costs and turned Toronto's core into an armed camp. Still, over 1,000 people were arrested as the protests widened their focus to encompass not only global institutions like the IMF, but the legitimacy of the governments of the leading industrial nations. The WTO meeting in Seattle took place at the high tide mark of a new, hypercharged form of free market[1] economics that established the template and pace of global economic development. In fact, the rising crescendo of protests that commenced in Seattle are only the most recent outcries against a model of economic and social organization that has drawn determined opposition and resistance for the last two hundred years.

The tangible effects of this global economic order, the marks it scribes on the lives and livelihoods of billions of people the world over, are felt not in the realm of ideology, trade policy or politics. The effects are visible in the wages people earn if they are lucky enough to have a job, in the prices they get for their coffee beans, in the cleanliness of their drinking water, in the quality of their shelter and whether or not their children will go to school. These are the battles for survival and the prospect of life with dignity that billions of people the world over have to wage day in and day out. Today, with a global economic crisis destroying the livelihoods and pulling the foundations from under millions in developed and poor economies alike, the pitfalls of the new economic order are plain for all to see.

This book is about an alternative. It is a story about how a revolution in human society that began with the rise of democracy in politics continues to unfold as the democratic idea struggles to find its place in the world of economics. If economic democracy is the hidden face of this ongoing revolution, then the history of the co-operative idea is its most durable expression.

Today, the global co-operative movement appears to have arrived at a crossroads. With the collapse of communism, and with the capitalist system in crisis and facing unceasing demands for reform, the case for the expansion of economic democracy has never been more relevant or more urgent. More importantly, there is a need for a middle path that avoids the extremes of market rejection on the one hand (as in the case of Marxism) and the unbridled power of capital as expressed in neoliberalism on the other.

To what extent an alternative will prove possible will depend on many factors, not the least of which is the willingness of co-operative leaders, thinkers and practitioners to take up the challenge at an unprecedented level of action both locally and globally. A key purpose of this book is to show that, in fact, the popular drive to democratize economies is a force that is working to transform virtually every economy in the world today. And for those who are willing to look, the evidence of a new, more humane economic and social order is there to see.

With over 800 million members in 85 countries the co-operative movement is by far the most durable and most powerful grassroots movement in the world. Co-operatives employ more people in democratically run enterprises than all the word's multinational companies combined. Although the forms co-ops take and the uses to which they are put display an astounding variety their essential structure remains what it was when they were first organized in the mid-1800s — enterprises that are collectively owned and democratically controlled by their members for their mutual benefit. As the global economic crisis continues to take its toll, co-operatives continue to provide livelihoods and essential services in the very places where established multinationals are shedding workers and shuttering plants. In its own quiet way, the co-operative vision continues to thrive and hold the keys to the emergence of an economic model that is capable of remaking and humanizing the current capitalist system.

Whether or not modern capitalism will make room for the emergence of democratic economies and truly open markets may well become the defining question of our age. For despite the banner headlines that compel our attention to the atrocities of terrorism and the violence of intolerance in all its shades, this is marginal to the lived experience of the vast majority of humanity the world over. What truly conditions how people live and what societies will become is the degree to which people can exercise control over their lives. Economics is central to this. This is the question that lies at the bottom of the resentment and rage that continues to fuel the resistance to globalization generally and the corporate model of free market capitalism specifically. This is true in rich and poor countries alike and the recent global economic crisis has brought this truth home with a vengeance.

What is far less clear is how those who seek change can respond constructively and concretely to this challenge, moving beyond protest to a vision of what else is possible and how to build alternatives. Convincing answers to this question have not been abundant. For many, the search for clear alternatives has been disappointing if not downright demoralizing. The collapse of socialism as a viable challenge to the capitalist idea has indeed left a vacuum where, at one time at least, there resided some hope of a more humane alternative. Most of those protesters on the streets of Seattle would be hard pressed to propose something that could truly replace the system they were protesting. But the policy makers and politicians who understand that something has to change are also in a bind. Beyond salvaging the status quo, very little has been proposed as a way of rethinking the philosophical, social and organizational foundations that underpin the capitalist systems that are now in such peril.

My purpose in writing this book is to help bring to light both the possibilities and the problems that the movement for economic democracy is contending with today. It is a movement that has a long and rich history — one that is little known yet whose effects are felt by millions the world over. It is a history whose seeds were sown in the great resistance that arose with the onset of capitalism at the dawn of the industrial age, and whose essential dynamics continue today both in the industrial democracies and in the societies where the rise of capitalism is still in its formative stages. And while it is certain that the co-operative idea will endure, it is far less clear whether the co-operative movement internationally will be able to meet the global demands of a world that daily grows smaller while the gulf that separates rich and poor, the powerful and the powerless, grows ever greater.

The story that follows encompasses three objectives. The first is to set out some of the historical and theoretical questions that surround the subject of economic democracy. These are summarized in the opening two chapters. I believe that a sense of history and theory must ground the search for alternatives, and I hope this book can help in this respect. Readers will notice that I have focused primarily on Europe to discuss the intellectual currents that nurtured the growth of the co-operative movement. I wish to stress that the figures I treat represent a particular interplay of ideas that were germane to the rise of the industrial age in England where, after all, the modern co-op form took shape. I do not wish to imply that the emergence of co-operatives in other countries depended on these ideas or a knowledge of these thinkers. People in all countries have been creating co-operatives, and advancing the cause of economic democracy, quite independently. The co-op model has deep roots, in an astounding variety of forms, in virtually every country and culture. Likewise, while I have concentrated primarily on the rise of European socialism I am also aware of other influences that played a formative role, particularly the movements for religious reform that were among the very first catalysts for the spread of democratizing ideas and practices on a mass level among the working classes.[2] In England these ideas were associated primarily with the Dissent movement that included groups like the Unitarians, the Baptists, the Quakers and countless other smaller sects that arose to challenge the authoritarian character of the established church and the class privilege to which it was allied. In Germany, the radical early roots of Protestantism found expression in the anti-authoritarian teachings of Moravianism, which found followers also in England. In these movements the yearning for liberty of conscience was mingled with the drive for political liberty. Both were shaped by a deep popular impulse to make the principles of democracy manifest both in the world of the spirit and in society. If Christ's poor came to believe that their souls were as good as aristocratic or bourgeois souls, then it was but a short step for them to embrace the revolutionary sentiments of Thomas Paine's *Rights of Man*. These ideas acted like a social leaven that shaped political consciousness by advancing notions of personal worth, egalitarianism, working class identity and the redemptive power of community. The co-op movement owes much to this tradition.[3]

My second objective is to flesh out how the ideas and aspirations introduced in the opening chapters have been realized in the stories of people and communities that have struggled to make a more humane economics respond to the needs of their time and their place. These stories of people and places dramatize in a very real manner fundamental questions of economic organization, human relations and social values that help to illuminate the meaning and message of the co-operative idea in our times. What I hope emerges is a glimpse of what is possible for the future if the principles and promise of co-operation are made real in the world as it is, not only in the world as we would like it to be. This is the third objective of the book.

What the future may hold is anybody's guess, especially in times as turbulent and unpredictable as our own. But how the co-operative idea relates to some of the economic and social issues that are already unfolding around us is the focus of the closing chapters.

Overall, my aim is to make this book useful to practitioners working in the fields of co-operative and community development, activists and laypersons alike. It appears to me that, in North America at least, the popular movements for economic and social reform, have been gravely weakened by a lack of contact with economics — as if anything might be gained by turning our backs on that discipline, flawed though it is, and reverting instead to arguments based solely on an appeal to values. There appears to be little serious consideration given to the practical basis on which these values might be realized. Even worse is abandoning the theoretical and intellectual contest and adopting instead a smug stance of moral superiority to those who view things in a different light. These are serious flaws and in themselves symptoms of the problem we most need to address — ceding economics to the class of vested interests that currently governs both its teaching and its practice. Rather, the underlying premise of this book is that economics is *everybody's* business.

Finally, I make no pretense to being impartial in what follows. Where I stand and how I feel about the issues I raise will be unapologetically obvious. But I try to be fair about the facts and the case I make will stand or fall on the evidence I present. The reader will decide how far I have succeeded.

We will cover a broad canvas. From the worker co-operatives of Emilia Romagna to the recovered factories of Buenos Aires, from small tea farmers struggling to make a living in Sri Lanka to the consumer co-ops of Japan, and from the lonely nursing home rooms of small-town British Columbia to the brothels of Calcutta, the co-op idea is an enduring vision that is being rediscovered and reinvented every day and in a thousand ways by people from all walks of life the world over. In times when the course of world events seems to leave little reason for hope, these stories are worth telling for they lend a hopeful light on human affairs and hint at a future worth striving for.

 CHAPTER 1

The Grand Delusion

I admit to a flaw in my ideology.
I could not have believed that the self-interest of banks
would not prompt them to better protect their stockholders.

— ALAN GREENSPAN —

On October 3, 2008, the United States Congress passed an $800 billion bailout package to stem a financial meltdown on Wall Street that threatened the collapse not only of the US financial system, but financial markets the world over. Only with the most extreme reluctance did the administration of George W. Bush accept the necessity of pumping over $250 billion into the purchase of equity stock in nine major American banks. In this, the US followed the leads of Britain and the European Union that had adopted similar strategies to protect the solvency of their financial institutions.

This was the largest market intervention by government in US history and it was only the beginning. It framed what appeared as the ignominious final act in the current reign of free market ideology in the United States.

It was a deep and bitter irony that in the closing days of the Bush era, the free market ethos that was epitomized in this administration should have failed so spectacularly. For it was a failure and an exposure not only of the particular follies of deregulation and *laissez faire* that had led to the crisis, but more profoundly, of the political and economic policies that had dominated the western world for a generation. It was not the validation of free markets that George W. Bush or his admirers would have hoped for.

And yet, with news reports in the United States and abroad providing blanket coverage of the crisis, the focus was almost exclusively on the financial collapse, the imminence of global recession and on the prospects for rescue by governments. Very few questioned the underlying assumptions of the free market system itself. Everyone, regardless of their place on the political spectrum, was quick to affirm their support for the free market.[1] Certainly this was true in Canada, where the world's least noticed federal election was underway. And predictably, just when Americans had awakened to the folly of free market policies in their own country, Canadians handed a second term to the party most committed to applying these same policies in Canada.[2]

The greatest resistance to the bailout plan finally passed by Congress was from Republicans who opposed any government intervention in the market as a "slippery slope to socialism." In their minds, and in the minds of many who felt compelled to support the measures, the only options were a choice between an imperiled free market system on the one hand, and "socialism" on the other. Thus, in the very act of announcing the partial nationalization of America's largest banks, President Bush felt compelled to assert that this was only a temporary measure. The government, he said, had no intention of taking over the free market. "These measures" he reassured Americans, "are not intended to take over the free market, but to preserve it." American taxpayers, it seemed, were to bear the cost of the bank bailout, but must not expect to profit from it. Once the banks returned to profitability, control would revert to them. The taxpayers also ended up covering losses for American International Group (AIG), the world's largest insurer.[3] The rationale was embedded in a follow up announcement by US Treasury Secretary Henry Paulsen who stated, "The government owning a stake in any private enterprise is objectionable to most Americans, myself included."[4] The strain on Paulsen's face as he had to make this announcement showed how much the decision had cost him. Henry Paulsen, free market warrior, former CEO of Goldman Sachs, had stared into the abyss and concluded that his beloved free market was teetering on the verge of collapse.

Three weeks later, as the extent of the cataclysm became clear with the plunge of stock markets the world over, Allan Greenspan appeared before the House Financial Services Committee to concede that, indeed, he had perceived a flaw in his ideology. He could not have believed, he said, that the self-interest of American banks would not prompt them to better protect their stockholders. It was a rare admission of error that put into question his entire approach to the management of the American economy as a test lab for free market ideology.

Over the course of this entire period no one pointed out that the choice between a hypothetical free market on the one hand and a demonic socialism on the other was always a false choice. Or that the failure to understand that free markets were not incompatible with a governmental role in the marketplace was the very mistake that had led to the crisis in the first place. It was the unceasing pressure to deregulate financial markets and repeal the safeguards designed to prevent a recurrence of the stock market crash of 1929[5] that led to the unrestricted speculation on unsecured, high risk loans that pulled the floor from under the American financial system. Even now, with the free market model in crisis, and with governments being called upon to intervene in ways not seen since the days of the Great Depression, the question that was uppermost in the minds of policy makers and politicians was how to save this free market system, not how to change it. Of course, it would have been sheer starry-eyed delirium to expect that politicians or the media should notice that among the *only* institutions to weather the storm were the co-operatives and credit unions that functioned on an entirely different economic model. Worldwide, almost none had to ask for government bailouts.[6]

In fact, the operation of a hypothetical free market has never really been the issue. Markets have never been "free" in the normal sense of the term, nor will they ever be. They have always been, and will always remain, subject to external constraints — legal, political, cultural, religious. The question is to what degree and for what ends these controls operate. Purely free markets exist only in the ethereal regions of *laissez faire* economic theory, along with such treasured notions as perfect competition, freedom of choice and the "invisible hand" that guides the market to produce the optimum outcome for all through the unrestricted pursuit of self interest.

To be fair, the *laissez faire* doctrine of free markets has been all but abandoned by most respected economists. But this has come late and only after a monumental accumulation of evidence and the sustained criticism of decades. No one, it seems, has informed the politicians and the policy makers. Throughout the crisis, pundits and political leaders continued to argue that these were extraordinary times calling for radical government measures. Under normal conditions, the free market functions best when left alone. But this has never been true. The free market system, such as it is, has been able to survive only *because* the state has been there to support it — and to salvage it. It happened during the depression of 1873–86, during the Great Depression of the 1930s, and the same pattern of state rescue in times of crisis continues today. The role of the state in sustaining the free market is constant and pervasive and has been so for well over a century.[7]

The regulation of financial markets, the regulation of banking and the insurance of deposits, the enactment and enforcement of commercial and corporate legislation, the maintenance of monetary policy, the management of labor policy, the negotiation and regulation of trade, the creation and administration of tax policy — all these are indispensable institutional supports for the operation of a market system in times of "normalcy." The collapse of any one of them would entail a crisis for the system, as it did with the unraveling of bank oversight that sparked the current crisis. All this is plain. And so, one might ask, what exactly lay beneath this continuing insistence on the sanctity of the free market system? Was it the residual force of an ingrained ideology? Was it blithe ignorance? Or was it a cynical ploy to protect the privileges of powerful vested interests? Probably, it was all three. In any event, with shameless jaw-dropping audacity, Bush continued to bang the free market drum in the closing days of his presidency, appearing all the while before international summits convened to clean up the colossal wreckage that resulted from his policies.[8]

The closing decades of this most delirious of economic times saw perhaps the most ambitious application of that grandest of all economic delusions, the self-regulating market. This cornerstone of classical economics is rooted in the belief that economics exists in a sphere of its own, that its laws are complete and sufficient to themselves, and that the broader social and human relations that constitute the day-to-day reality of our lives are not only apart from it but should be subject to its dictates. In substance, the collapse of the US financial markets and the wreckage of the global economic order that followed their fall was the price to be paid by enacting in the real world the insane dictates of this delusion.

Indeed, the grand delusion goes even further. Not only does it hold that the free market operates in a perfect order of its own but that the market itself is the *source* of free and democratic societies. When left to operate without interference, the market functions as a perfect democracy with free choice in the marketplace representing the summit of human achievement.[9] The supposed triumph of this idea over all competing worldviews in the late 20th century inspired one writer to claim seriously that human history had come to an end.[10] The unfolding of the human story as a continuous striving toward human freedom had now been fulfilled in the neoliberal order of the United States, Western Europe and the growing fraternity of free market countries. All that remained was for the perfected model of free market capitalism as realized in the US to be implemented in the backwaters of the world through the inexorable march of globalization.

Today, with global economic recession working its way like a virus through national economies it seems hardly credible that such a view might have been taken seriously. But in truth, it was only those already spellbound by the free market myth that were seduced. For just like the free market they believed in, the prophets and pundits of this Brave New World seemed to inhabit a world of their own devising—a world apart.

No amount of evidence to the contrary could shake their faith. One could point to the growing disparities of wealth at home and abroad. One could cite the declining conditions of work, health, education and social welfare that plagued the very countries that followed the neoliberal prescription. The obscene concentrations of power and money that were the predictable result of privatizing public assets in already impoverished nations were plain to see. None of this mattered. Always, it was dismissed as the harsh medicine that preceded the remaking of economies in the free market mould. As in all ideologies, the effects on actual people were secondary. What mattered was the advancement of the free market model. And if some became very, very wealthy in the process while others searched through heaps of rubbish for food, this was further evidence of the bounty for all that lay ahead.

The dogged allegiance of the free market faithful bore all the marks of a religious fervor—blind faith, supreme self-confidence, imperviousness to evidence, hostility to opposing views. Economics has, at the opening of the millennium, acquired the traits of a secular religion—a religion perfectly suited to a material age.

Of course, there is a long back story to this tale. The rise of the free market myth that has so enthralled politicians, policy makers, academics and a great swathe of the public in Western democracies owes its origins to the early 18th century and the onset of the Industrial Revolution. Here there arose a school of economic thought deeply influenced by the mechanistic model of the universe embodied in Newtonian physics and utilitarianism — a philosophy in which the individual came to be regarded not as an integral part of a social whole, but as an isolated social atom struggling with impersonal and unchanging market forces.[11] Utilitarianism, and the repressive doctrine of submission and work that defined Methodism, worked together to forge the reigning ideology of the Industrial Revolution.

Homo Economicus

In the view of Jeremy Bentham, the founder of this philosophy, the human individual is an egotistical, selfish, competitive being whose sole criterion for action is the maximization of pleasure or the avoidance of pain. All human motives are traceable to this impulse and its expression in the marketplace is the definition of rational choice. This is what economists mean when they speak of "maximizing one's utility." Indeed, all true social interaction takes place *only* in the marketplace. In this view of utilitarianism, social life considered as a collectivity, embodied in community, social classes, mutual aid societies, trade unions or the myriad other forms of social association are simply discounted. It was as if Jeremy Bentham had first asked himself, "What type of human personality and human society is most conducive to the psychological and material needs of industrial capitalism?" and then proceeded to ascribe to the *homo economicus* of classical economics precisely those attributes.

The other influence that helped shaped the philosophic temper of the emerging economics was the English philosopher Thomas Hobbes's deeply pessimistic view of human nature as essentially bestial, an aggressive, self-aggrandizing impulse that reduced the human community to "a war of each against all."[12]

Bentham at least meant well. He believed his philosophy would result in the greatest happiness for the greatest number. And this sounds very good. But in practice this means that actions are judged solely from the standpoint of their effects. The problem is that it is impossible to know what the effects of certain actions might be. What seems good in the present may turn out to be catastrophic in the long run. The practice of utilitarianism also allows the ends to justify the means. It instrumentalizes human beings. The untold suffering that was visited on people during the Industrial Revolution was justified in exactly the same manner as free market ideology — indeed all ideology, whether we speak of Communism on the left or Fascism on the right — justifies the pain that is inflicted today for the sake of progress in the future, however that may be defined. Consider only the inhuman sacrifices exacted in the name of "the socialist revolution."

In his time Bentham was a tireless advocate for political and social reform, a voice for universal education and women's rights, an opponent of the death penalty and a supporter of early socialist experiments including the co-operative communities of Robert Owen. Bentham passed on to posterity not only a hugely influential moral philosophy, but also on a more material plane his own preserved body which may still be viewed perched inside a case of his own design at University College of London.[13]

That such a one-sided and impoverished conception of human nature should find such ready acceptance among economic theorists is itself cause for reflection. But its ultimate triumph as the cornerstone of conventional economic theory has provided intellectual cover to a revolutionary process of social engineering that succeeded in fundamentally changing both our notion of what it means to be human and the ways in which human life is lived.

Acceptance of such a view outside the lecture hall and the boardroom has not been smooth, however. Its catastrophic effects on society, on the security and sustenance of the individual and the community, were bitterly contested from the start.[14] In the 19th century, there was a lively interest in co-operative theories of economics that blended social with economic values.[15] William Thompson, perhaps the foremost intellectual figure of early socialism, formulated a political economy of co-operative socialism that provided a scathing critique of the capitalism of his day and a very different view of utilitarianism from that taught by Bentham. We shall have occasion to examine Thompson's seminal influence in more detail in the following chapter. But the victory of economic man as viewed by Bentham and Hobbes was hard won by its advocates through a blend of brute force and a constant, unrelenting assault both on the public mind and on more humane ideas of economics that vied with this view. During the late 1700s and throughout the 1800s a stifling repression of both political and economic freedoms was the government's primary means of enforcing the privileges of *laissez faire* for the propertied class. The Combinations Act of 1799–1800 made it a capital offence for workers to organize, trade unionism and the movement for political reform were driven underground, and in the early 1800s the overwhelming majority of executions in the United Kingdom were for crimes against property. Naturally enough, it was those who had most to gain from such a view that did their most to propagate it. Thompson himself made this same point in his own day.

In the United States, the current epicenter of free market ideology, the transition from a deeply conservative, frugal, agrarian Protestantism in which community life and the values of thrift and mutual help had deep roots, to a culture of compulsive individualistic consumption was slow — over a century in the making.[16]

Severing the social dimension of economics, including the role of public institutions such as government, from the supposed "pure" operations of commerce violated both common sense and the traditional operations of market economies since their inception in the 14th century. The role of collective interests — the public good — in regulating the operation of markets had never been questioned until the advent of the Industrial Revolution in England. It was here that the notion of the autonomous economy was first articulated as a corollary to the social transformations attending industrialization and the growing influence of capital. And it was here, too, that the traditional relations between markets on the one hand, and the underlying economic organization of society on the other, were entirely recast.

In the past, markets were closely monitored and controlled by social and political forces that acted to protect what was conceived as the public interest from the negative effects of market forces.[17] The meticulous management of markets was thus a familiar feature of medieval city life. State regulation and local custom combined to protect the public interest. In local trade, there was careful regulation of food supplies through the transparency of transactions. Middlemen were strictly prohibited in order to protect the populace against the inflation of prices. Later, when the state played a central role in the development of internal markets between cities, the social interest was again paramount in the control of competition to avoid the emergence of monopolies. It was well understood that unrestricted competition leads to monopoly, a truth that seems lost on conventional economic thinking. Indeed, this conception of market forces operating within recognized social and moral limits persisted well into the 18th century. During the late 1700s in England, there were regular outbreaks of riots when food prices transgressed these limits. As noted by E. P. Thompson, in the popular mind the prevalence of what he termed a "moral economy" still governed the rules of the marketplace. People expected to buy their provisions in the open market, and even in times of shortage they expected prices to be regulated by custom. Here is John Wesley's contemporary account of what happened in James' Town, Ireland, when this custom was violated.

> The "mob had been in motion all the day; but their business was only with the forestallers of the market, who had bought up all the corn far and near, to starve the poor, and load a Dutch ship, which lay at the quay; but the mob brought it all out into the market, and sold it for the owners at the common price. And this they did with all the calmness and composure imaginable, and without striking or hurting anyone." [18]

Similarly, in Honiton in 1766 lace-workers seized corn on the premises of the farmers, took it to market themselves, sold it, and returned the money and even the sacks back to the farmers. [19]

Economic systems that preceded the Industrial Revolution were inseparable from the broader realities of social relations; the regulation of markets was essential for the delicate balance between commerce and the social system that surrounded it. The same principle held true for primitive economies. The primacy of social relations and the individual's identity as a social being was the basis of human society and the economic systems that sustained it. The conduct of economics as an expression of social values was also an integral part of the civic humanism that was epitomized in the great urban cultures of central Italy at the dawn of the Renaissance era. Three principles stand out in this conception of urban civilization: the social identity of the individual as expressed in the notion of citizenship; the sovereignty of the people in a free society; and the orientation of economic activity to the common good, which alone justifies it. It was this humanistic view of economics as a social good that was supplanted by the Industrial Revolution and the utilitarian philosophy of Bentham that was its intellectual expression.

Contrary to the common view that modern market society grew out of humankind's natural propensity to barter and engage in commercial exchange for profit, the organizing principles for economic systems right up to the advent of the Industrial Revolution were reciprocity, redistribution and family-based farming, or some combination of the three.[20] In this framework, the orderly production and distribution of goods was secured by a wide range of personal motives that were guided by well-established rules of social conduct. The profit motive was not prominent among them. This is not to say that there was not a class of individuals that pursued gain just as avidly as businessmen do today. Iris Origo's illuminating study of merchant life in 14th century Italy makes this clear.[21] Her protagonist, the Prato merchant Francesco di Marco Datini, pursued profit with a gusto that would be perfectly at home on Wall Street today. His life's motto, "In the name of God and of Profit," appeared like a talisman on the first page of his business ledgers and was a quintessentially medieval marriage of the pious and the profane. But this single-minded drive for profit was still restricted to a relatively small class of merchant specialists. It did not serve as the founding principle of the economy as a whole. As will be illustrated over the course of this work, the principles of reciprocity and redistribution that shaped the contours of economic life remain vital, if unnoticed, in modern economies as well, each playing a central role in forms of economic activity embodying social values that are once again coming to prominence.

Some readers may object that in describing this social immersion of economics in pre-industrial societies I am idealizing pre-industrial life. This would misread my intention. Who would want to advocate a return to a time when by almost any measure, life for the average individual was unimaginably harsher, shorter and more precarious than what we know today? Rather, my purpose is to correct some received assumptions about the history and nature of economics as a body of thought and practice. I wish to stress that the splitting off and ascendance of economics over social values has not been the inevitable process that some would have us believe, and that the balance of social and spiritual values with those of commerce that was a feature of pre-industrial life is a matter of the utmost importance. The nurturing of a spiritual life is inseparable from the cultivation of social and personal values that supersede those of commerce. I am arguing that the loss of this balance has cost humanity dearly.

The great economic historian Karl Polanyi argued that the emergence of the market system we live with today required the devaluing of all those patterns of social organization that were embodied in the production and exchange of goods for motives other than personal gain. When all transactions are turned into monetary transactions, all incomes must derive from the sale of something; it was precisely this reduction of all societal transactions to a commercial purpose that marks a radical break and discontinuity with everything that came before. For this to happen, people's motivation had to change from subsistence, or mutual benefit, or the welfare of society as a whole, to the single motive of personal gain.

For Polanyi, the conflation of narrow market operations with the broader economy and social life as a whole was a direct consequence of re-imagining society as an analogue to the industrial process of machine production. In what can only be described as a mechanics of dehumanization, the essential elements for the sustenance of an organic human life — shared use of land, meaningful labor and socially embedded personal identity — were deprived of their social meaning and turned instead into commodities to supply the needs of an autonomous market system. As the nature of that market system evolved, so too did the manner in which these elements come to be manipulated.

The insecurity and disorder of the times made the threat of hunger ever present and real. The mobilization of that threat by employers and their proponents in parliament in order to induce the selling of one's labor at the lowest possible price was one of the most debased aspects of the transition to the market system. It also flowed from the callous political economy of the Rev. Thomas Robert Malthus and became an operating assumption of classical economic theory thereafter.[22]

But there was also in this period a conscious and sustained effort to erase any semblance of the artisan's traditional independence. The transition from artisan to worker entailed two tasks: the progressive elimination of skill and the internalization of those submissive attitudes that fitted the man to the discipline of the machine. The factory's demand for a fundamental transformation of human nature was stated explicitly by Dr. Andrew Ure, the Scottish chemist and inventor who became the pre-eminent theorist of industrialization. In his truly Satanic work, *The Philosophy of Manufacturers*, Ure boldly states that the main difficulty of the factory system was not technological, but rather "in training human beings to renounce their desultory habits of work, and to identify themselves with the unvarying regularity of the complex automaton [the factory]." "It is in fact the constant aim and tendency of every improvement in machinery to supersede human labor altogether, or to diminish its cost, by substituting the industry of women and children for that of men; or that of ordinary laborers, for trained artisans."[23]

Skill in this context was a threat to mindless efficiency. Thus the manufacturers aimed at withdrawing any process that required "peculiar dexterity and steadiness of hand...from the cunning workman" and placing it in charge of a "mechanism so self-regulating, that a child may superintend it."[24] To remake human character by internalizing attitudes that served the factory system, he enlisted the indoctrinating power of religion. "It is...excessively in the interest of every mill owner to organize his moral machinery on equally sound principles with his mechanical, for otherwise he will never command the steady hands, watchful eyes, and prompt co-operation, essential to excellence of product... There is, in fact, no case to which the Gospel truth, 'Godliness is great gain,' is more applicable than to the administration of an extensive factory."[25] The malleability of human nature for selfish ends is an old and awful truth. Ure foresaw an explicit science of exploitation, but even he would have been left breathless at its final fruition in the dark arts of advertising in the latter part of the twentieth century. Andrew Ure was a brilliant and malign force, exerting his influence on both Marx and Engels and the entire class of England's industrialists. And, in one of those happy coincidences that are literally impossible to invent, it turns out that our Dr. Ure was Mary Shelley's model for Victor Frankenstein.[26]

Of the three elements of the pre-industrial economy, land and labor were the first to be subjected to the demands of industry. The third, personal identity, was undermined at a theoretical level by utilitarian economic theory and then by the dehumanizing realities of landlessness, wage labor, destitution and social alienation. But the *individualization* of identity remained only a precondition and corollary for the creation of a market for labor. It took two centuries before the conditions were ripe for the ultimate manipulation of personal identity as a driver of consumption.

Despite its enormous influence (largely outside economics) and its role in challenging the assertions of economic liberalism, Polanyi's thesis on the market and its relation to society has not been without its critics. His critique of *market society* and of capitalism also led to a rejection of the market *itself* as a means of realizing democratic ideals. In this, I would argue, Polanyi failed to acknowledge the possibilities of his central premise — *the economic system is, in effect, a mere function of social organization.*[27] This need not mean that an economic system derives solely from the state. Polanyi underestimates the generative power of civil society — the co-operative movement itself is evidence of this. And while the co-operative model parts company with capitalism, it remains firmly connected to the notion that the market can be made responsive to human needs — *without* the need for a planned socialist economy as Polanyi believed.[28] Democracy and the market are not antithetical. Democracy and the *market society*, in which social principles are subordinated to economic ones, as in the neoliberal doctrine of the free market, is another matter entirely.

In our era, the horrors of the transition to market society are behind us. They have long receded from our consciousness. But they are painfully real to those millions who today are suffering through the same traumatic transition to market systems now underway in China, Asia, Latin America and eventually in every forgotten haven of the pre-industrial world.

Bitter, prolonged, often deadly struggles were fought over the social impacts of these ideas. The real question that confronted market economies over the last two centuries, and the bedrock issue over which the social and economic battles have ultimately been fought, is how to limit the catastrophic damage this free market model does to society.[29] Which ultimately has come to mean how, and to what extent, to constrain the power of capital. In the end, the free market worldview boils down to this: the claims of capital to be sovereign and the exercise in the field of economics of that despotic power that was only recently ceded in the field of politics. The exercise of democracy that *laissez faire* capitalists now celebrate as good and holy in politics must be banned from economics. This is a rich terrain for irony. For while maintaining the principle of authoritarian control of markets and enterprises by capital in the economy, free market mythology also claims that free markets — and by extension capitalism — are the foundation of democracy.

The claim is ludicrous, incoherent and almost universally accepted. One reason is that there are certain analogies between democratic values such as equity and dignity and a particular view of markets. Unlike closed caste systems where a person's status is determined at birth, markets can display features like openness, access of opportunity and freedom of action that are features of democratic systems. But markets do not, and cannot, guarantee equitable or dignified outcomes.[30] The conflation of markets with democracy is a confusion at the most elementary level. It is the kind of mistake that could only be made — and this is being charitable — by the willfully ignorant.[31] Capitalism is neither synonymous with the market nor is it the source of free and democratic societies. Anyone with even a passing knowledge of political history will know that democratic societies preceded capitalism and market societies by many centuries, commencing with the Greek city-states in the 4th century BC and continuing up through the rise of civic humanism and the Italian democratic republics in the 14th century. The identification of free markets with democracy has become another element in the prolonged self-delusion of Americans who believe that the United States is the founding home of democracy. And this is not restricted to the reflexive free marketers some might wish to associate with a particular breed of Republicans. It is a pervasive conceit. On her first state visit to Europe as Secretary of State, Hillary Clinton, who no one could claim is either ill educated or stupid, was pleased to inform a stunned European Parliament that America's democracy "…has been around a lot longer than European democracy."

The relation of the free market to democracy is more accurately the annexation and distortion of the democratic idea by free market proponents as a cover for the distinctly undemocratic economic realities of capitalist systems. The rise and rule of administrative bureaucracy was one of the first, and most characteristic, features of a society based on the free market system.[32] From the very beginning, the banner of utilitarianism had *laissez faire* emblazoned on one side and state control for the protection of property on the other. The patrician classes have always enlisted the power of government to advance their interests and the fight for democracy has always been the struggle to break this nexus. Despite free market rhetoric to the contrary, this co-dependence of state control with the market system is one source of the tension between democracy and capitalism. It is even more pronounced in state attempts to control the market with centralized command models, as was the case with Marxist brands of socialism.

The alleged affinity for democracy on the part of economic liberalism is belied both by the historical record and the everyday evidence presented by the conduct of its institutions. Nowhere is this more obvious than the suppression of democracy in the marketplace. The freedom and equality that were achieved at such cost in politics through the democratic revolutions have been steadily eroded by the pervasive and growing influence of corporate economic power. In any society, authoritarian power in economics ultimately trumps democratic power in politics. Therefore, the absence of democracy in economics is a permanent threat to the survival of democracy in politics.

In truth, the human striving for equality and dignity that lay at the foundation of the democratic impulse was derailed in its extension to economics just when it was most needed, when the power of capital and the property-owning classes was consolidated during the period of the Industrial Revolution. But there has never yet been a convincing answer to the question: "If democracy is good for politics, why is it not equally good for economics?" After all, the operations of the economy and the connection that people have with its institutions on a daily basis have a far more significant impact on the quality and conduct of their daily lives. We exercise our democratic right to vote for public officials once every three or four years. Yet we spend most of our waking hours in our workplaces, which are still run like dictatorships, day in and day out. And finally we might ask, "How is it that a *free market* is run along authoritarian systems of command and control and personified by tyrannical models of power in the individual firm?" It is a fundamental contradiction so elementary a child could see it, and one that free market mythology cannot resolve. If markets should be free, they must also be free in their constituent institutions.

Admittedly, the democratic principle has found a fragile foothold in our economies, mostly through trade unions and sometimes in democratically controlled enterprises in the form of co-operatives. But even this was the result of bloody battles waged over decades with the captains of industry and their willing aides in government. From the very beginning, the establishment of the free market system and the transition from pre-industrial to industrial society was accompanied by a brutal repression of democratic rights both at the political and the economic level. The current claim that free markets are the source and guardians of democratic societies would be laughable if history didn't present such a dismal record showing exactly the opposite. The capitalist free market is not, and never has been, a friend to democracy.[33] But the reverse is certainly true: it was free and democratic societies, and more particularly free cities, that generated the conditions for what we have come to call free markets.

A free market in the proper sense means essentially three things: a division of labor, the accumulation of wealth through economic development and the freedom of enterprise. As Stefano Zamagni has so eloquently described this, the division of labor allows everyone the possibility of work, even those less gifted, while allowing greater productivity through specialization. In practice, the division of labor obliges people to recognize their reciprocal ties. It underscores reciprocity as an economic value and it makes explicit the interdependence of specialized forms of work as components of a production process. It also enables those who are less gifted to contribute to the work of society, providing a fundamental component of self-worth. Development means the accumulation of wealth as a social good — not as a private end, but as a contingency against future misfortune and ultimately, as a responsibility for future generations. Freedom of enterprise, according to Zamagni, means:

> Those endowed with creativity, a good propensity for risk and the ability to coordinate the work of many others — the three essential qualities of the entrepreneur — must be left free to undertake initiatives without the need for prior authorization from a sovereign or underling, because the active and industrious life (*"vita activa et negociosa"*) is a value in itself, not just a means to other ends.[34]

Freedom of enterprise is here understood as the freedom to engage in a productive and useful life in an open economy — one not controlled by a sovereign power (or in our day, a monopoly power). It does not entail the notion that an entrepreneur, or a business, may do what they please regardless of the effects on others.

The Franciscans presented the idea of the free market in precisely these terms as early as the 15th century.[35] All these conditions existed in the market economies that preceded capitalism. None of them presuppose the form that individual enterprises might take, whether privately owned firms, joint stock companies or democratically controlled co-operatives.

It was in the city republics of Tuscany and Umbria between the 14th and 16th centuries that market economies first flourished in Europe, giving rise to the institutions of banking, notes of credit, the joint stock company and a merchant class that, among other things, inaugurated the first truly global trading systems that in turn helped finance the Renaissance. It was only during the Industrial Revolution that the notion of profit maximization was added as a condition of market economies. This pre-eminence of profit really marked the transition from traditional market economies to capitalism.

I dwell at some length on this economic history only to show that the notion of capitalism as being a precondition of free and democratic societies is a fallacy, although an article of faith of the free market creed. And if one were in need of more bracing contemporary evidence, one need look no further than the rise of capitalism in China and Russia and the truly dispiriting spectacle of a state capitalism combining unfettered market development with totalitarian power in the first case and the consolidation of a corrupt, kleptocratic dynasty in the other.

The one thing that emerges in this endless contest over economic ideas and values is that the nature of economics in general and the market in particular remains an open question — a continuously contested arena of claims and counterclaims. What is very clear is that the market and the larger notion of the economy of which it forms a part is in its nature a social and public concept. The notions that any one class can own the market or that the market has a natural organizational form such as the corporation, are false. And despite the assumptions of the free market faithful, the market does not belong to capital; the forms of enterprise that make it up and give it its vitality are as varied as the uses to which they are put and the values they embody. These values may be just as committed to social goods and ends as they are to commercial ones. Moreover, the forms that capitalism itself may take are astonishingly diverse. Free market doctrine makes it sound as if true capitalism comes in just this one "pure" form. This is also false and belies one of capitalism's singular strengths — its chameleon-like ability to adapt. There are many capitalisms, many ways that capital can mobilize and co-ordinate the process of economic production.

Industrialization and Social Defence

What has been well and truly buried from view this last two centuries and more are the uses of the market for the pursuit of social ends. However, the social dimension of economics was acknowledged at the very dawn of economics as a discipline. The first chair of economics in

Europe was established at the University of Naples in 1776 under the title Chair of Civil Economy. Antonio Genovese, who first held the chair, was a pioneer in the study of social economy and had a direct influence on his contemporary, Adam Smith. It is only now that the hidden history of social economy is coming to light. The exclusion of society from the development of economic theory has had profound, lasting and deeply damaging effects.

Society's survival response to the plain idiocy of the autonomous market doctrine asserted itself from the first attempts to enforce market logic on human systems. The struggle continues to this day. The great experiments in socialism and co-operativism, the emergence of trade unions and the battle for democratic rights in the economy as well as in politics were all part of this human response to an inhuman system. They appeared as soon as the first hammer blows of the machine age were felt. And while the forms of this struggle first evolved in our own industrial societies, the models of resistance and reform that are now un-folding in developing countries mirror the social and collectivist models that arose in the early stages of the Industrial Revolution. As Polanyi put it, the overarching dynamic of western history since the rise of the machine age has been a double motion: the attempt to subject society to the mechanisms of the market system, and the corresponding responses by society to defend itself against the damages wrought by this system. This same dynamic is now being played out on a global level.

The integration of economic activity within the broader frame of so-cial values is still a feature of societies that are today struggling to protect these values from the corrosive effects of capitalism. Were Western at-titudes less blinkered, there would be greater recognition of the urgent need to learn from societies that have retained something that Western culture has lost over the last two hundred years. But herein lies the trag-edy. It is precisely *because* Western culture has lost this knowledge that it fails to recognize its value. It is a case of cultural amnesia and its effects are felt at the deepest levels of modern living.

In our time, the issues attending the long domination of market logic in Western society have become subtler, more complex and more dif-ficult to perceive because the problems are now as much questions of ideology and the patterns of popular consciousness as they are of mate-rial welfare. Any attempted solution or alternative to the prevailing form of free market capitalism will have to contend with these non-material realities.

The submersion of our social identities entailed in the creation of "economic man" has prompted the emergence of two contradictory realities in the human experience. The first is the growth of material wealth to a scale beyond imagining in any age previous to our own. It is the undeniable and crowning achievement of capitalism in all its forms. The second has been the spiritual and social impoverishment that lies at the bottom of a profound sense of unhappiness and longing that has become a defining feature of modern industrial civilization. This is the great paradox of our age — the happiness paradox. It would appear that such unhappiness, and the illusion of material gratification on which it rests, is the psychic price to be borne for the type of wealth we have created.[36]

The severance of the individual from society, and the pathological inflation of individualism that is its counterpart, are at the foundation of free market psychology. These are essential conditions of our material wealth and at the same time the source of a profound spiritual malaise that makes us incapable of deriving the happiness we seek from the wealth we consume. It is as if the myth of Tantalus has materialized in the spiritual condition of our culture. Happiness recedes as we stretch our hands to the material wealth we desire. And perhaps it could not be otherwise, for the disjunction between unlimited material acquisition — avarice — and personal happiness is a fundamental truth of moral philosophy and religious teaching leading back to ancient times.

But never before has this tension between the material and the spiritual been institutionalized in an economic system that so devalues the social and the spiritual in favor of the material. By "spiritual" I mean simply the sensibility to a value or meaning that transcends material pursuits. The poisonous consequences of such an obsessively materialistic worldview — the social and spiritual corrosions that flow from it — are apparent everywhere. They show in the insatiable appetite for consumption that drives us compulsively to satisfy material desire as a solace to sadness; in the demonization of "socialism" and the mistrust of collective action and the pursuit of shared benefit; in the contempt of government and the idea of the public; in the unraveling of the very social bonds and fellow feeling that are, in times of crisis, the final security against danger; in the perverse sense that our self worth is bound up in the things we buy; in the utter lack of comprehension in the minds of those who, like Margaret Thatcher, truly believe that society is a fiction and nothing more than a collection of individuals; and most disturbingly, in the difficulty people have in imagining any alternative to the present system.

This inability to imagine an alternative is the final triumph of ideology. As William Leach put it so well, the enthronement of consumerism and the acceptance of corporate capitalism as its social mechanism has diminished public life, denying people everywhere "access to insight into other ways of organizing and conceiving life, insight that might have endowed their consent to the dominant culture…with real democracy." [37] It is here that the most difficult, the most necessary work must be done to advance a more fully human vision of what economies might be and how such economies might be constructed.

Alternatives do exist. The effort to construct economic systems with a more human face has been attempted since the dawn of the industrial age. And the impact of these attempts on capitalism has been decisive in making our own market system more humane. For the task has been not only to construct a more humane alternative to the free market model, but also to humanize the model we do have.

The effort to socialize economics through the creation of collective models of production and exchange has been at the center of a reform movement stretching back for two and a half centuries. All these efforts, embodying the idea of socialism in some form, reflect the attempt to transcend the self-regulating market by consciously subordinating it to the needs of society through democratic means. [38]

This book argues that the most enduring and the most promising of these efforts is the use of co-operation as a model for economic and social exchange and the use of reciprocity as the basis for both economic and social reform. The following chapters will attempt to show why this is true, how the co-operative experience is being played out in both advanced industrial societies and in developing ones and in what ways the co-operative movement worldwide is succeeding—and failing—in its mission to construct a humane alternative to free market capitalism.

CHAPTER 2

The Materialization of Dreams

England is a chopping machine,
and the poor man is always under the knife.
— GEORGE JACOB HOLYOAKE —

When Robert Owen was assigned by the British House of Commons to coordinate the parliamentary commission of inquiry into the application of the Poor Laws in 1817, England was caught up in a transformation that was cutting loose the social moorings of an entire class in the name of progress. The small landholders of the English countryside, evicted by enclosures from land that had been used in common for centuries, were descending on the cities in their thousands to seek work in the factories and mills of the nation. Entire villages were depopulated as common land was turned over to raising sheep or large-scale farming that was more profitable to landowners. At the same time, the artisans and craftsmen of the towns were watching their livelihoods disappear as machine production used unskilled labor to replace the human skills that had been the foundation of the traditional craft economy. The destitution and misery that accompanied this process was on a scale unlike anything seen before.[1] It was the time of Dickens, the poorhouse, child labor, stalking hunger, and the swelling, festering slums populated by the displaced and the dispossessed.

The Age of Revolt

These were the years the modern workers' movement was born. In the years following the end of the Napoleonic Wars and culminating in 1848 a wave of revolution swept over Europe. In England in particular, the great social uprising of the Luddite movement that erupted episodically from 1808 to the 1830s involved hundreds of thousands in the struggle to turn back the social wreckage prompted by automated production in the textile industry. At its height, the revolt was so strong and so well organized 12,000 men-at-arms were needed to put it down in a series of bloody battles. The popular impulse for social reform in these years also crystallized in other quite distinct forms — in the demand for popular suffrage by the Chartists, in the first stirrings of the movement for women's rights and in the many worker education and self-improvement societies that for the first time provided workers with the ideas and the organizational means to frame their own future and establish the foundations for an organized labor movement. A further outcome of these societies was their coalescence in the co-operative movement, given form and direction by the work and teachings of figures like Robert Owen, William Thompson and William King.

Robert Owen was already well known as a successful industrialist, one of the most prosperous men in England, but even better known for his advocacy of reforms to alleviate the desperate conditions of the poor. His charge for the British House of Commons was to report on these conditions and on the ways and means of addressing a host of afflictions that immiserated such a huge percentage of the English population. It was to be a turning point in the long and bitter struggle for social and economic reform in that country.

Owen was an improbable revolutionary. The son of a saddler and ironmonger, he was born in Newton, Wales, and at the age of ten was sent by his father to work as a draper's apprentice in Lincolnshire. At 16 he moved to Manchester to work in a large drapery firm, and by the age of 21 he was a manager in one of Manchester's largest spinning factories. A model of the self-made man, Robert Owen seemed destined to pursue the conventional destiny of a gifted and ambitious businessman caught up in the full flow of England's Industrial Revolution.

Owen had earned his reputation as a reformer by pouring his substantial wealth into the improvement of the nation's underclass and lending his unquenchable energy to a host of causes including the creation of Britain's first labor organizations, the reform of the child labor laws, the movement for universal suffrage and the creation of Britain's earliest childcare system. But it was in his *Report on The Poor* that Owen first outlined a comprehensive vision for a revolutionary reform of Britain's economic and social order as the only means of addressing the endemic social ills that accompanied the capitalism of his era. The report he drafted centered on the creation of "Villages of Co-operation" as the means to end poverty. And while his report was rejected by the House of Commons,[2] its co-operative ideals crystallized a movement that at its height spread through the length and breadth of the nation.

Owen's ideal socialist society was based on the establishment of co-operative communities and on the conviction that man's character was a product of his circumstances. His communitarian plans were encouraged by the success of the Shaker communities that forty years earlier had taken root in the United States as an offshoot of a small band of dissenting Quakers who were at that time disseminating their egalitarian teachings in Manchester. Owen believed the essential goodness of man was corrupted by the harsh ways in which he was treated and the dehumanizing effects of inhumane environments. In this he was close to French Enlightenment philosopher Rousseau. But instead of rejecting civilization as a corrupting influence on man's nature, Owen's solution was to create the external conditions that would remake human character and produce good, rational and humane people. More importantly, Owen linked this social formation of character to an economic model in which the social element was paramount. He refused to accept the division of society into an economic and political sphere and the social nature of the solution he proposed set him apart from his contemporaries.

Robert Owen saw in co-operation the key to both wealth creation and a just society. Unlike later Marxism, co-operativism did not reject the market as a source of social evil. Instead, Owen saw in co-operation a means of using the market to meet the needs of all members of society, not just the privileged few. As owner of Britain's largest spinning business, the Chorton Twist Company located in New Lanark, Scotland, he had the perfect opportunity to act on his ideas. Owen sought not just to run a successful business but to create also a new type of community. Owen's first concern was the molding of character through the transformative power of humanistic education. The creation of co-operative communities and humane workplaces was an extension of this primary principle. It was also the foundation for one of Owen's most signal contributions to England's social and cultural development — the rise of education, especially among adults, as a mechanism of social change.

When he arrived in New Lanark in January of 1810, over 2,000 people lived in the village. Among his first decisions, Owen ordered the building of a school and limiting the workday for children. He also refused to employ children under the age of ten. At the time, children as young as five were working in the textile mills. Five hundred of these children had been taken from the poorhouses, primarily in Edinburgh and Glasgow, to work in the New Lanark mills. It was common practice for poorhouses to provide factory owners a regular supply of this cheap labor, to ensure employment for all their wards, children included, in order to prevent them falling into the vicious habits induced by idleness. This hateful philosophy was only one of the enduring evils promulgated by Methodism at this time.[3] Stunted, many with deformed limbs, children were on their feet 13 hours a day, often sleeping beside the machines they served. One harrowing explanation for the appalling infant mortality rate among the working poor during this period — upwards of 50 percent for children to the age of 5 — was the characteristic deformation and narrowing of the pelvic bones in girls who had worked since childhood in the mills.[4] After serving an "apprenticeship" of six, seven, eight years, they were turned loose — uneducated and untrained — to take up their place in Britain's permanent underclass.

Owen had hoped that his treatment of children and the other reforms he introduced at New Lanark, including a pension scheme for workers, would induce other industrialists to follow suit and he campaigned vigorously to promote his ideas. He was an indefatigable propagandist. Yet he did not succeed. His courting of powerful patrons and governments across Europe was to no avail, and his belief that the rich would eventually support his plans for the alleviation of poverty through co-operative communities proved entirely groundless. It was a product of an almost childlike faith in the persuasive power of reason and an almost total absence of political acumen. Owen had not an ounce of aptitude for political reality. As E. P. Thompson remarked in his treatment of Owen's role in this period, Owen simply had a vacant place in his mind where most other men had political responses.[5] Moreover, his attempts to engineer model co-operative communities from the standpoint of the benevolent patriarch drew suspicion and ridicule from many critics — some charging him for being a dangerous radical and a menace, others for not being radical enough. This was a time, let us remember, when the popular temper was long past expecting any favors from the rich. Among these latter critics was William Thompson, a fellow reformer and political philosopher who, even more than Owen, helped establish the intellectual foundations of the co-operative movement and early socialism.

Today, Thompson is an obscure figure, someone whose achievements have been largely lost to the mists of time. In his day his influence was profound. His writings, in particular *An Enquiry into the Principles of Distribution of Wealth Most Conducive to Human Happiness*, written in 1824 when he was already 50, are among the foundation stones of socialism.[6] Thompson was born in 1775 in Cork, Ireland, a son and heir to one of the most prosperous merchants of the Anglo-Irish aristocracy. After his father's death in 1814, Thompson inherited a trading fleet and a landed estate in Glandore, West Cork, where he promptly rejected the role of absentee landlord. He moved onto the estate and worked to improve the living conditions of the tenant families, educating the children and introducing innovations in agriculture. In this, he recalls the figure of Leo Tolstoy who attempted the same on his own estates in Russia a short time later. The parallels between the two even extend to Thompson's attempts to leave his property to the co-operative movement after his death, prompting the longest legal battle in Irish history as other branches of his family fought to have the will annulled.

Like Owen, Thompson was a friend and disciple of Jeremy Bentham. But his approach to utilitarianism and the problem of human happiness was entirely different. Unlike Bentham, Thompson saw happiness as a social phenomenon, not a personal pursuit. It arose as a consequence of specific social conditions and from the nature of one's relations with others. And whereas Bentham defended private property and social hierarchy as preconditions to liberty and security, Thompson was a fierce critic of capitalism and all forms of subordination. He argued for the principle of common property, claiming that private property was the basis of competition and the mechanism by which one person is pitted against the other. For Thompson the key to a just society, and to personal happiness, was the alignment of self-interest with the interest of society, not the subordination of one to the other. And unlike Bentham and Owen, Thompson fought for the practice of participatory democracy in social institutions. In this, Thompson was a prophetic forerunner of contemporary theorists of social capital. His explicit linking of happiness with social relations, and both with co-operation and the extension of democratic practice, established the moral and methodological foundations for a modern understanding of co-operation as a remedy to the corrosive effects of capitalism. These are key themes that we will explore in the concluding sections of this work.

By the time of his death from a chest affliction at the age of 58, Thompson's influence inside the co-operative movement had grown steadily and was beginning to overshadow that of Owen himself. Their differences, particularly on the questions of democratic practice and Thompson's belief that workers in co-operative communities should have ownership and control of the community's land and capital property, led Thompson to distinguish his more radical views from that of other Owenites by adopting the term "socialist." Thompson's use of "socialist" in a letter to *The Co-operative Magazine* in 1827 is the first documented use of the term.[7]

At the time, the rise of co-operative communities of one form or another was not restricted to Owen's experiment at New Lanark. Dozens had come into existence both in England and abroad, brought into being by a common impulse to forge an alternative and a growing class consciousness and self-confidence on the part of working people. All attempted to realize some socialized form of the ideal community. Eventually all failed, including Owen's own efforts to extend the New Lanark model to a new co-operative community called New Harmony in Indiana. Why did these efforts fail?

In Owen's case failure resulted both from the paternalistic (and, indeed, authoritarian) nature of his model and his philosophy of human nature. His cast of mind is illustrated in the tone of his writings. He wished (he said in 1817) to "…remoralize the Lower Orders" and the words most encountered in his early writings are "benevolent" and "provided for them." It would be hard to find a tone more perfectly calibrated to annoy the Radicals and the leaders of the emerging trade union movement. The notion of the working class advancing by its own efforts and toward its own goals was alien to Owen, even though he was eventually to find himself at the head of precisely such a movement.[8] Owen's co-operative communities depended on his personal prestige, presence and philanthropic support. In New Harmony, when he left the leadership of the community in the hands of his son Robert Dale Owen, the community came apart, showing the degree to which his successes were dependent on his own considerable leadership gifts and charisma.

The second cause of failure was a fundamental flaw in Owen's philosophy. People are not simply passive creatures of circumstance. They are not born as blank slates. They carry something of their own into the world and the individuality of the person is ultimately the interplay between what is social and environmental and what is inherent. Owen deserves great credit for understanding the contribution of environment, education and humane treatment to the formation of character. Unfortunately, his optimism concerning the effects of environment on people wasn't enough to overcome the differences and divisions among incompatible individuals that eventually undermined New Harmony. Nevertheless, his co-operative experiments helped to consolidate and give form to the new movement.

The third cause of failure was more prosaic — a simple lack of practical experience in the operation and management of co-operative enterprises. A great many of the co-operative societies that preceded the first success at Rochdale (estimated at some 250 in 1830) foundered on the mishandling of credit, a natural effect flowing from the propensity of those societies to extend credit to members who either had no money, or had little incentive to repay their loans. Another problem was the utter absence of any legal recognition or protection for the co-operative as a legal entity; its funds could be embezzled by anyone with total impunity. The legal obstacles to success were in themselves enormous.[9]

Despite these weaknesses and setbacks, Owen's ideas provided something indispensable to the rise of an organized working class movement for reform — the formulation of an organized system of thought, a *social theory* that could offer a counter vision to the capitalism of this time. Owenism was the first of the great social doctrines to grip the imagination of the masses in this period, both embracing and recasting the industrial epoch. What was at issue "…was not the machine so much as the profit motive; not the size of the industrial enterprise but the control of the social capital behind it."[10] Owen's ideas were general and imprecise, but they lent themselves to adaptation and innovation. From their stock countless working class efforts were able to adapt the key notions of co-operation and self-help to suit their own purposes. *Owenism* — that great tide of economic and social reform that swept across England — in the end came to signify far more than Owen. Many working people had ideas about what needed to be done and took the initiative in their hands. Owen reflected this ferment and championed reform in polite society. But on the ground, co-operatives were among the most enduring creations of the workers themselves.

Rochdale

As so often happens, the ultimate realization of Owen's vision came in a form that he would not have predicted. The first successful market-based co-operatives did not even receive Owen's support. He rejected the commercial basis of the co-operatives arguing that the societies were "not the social system we envisage." His ideological opposition to private ownership in favor of a "pure" co-operative model based solely on communitarian principles blinded him from perceiving how co-operation could succeed in another form.

The breakthrough success of the co-operative model came in the form of a co-operative business, not a co-operative community. It was given impetus through the work of Dr. William King, a crucial transitional figure who bridged the co-operative ideals of both Owen and Thompson with the pragmatic task of making these ideals plausible in the real world of the marketplace. King had his own ideas about how a co-operative community should function and his greatest contribution was in applying his considerable talents of practicality and realism to the task at hand.

William King was born in Yorkshire in 1786, the son of a vicar. Unlike Owen, who was largely self-taught, King was a distinguished academic who studied political economy, moral philosophy and modern history at Cambridge and then became a doctor and Fellow of the Royal College of Physicians. He settled in Brighton and gained valuable experience as a doctor ministering to the poor, but went from doing charity work to organizing a friendly society that he hoped would eventually allow the poor to do without charity and to meet their own needs through mutual insurance. Friendly societies were at this time among the most important creations of working class communities, using mutual aid to provide for their members in times of sickness or other hard times. One of their key functions was to cover the cost of burials.

King believed in the ultimate aim of a co-operative community building its own homes, on its own land, and employing its own members in productive work. But unlike Owen (who had said a community might build a store, but a store could never build a community), King was a gradualist. He believed it was better to begin small, to accumulate modest victories, than not to begin at all. He also perceived that the working classes would have to do this work by themselves, and set about instructing them. He started a monthly publication *The Co-operator*, which sold at a penny and reached a circulation of 12,000 copies. In the pages of *The Co-operator*, King provided a systematic exposition of the co-operative philosophy and some realistic advice on how to set up and run a co-operative shop. This magazine became the textbook of the new movement.

In working out his co-operative philosophy, King responded directly to the dominant ideas of his time. Like Adam Smith, he accepted that in the "original state of things... the whole produce of the labour belongs to the laborer." Unlike Smith however, he did not accept that the growth of landlords and masters is inevitable, and that in a market society a laborer must get only a fraction of the value of his labor in the form of wages. He saw clearly that wages are determined not by the value of the product but rather by the ruthless play of competition between capitalists. Moreover, workers were trapped by the logic of a market in which they functioned as mere appendages to the machines they ran. Eventually, through overproduction, these same machines would put them out of work altogether.

How can the worker break out of this trap? First, King proposed that without labor, capital is nothing; capital is really only stored labor and has no utility until the worker makes use of it. But workers are prevented from taking all the value of their product because they remain dependent. While they are working to produce goods, they must also live. The capitalist merely advances capital in order to keep the workers alive. However, if the worker has enough capital to do this, then the value of the product would all go to the worker. The key for King was for workers to store up enough capital to gain control over their own labor. They must also generate enough of a surplus to be able to invest in their enterprise. Possessing both labor and capital the workers can then do away with the capitalist altogether. But co-operation is essential to this. Individual workers cannot do this on their own; there is too much risk, their condition is too fragile, and the time required to accumulate sufficient capital takes too long. It is crucial therefore, that workers learn to share their risk by co-operating to pool their capital.

How to start?

King advocated the establishment of a shop. Since people have to go to a shop every day to buy food and necessities, why not go to one they owned? The surplus from the co-operative shop would then go toward building the co-operative community that is the ultimate aim.

Ever the pragmatist, King proposed that capital be accumulated partly through weekly subscriptions (as in the friendly societies) and partly through the surplus generated from running the shop. Work can then be found for other members until all are employed. Finally, the co-op can afford to pay sickness benefits, pensions and schooling for the children; it can purchase land, build housing and keep unemployed workers in employment growing food. Eventually, a whole new society-within-society will emerge independent of both capitalists and welfare. The Owenite vision of a co-operative community is thus achieved gradually, from the patient accumulation of capital that comes from using the market in the interests of workers.

King's great achievement was not merely to present a vision of the future (at this time there was a surplus of utopian visions to choose from), but much more importantly a way to translate this vision into a reality. What was needed to make such a plan work? Unromantically, and at the most basic level, there was a need for rules on how such a co-operative shop should be run: no credit; the selection of three people to act as trustees; a weekly accounting of the business; acceptance as members only people that can be trusted; and the very wise advice that meetings be held in a room, not a pub, otherwise members will be tempted to drink the surpluses before they are earned. On this basis, (save the last — their directors, showing remarkable restraint, would meet in the committee room of the Weaver's Arms) a group of weavers and cobblers in the old industrial town of Rochdale created the seed from which the modern co-operative movement would grow. It was on account of King's practical and sage advice on the proper manner of running a co-operative business, especially on the importance of carefully limiting credit and a dividend system based on the amount of business that a member conducted with the co-op, that the Rochdale store succeeded where so many others had failed.

Much has been written about Rochdale and the name has now acquired a semi-mythical status in the co-operative corpus. All movements need their symbols and Rochdale is one. But it marks a milestone in the movement for economic democracy because the Rochdale story shifts the focus from the creation of socialized communities as the means to reform society to the transformation of market relations in the service of social ends.

With the guidance of King's rules for co-operation, Rochdale helped transform economics by formalizing reciprocity as an economic principle. When it proved successful, the model became the blueprint for the largest, most durable and most successful mass movement for economic reform in history. It was here that the modern conception of the cooperative as a democratically controlled enterprise took form.

Its beginnings were memorably (and very humorously) recorded by George Jacob Holyoake:

> At the close of the year 1843, on one of those damp, dark, dense, dismal, disagreeable days, which no Frenchman can be got to admire — such days as occur towards November, when the daylight is all used up, and the sun has given up all attempt at shining, either in disgust or despair — a few poor weavers out of employ, and nearly out of food and quite out of heart with the social state, met together to discover what they could do to better their industrial condition. Manufacturers had capital, and shopkeepers the advantage of stock; how could they succeed without either? Should they avail themselves of the poor law? that were dependence; of emigration? that seemed like transportation for the crime of having been born poor. What should they do? They would commence the battle of life on their own account. They would, as far as they were concerned, supersede tradesmen, mill owners, and capitalists: without experience, or knowledge, or funds, they would turn merchants and manufacturers.[11]

And so it was. The small shop, stocked with a tiny inventory of butter, flour, oatmeal, sugar and a few candles opened just before Christmas on 21 December 1844 for two days a week. It had a founding capital of 28 pounds sterling collected from its members on a subscription of two pence a week. It took the 28 founding members four months to pool the money. But despite these humble beginnings there was no dampening the reformist fervor of the society's founders. Included in the charter, along with the mission to open a shop and to build homes, was the following modest aim: "That, as soon as practicable, this Society shall proceed *to arrange the powers of production, distribution, education, and government; or, in other words, to establish a self-supporting home-colony of united interests, or assist other societies in establishing such colonies.*" Not to neglect the moral side of things, the proposition followed: "That, for the promotion of sobriety, a Temperance Hotel be opened in one of the Society's houses as soon as convenient." It was a grand vision, founded on a two pence subscription. And while the rearrangement of the national means of production, distribution and government had to wait a while longer, ten years later the British co-operative movement had grown to nearly 1,000 co-operatives. The original shop still stands preserved as a museum at 31 Toad Lane.

Located on the boundary of Lancashire and Yorkshire, Rochdale had a long history of activism and labor unrest. It was a tough political town. In 1808, a bitter strike resulted in the stationing of regular troops in the town, which remained there until 1846. In particular, Rochdale hand-loom weavers were a highly politicized group, born troublemakers, that could be counted on to lead the strikes and be key activists in organizing the community. Reform meetings often attracted ten thousand or more people.

Rochdale's woolen and cotton industries brought it within the influence of other textile districts like the West Riding of Yorkshire and South East Lancashire, both areas of social unrest, and seedbeds of various reform movements. The strategic importance of Rochdale was attested by the fact that a major effort to organize a National Trade Union took place here, and the town played a central role in both the Chartist movement and the Ten Hours movement.[12] The town became an important center for Owenite activity. In the midst of this tumultuous reform atmosphere there were concerted attempts at co-operation.

The 1840s were a grim time in Rochdale. Economic depression had hit the weaving town particularly hard. Hunger and privation among workers and their families left them vulnerable to disease and of those hardest hit five-sixths had scarcely any blankets to keep them warm, while over a hundred families had no blankets at all. Starvation was in the air. In 1837 for example, an average of one hundred eighty animals were killed weekly to provide for the town's food needs. In 1841 this number was down to sixty-five, a reduction of caloric intake of nearly 60 percent.

The conditions of most weavers from the 1820s to the 1840s and beyond were commonly referred to as "indescribable." But described they were. Here is an account from the evidence gathered by the Select Committee on Emigration (1827) of conditions in Lancashire where in the space of 20 years industrialization had driven weavers from relative prosperity to the edge of starvation:

> Mrs. Hutton and myself, in visiting the poor, were asked by a person
> almost starving to go into a house. We there found on one side of the

fire a very old man, apparently dying, on the other side a young man about eighteen with a child on his knee, whose mother had just died and been buried. We were going away from that house, when the woman said, "Sir, you have not seen all." We went upstairs, and, under some rags, we found another young man, the widower; and on turning down the rags, which he was unable to remove himself, we found another man who was dying, and who did die in the course of the day. I have no doubt that the family were actually starving at the time...

In Rochdale, the economic backdrop to the crisis was the crumbling of the town's industrial heart. The new factory system had turned once proud and independent artisans into dependent outworkers for large manufacturers. Employers succeeded in ratcheting down wages while simultaneously defeating attempts to introduce a minimum wage. By the 1840s automation was putting handloomers out of business and the industries of cotton manufacturing and machine making were supplied by imported, cheap labor, composed mostly of desperate Irish workers fleeing famine back home only to face the hatred of the local townsfolk. The hat industry that used the felt produced in the town was in decline. Making matters worse, the cotton factories had to compete with imported cloth produced at a fraction of the cost with slave labor in the United States. Globalization then, as now, was linking the fates of workers half a world apart. These then, were the material conditions that immediately preceded the establishment of the Rochdale Society of Equitable Pioneers in 1844.[13]

But the factors that gave rise to the co-operative movement at this time and in this place extend far beyond immediate economic hardship; the deeper roots of the movement arose from the human qualities that made up the unique character of the weaver communities from which it sprang. Understanding this is more than a simple appreciation of historical conditions. It goes to the heart of what gave the co-operative movement its galvanizing power during the latter part of the 1800s and its continuing relevance to the conditions of globalizing capital today.

The weavers that led the Lancashire Radicalism of 1816–20 were a product of the clash between two conflicting ideologies and ways of life. One was the rising swell of industrial *laissez faire* capitalism which we have already described. The other was the disappearance of an ancient way of life that was characterized by the artisan tradition and the weaver communities this tradition had woven[14] — a deep social egalitarianism, a spirit of independence, an immense pride in personal skill and a profoundly interdependent community life in which fate's fortunes were shared by all, in good times and bad. The sufferings of the weavers that resulted from the rise of industrial exploitation were those of the whole community. The deliberate erosion of trade union protections by the state, the loss of status and self-worth that came with de-skilling and factory production and the flood of unskilled labor that employers used to depress wages gave their resistance a particular moral force. The Owenite frame in which they voiced their protest appealed to essential rights and elementary notions of human fellowship rather than merely economic or sectarian interests.[15] They demanded betterment as a whole community and Owen's ideas provided them the framework that would at one stroke recast the social architecture along lines that they already recognized. Their dreams, which also incorporated the political demands of Chartism, land reform and free trade unions, were centered on the protection of human dignity. They envisioned a mutually supportive community of independent small producers, exchanging their products without the manipulations of middlemen, free of the control of masters. At its heart, this is still the vision that speaks to the aspirations of millions caught in the exploitative web of capitalism today. It is very simply a vision that asserts the primacy of human and social values over those of commerce. And it was precisely these values that were unraveling as industrial capital consolidated its control in the middle decades of the 19th century.

A Brief History of Nowhere

Owenism was only one among a great variety of utopian visions that had been formulated in the political and social ferment that characterized the 19th century. What set this era apart from earlier periods, however, was that what were once mere dreams now found in the crucible of the industrial revolution the social and economic conditions that allowed them to be materialized in the real world. Their antecedents could be traced back through the late Middle Ages to the writings of Thomas More in his work *Utopia* — a Greek term meaning "no place" or "nowhere" — and Catholic philosophers such as Campanella and Ludovico Agostini in the 16th century. Much earlier, in the 4th century BC, Plato visualized in *The Republic* a utopian society in which the individual was wholly subservient to the needs of society. In the Platonic Republic the individual was destined to live out his life in a strict caste system at whose apex was a class of aristocrat-warriors, with the whole governed by a philosopher king.[16] Later medieval visions of an ideal society were based on the Christian concept of society as a mystic body through which the individual is united to God. This was formulated in St. Augustine's *City of God*, in which God's love, acting through the Holy Spirit, is the source of all social relations. This is why community, conceived as the fulfillment of God's grace, is so central to the mission of the church, to personal salvation and to the later evolution of liberation theology as a Christian injunction to fight for social justice.

Indeed one of the first and most successful versions of such a utopian Christian community outside the confines of monastic life was in the mission communities, portrayed in the 1986 film *The Mission*,[17] that the Jesuits established in the early 1600s among the Guarani Indians in what is today Paraguay. In addition to winning souls these communities, called Reductions, were a remarkable attempt by the Jesuits to provide refuge against the enslavement and maltreatment of the Indian population by the Spanish and Portuguese colonizers of the region. Between 1609 and 1780, 32 Guarani Reductions had been organized into a "Christian Indian State" that, at its height, numbered over 100,000 souls. The economic and social foundation of the communities was a theocratic commonwealth in which all property was held in common, including the buildings and livestock. Tools for work were loaned from a common supply. In addition to allocations of private plots to the Indians for agricultural production, common plots were also set aside and cultivated by common labor to provide for the sick and needy, to collect seed for next year and to stock a common storehouse as a reserve food supply and as a means to exchange produce for European goods. A thriving socialist economy was built, including a highly developed craft industrial system, all under the watchful eyes of the Jesuit missionaries. This was a religious socialism, in which the whole community was understood as an expression of Christian teaching and whose members all attended Holy Mass and the evening devotions daily. This extraordinary chapter in Christian mission history came to a sad and bloody end when on 2 April 1767 Charles III of Spain signed the edict expelling the Jesuits from Spanish possessions in America and transferring the missions to Portuguese control.[18]

Ultimately socialism, for all its variety of forms, embodied two distinct and opposed conceptions of the relation between the individual and society, the one authoritarian, the other libertarian. The first stressed Utopia-as-order and was embodied in the systems of Plato and More and, later, in the theoretical system of Saint-Simon. The second focused on the ultimate value of freedom and found voice in the works of thinkers such as Rabelais, Proudhon and Fourier.

Almost all the socialist systems that were formulated in the early to mid-1800s as a response to early capitalism oscillated between one or the other of these two extremes.

The tension between authoritarian social order on the one hand and individual liberty on the other have continued to color the development of collectivist alternatives to market capitalism to our own day. In the twentieth century the two poles of socialism were epitomized in the state socialism established in Soviet Russia and Eastern Europe, while the more libertarian vision flowered for a brief time in Republican Spain before it fell to Franco's fascism. It is still present in the thriving co-operative economy of Mondragon in Spain's Basque region where a network of 200 worker co-operatives form part of COOPerativa Mondragon, Spain's largest industrial enterprise. Between these two extremes there developed the social democratic movement that was to have a lasting impact on the evolution of modern Europe, and the co-operative movement itself which took hold not within the formal institutions of state but in the organizations and institutions of civil society.

In their volume on the history of economic thought Ernesto Screpanti and Stefano Zamagni draw out the source of this polarity in socialist thought.[19] In their view, it is rooted in ambivalence to the economic principles present in the social relation between labor and capital. In the traditional socialist view, the liberation of labor entails the abolition of this social relationship. But the project has two faces. On the one side it can be seen as a plan for the abolition of profit and capital. On the other, as a project for the liberation of wages and labor. In the first case emphasis is placed on capitalist exploitation while in the second on the alienation of labor.

Systems focusing on the exploitation of labor by capital aspire toward an ideal society capable of ensuring distributive justice (economic equality). Conversely, in models that focus on the alienation of labor the ideal society is one that maximizes individual liberty. Liberty is not a value in the first case. On the contrary, once authority is freed from an association with arbitrary power as personified by the owners of capital, it becomes exalted and purified when related to a centralized organizing command whose purpose is to maximize equality based on merit. In the libertarian conception of socialism, economic equality is a negative value as it is associated with the suppression of natural difference and the unique aspirations of individuals on which a free society is based.

Needless to say, it is the first model of state domination over both the individual and economic life that most often springs to mind when socialism is mentioned. It is the model that dominated socialist philosophy and practice in the twentieth century. But it is not the only one. Libertarian and communitarian alternatives to free market capitalism have also been developed. The most instructive way to understand where a genuine alternative to market capitalism may lie in the long run is to look at how the co-operative model has addressed this classic tension between capital and labor.

Co-operativism and Socialism

The co-operative teachings of Robert Owen, William Thompson and others preceded Marxism as a system of thought advocating collective responses to the problem of wealth creation and distribution. And while the immediate source of the co-operative movement was the effort to redress the injustices of the Industrial Revolution, the overarching intent of the movement was the creation of an ideal society, one that was inclusive of all social classes and freed of the inequities associated with unbridled capitalism. It is for this reason that Marx and Engels coined the term Utopian Socialism to describe Owenism and the other precursors to the "scientific socialism" embodied in Marxism.

Despite their criticism, Marx and Engels respected Owen. Like Owen, Engels was himself an industrialist whose family owned spinning concerns in Manchester. When he arrived there in 1842 to serve his apprenticeship in his father's cotton factory, Engels became acquainted first hand with the desolation and misery that defined the living conditions of the working class in Victorian England. He chronicled his experiences in *The Conditions of the Working Class in England in 1844*, a classic of social anthropology and the foundation for what later came to be his long collaboration with Marx. It was in Manchester that Engels came in contact with Owen's co-operative work. Manchester at this time was the epicenter of industrial England, its factories and mills the laboratories where the Industrial Revolution was invented. It was also here, during a visit to the city, that Marx encountered and was influenced by the ideas of William Thompson.

By this time, New Lanark had been operating for some 30 years. It had become a place of pilgrimage for reformers, educators, politicians and philosophers not only from England but from across Europe and the United States. It was on the itinerary of genteel tours that brought the curious and the socially concerned alike. Owen's followers had been propagating the co-operative message in a kind of religious zeal that included the building of Halls of Science where lectures on Owen's ideas were held along with the singing of socialist hymns. Engels visited one of these and was thereafter much influenced by the idea and practice of co-operativism. It was Engels who introduced Marx to the movement.

Marx and Engels initially saw the co-operative experiment as a practical and realistic step toward the realization of a socialist society. What they criticized was the absence of a class dimension to co-operativism. In its time, they thought, the co-operative idea was appropriate because the conditions for a class-based strategy for revolution were not fully developed. Once they were, by the time they wrote the Communist Manifesto, Marx and Engels considered Owen's co-operative vision obsolete. And so the distinction for them was one of methodology. The differences, however, ran far deeper and they centered on the concept of man and the place of social relations in economics.

In most respects, Marx accepted the operating premises of classical political economy. This included the manner in which the classical theoretical system was based on the analysis of classes and class conflict as depicted by David Ricardo and his contemporaries.[20] Marx followed the classical economists in defining man and classes in strictly economic terms. However, Marx argued, once the capitalist class had secured political power and had put down the revolutionary movements, the situation changed. For the capitalists the threat was no longer the landed aristocracy against which they had revolted, but the working class. This changing political dynamic was then reflected in the theoretical premises of classical economics.

Marx felt that after 1830 a shift in economic thought took place in which it was claimed that the Enlightenment goal of a free society had been achieved since exploitation had come to an end.[21] Class conflict now had no reason to exist. For Marx, the historical role of representing the interests of the whole of society had been betrayed by the bourgeoisie and the mantle of leadership had now passed to the working class and to the socialist economists that spoke for them. But it was a curious inheritance that Marx now claimed. Aside from the transposition of leadership for man's liberation from one class to another, the essential principles that defined the terms of this liberation — the subjection of social and individual reality to the iron rule of economic laws — had not much changed. The dictatorship of the proletariat, that brutal phrase, was only a distorted mirror image of capitalist society. Aside from that, one might ask what kind of liberation it is that subjects humankind to laws over which it has no control. This fatalism remains an enduring element of economics to our present day.

Marx, it turns out, was too alike his economist predecessors to offer a conception of man and society that was truly transformative and capable of humanizing economics. In effect, by upholding the viewpoint of opposing classes, liberals and Marxists stood for identical propositions.[22] Marx's revolutionary manifesto was a mechanism for freezing forever, through the logic of class, the forces that subjected all human and social life to economics.

Marxism and co-operativism were to take two very different paths in the long march toward a truly social economics. Marxism, rooted in the ideas of historical materialism on the one hand and revolutionary class struggle on the other, rejected the market as an instrument of capitalist exploitation. In this, it broke radically from the liberal tradition. But it was a move that drove Marxism headlong into the authoritarianism that was later embodied in the state's centralized control over markets and its waging of a futile — one might say mythical — class war. The Marxist view of society as a battleground of permanently opposing, and mutually exclusive, classes was an apocalyptic vision that demanded the extinction of all opposition. Authoritarianism and class violence were, and remain, the twin plagues of Marxism as its ideology became flesh in the real world. Indeed, Marxism's claim that it was "scientific" was from the start an attempt to monopolize socialism. That terrible claim to absolute truth that was later to warp the hearts and minds of millions through ideology was also the rationale for the atrocities of Lenin, Stalin, Mao and countless other lesser tyrants. The ideological seeds of that unspeakable violence were there from the beginning. Marxism, and its various

anti-market derivatives, was never interested in democratizing economies. It merely dreamt of replacing the dictatorship of capital with a dictatorship of labor, as if having suffered exploitation conferred on labor
an intrinsic virtue. It was yet another in the long chain of populist myths
that deferred the hard, patient work required for making economics an
open, democratic and ethical field for human endeavor.

The failure to understand the essential value of the social dimension
by the later socialist projects that eclipsed co-operativism proved to be
catastrophic when combined with the coercive power of the state. The
devaluing of society as a whole in favor of class was a precondition for
human suffering on a scale that exceeded the evils of the capitalism that
socialism sought to replace. The contempt for the principle of democracy
and the value of the individual also flowed from the adoption of a class-
based ideology and this, in turn, justified the worst excesses of socialist
totalitarianism.

The trajectory of the co-operative movement was entirely different. It
was characterized by localized, smaller-scaled efforts to understand and
control market forces toward social ends. Co-operativism viewed the
market as an instrument equally amenable to social and communitarian
control as it was to control by capital. Co-operativism, in general, stayed
away from a program of political control. It had little interest in state
power. Its focus was social and practical. But avoidance of confrontation
with established power, the refusal to acknowledge the inevitable need to
use force in the struggle for social change, the fatal evasion of the realities
of political power which traced back to Owen himself, were signal weaknesses of the movement. They remain weaknesses still. Nevertheless, it
was this more modest, pluralist, apolitical aspect of the movement that
in the end carried it farther and made it more durable than Marxism's
more militant strategy. At the time, it would have been hard to predict.
There was an undeniable power and magnetism to the Marxist message
that favored its ascendance during the political ferment of the time.

The appeal of Marxism lay ultimately in the compelling power and
simplicity of its narrative. Marxism claimed to be a theory that seemed
woven into the sinews of history. Historical materialism was a story in
which the emancipation of the working class was a historical certainty.
Capitalism was destined to collapse and the seeds of its destruction lay
in the nature of the system itself, like a disease. History itself was on the
side of the oppressed and their triumph was only a question of time. It

was the millennial religious myth secularized and tethered to the operations of economics. This grand, unifying narrative provided a huge advantage over co-operativism which never produced an emancipation story on such a scale. Neither did the gradualist and pacifist quality of co-operativism answer to the primal lust for retribution. For those who required a redemption story and a rationale for action on an apocalyptic scale, Marxism was potent fuel for revolutionary fire.

The second advantage of Marxism lay in how its teachings lent themselves to a mass movement. It conceived of social reform as a phenomenon that transcended individual relationships and was played out as a titanic struggle between classes on the canvas of history. By contrast, co-operativism was a project of reform proceeding from the transformed nature of relationships between actual people. Its scale was of necessity local and communal, and required the interplay of face-to-face relationships. Even today, this is the one feature that represents the co-operative movement's greatest strength and also its greatest challenge in a global era.

Despite its ascendance to political power across geographic regions representing billions of people, the Marxist project failed. Today this failure symbolizes vindication for capitalism on the one hand, and an eclipse of hope for an alternative on the other. But neither is justified. Capitalism has entered an era of deep disaffection in the industrialized west where its sharpest critics have received in full measure what capitalism has to offer and, more urgently, in those developing nations where the struggle for alternatives echoes the same struggles that characterized the rise of capitalism at the dawn of the industrial age in England.

The reasons for socialism's collapse have been pondered over endlessly since the fall of the Berlin Wall. They are worth recalling here, in at least one version of them, if only to reflect on where the prospects for humane, lasting avenues for reform may lay for the future. And it is also worth remarking that unless such alternatives are found, socialism will not have collapsed for long. The rise of neo-socialist regimes in Latin America such as that of Hugo Chavez in Venezuela display all the familiar trappings of the authoritarian impulse — the rhetoric of class struggle, the military attire, the recasting of Cold War animosities. It would appear that if history has one lesson to offer it is that the sufferings of the past, no matter how appalling, are always preferable to the sufferings of the present.

The first cause for the demise of socialism was the demise of the working class itself. Contrary to Marx's prediction, the working class in industrialized nations did not grow — it morphed into a middle class that benefited from what capitalism offered. Traditional class divides blurred. And even as the distance between the rich and the rest grew to astronomical proportions, there arose a degree of mobility that was unthinkable in the Victorian era. True, the middle class was still a wage-earning class and a permanent underclass came into being as well. But the conditions of wage earners today are not those that sparked the revolutionary discontent of the 1800s and the early 1900s.

Second, society has changed and so have our ways of living. One of the most revolutionary aspects of the twentieth century was the individualization of society. People stopped seeing themselves as members of a class. Life came to be lived as a personal pursuit in which the individual controlled the outcome. The language of class no longer seemed relevant. What is more, individualization resulted in the rejection of conformism — a fatal shift in attitudes that doomed a system that was based on crude paradigms of mass psychology.

Third, a spirit of anti-authoritarianism had steadily grown not only in industrial societies but also in socialist states. The suffocating control of the state became an unbearable, and ultimately unsustainable, psychological weight. The growing exposure of the socialist populations to the cultural products of the West proved to be a deadly corrosive to state control. They were banned but still seen and heard, all the while remaining tantalizingly beyond reach. (The Beatles' *White Album*, smuggled into the Soviet Bloc and listened to in clandestine gatherings, had a pivotal effect on the evolution of values that contributed to the fall of the Soviet Union.)

Finally, and perhaps most fatally, the socialist economies simply failed to produce the goods. The economies of the Soviet Union, the Eastern Bloc, China — they all failed to develop beyond the first machine age so long as they pursued the traditional socialist paradigm. Vast acreages of heavy industries churning out tractors, bad cars, exploding television sets,[23] and military hardware were not equipped to generate the transition to an electronic and digital world and the wealth that seemed to accompany it. People simply wanted what the West had.

In short, socialism in the Marxist mould became fossilized. It was unable to adapt to a world that was changing in ways its ideology could never have predicted. By contrast, capitalism proved to be infinitely more flexible, more creative, more adaptable to the changing conditions of the times. And this is not surprising. Most of these changes were prompted by the expansion and consolidation of capitalism itself. This capacity for self-reinvention and -regeneration remains among its greatest strengths.

The movement for social democracy, however, fared far better. It did so because, unlike Marxism, it recognized that markets had a role in economic and social progress, and because it accepted the possibility that common cause might be made with liberals and that through the democratic process a more humane economic order might be brought into being. It was a strategy that transformed and ultimately humanized the face of Europe.

Socializing Capital

The intellectual father of the movement for a peaceful or evolutionary path to social democracy was Eduard Bernstein. Born into a Jewish family in 1850 in Berlin, the son of a railway engineer, Bernstein was the first prominent socialist to question Marxist theory and subject it to a critique based on close observation and analysis of the actual economic and social conditions at the close of the nineteenth century. He too was a political exile, first from Germany and then from Switzerland, ending up finally in London where he became a close friend and collaborator of Engels and the Fabian socialists. Trusted implicitly by Marx and Engels, Bernstein was asked by Engels to edit a fourth volume of *Capital* after Marx's death.

The three were a study in contrasts. Marx, uncompromising, irascible, intellectually merciless and sectarian, was a natural leader and not a little tyrannical. He had no compunction about excommunicating anyone who didn't toe his line. Engels was far more affable. He was also more given to the comforts and pleasures of bourgeois life. He loved fine wine, women, pubs, horse riding, rifle-shooting, was an expert fencer — a sports enthusiast and bon vivant with means. He was also a bohemian, taking a mistress from the working class and ultimately marrying her. Engels was less doctrinaire than Marx and more open to the varieties of ways in which socialism might be realized, including the co-operative communities of Robert Owen. Bernstein was an outgoing, candid, genial man who was averse to violence, whether between nations or between classes, and strove to seek common cause with opponents. Photographs of him reveal a slight, bespectacled, studious-looking man.

Bernstein was a careful observer of the growth of the co-operative movement, both in England and the Continent, and provided a perceptive analysis of the movement's dynamics and its prospects. Unlike the usual belittling treatment of co-operative societies in Marxist literature, Bernstein's analysis was far more objective. He saw in the co-operative movement a means of not only rendering real benefits to workers through the retail of affordable goods by co-operative stores, but more importantly, serving as a means whereby working people might participate in a form of socialism that was amenable to existing values and ideas. This was precisely what other socialists had criticized — the "bourgeois nature" of the movement. Co-operatives had salaried officials, their employees worked for wages, profits were made and dividends were paid out — the conventional trappings of bourgeois enterprises. But it was precisely this quality that made co-operatives accessible. Bernstein recognized that to expect the average working person to suddenly jump into an association that was radically different in its precepts and ways of operating than what he was accustomed to was in itself utopian.

Bernstein was equally perceptive on the failure of the co-operative societies to invest in new production facilities capable of extending the co-operative commonwealth into the wider economy. Unlike other commentators, he shows that lack of capital is not the issue. The British co-operatives were in possession of 24,000,000 pounds — a phenomenal growth in a little over 50 years from the time 28 pounds was invested to create the Rochdale store. This did not take into account the very substantial sums owned by the various friendly societies, mutual associations, building societies, and trade unions. The problem lay elsewhere:

> ...financial means alone will not solve the problem of co-operative work. It needs...its own organization and its own leaders, and neither are improvised. Both must be sought for and tried, and it is, therefore, more than doubtful whether a point of time in which all feelings are heated and all passions excited, as in a revolution, can be in any way conducive to the solution of this problem which has already proved to be so difficult in ordinary times. In human judgment the contrary must be the case.[24]

The task of transforming the co-operative movement from one of merely local or sectoral influence to a force for broad economic transformation raised a problem of competent leadership, trained management, superior organizational capacity and, above all, an autonomous co-operative culture capable of inspiring leaders to lead and followers to follow. Hard enough in times of peace, such a work is unthinkable in times of revolutionary turmoil. It is a process that takes time and painstaking work. As Bernstein remarked, "Co-operative associations capable of living do not allow themselves to be produced by magic or to be set up by order; they must grow up. But they grow up where the soil is prepared for them."[25]

Bernstein might have used these very words to warn against the forced establishment of co-operatives by socialist states in the years that followed. The effects were disastrous. Co-operatives depend for their existence on the willing and informed collaboration of their members for purposes of mutual benefit. Enforced co-operation is not just a contradiction in terms. It reveals either contempt for, or incomprehension of, the nature of freedom and reciprocity in democratic associations. In either case, the result is the destruction of the co-operative form and the collapse of the enterprise once state patronage comes to an end, as it always does.

Bernstein stood at the transition point between the end of one stage of the co-operative movement and the start of another. He was witnessing the first flowering of the co-operative ideal as a practical possibility.

Stages of Co-operation

The co-operative model, and the movement more generally, has always been in a state of evolution, adapting and transforming according to the conditions and contexts in which it finds itself. In its first stage, lasting from 1817–1840, co-operation was at the heart of a visionary social impulse.[26] Philosophers and activists struggled to develop the co-operative ideal of the good society and to put this ideal into practice. It was a period when many were persuaded that co-operation was the gateway to a new millennium, a kind of paradise on earth. To this end, hundreds of co-operative communities were established in a grand social experiment spanning countries and continents to discover a model for a just and humane society. Robert Owen was one of these pioneers and his own efforts to create a functioning co-operative community became the model for others that followed in the United Kingdom, France and other parts of Europe, and the United States. Most of these efforts failed.

The second stage of the movement was marked by a shift from the ideal to the pragmatic and by the successful application of the co-operative idea directly to the market by groups like the Rochdale Society of Pioneers. This was in the period between 1844 and the turn of the century. It was at this time that large segments of England's working and artisan classes felt the impacts of the international commercial systems that were to form the first wave of a globalization process that has today become the dominant reality of world markets. Then, just as today, capital sought the cheapest means of producing goods through automation and by locating production in low cost areas, close to cheap labor and resources. The effect of this process on the textile industry in England was profound and the displacement of skilled weavers by machine production was the spark that ignited the start of the consumer co-op movement at Rochdale. Prior to World War I the Raiffeissen movement in Germany also took root, creating the co-operative credit societies that became a model for credit unions that spread around the globe.

The third stage of the movement was the period from World War I to the 1960s when the co-op model took root in countries the world over and expanded to fuel the creation of thousands of co-operatives in every sector of national economies. In the Netherlands and Scandinavia large sections of agriculture were transformed through co-operative forms of production that to this day maintain a major share of agricultural production. In France industrial worker co-operatives finally established a bridgehead in manufacturing and a sizeable consumer co-op movement also arose. In Italy the co-operative movement developed a unique capacity to bridge sectors and to transform the manner in which the mainstream capitalist economy functioned across entire regions of the country. It was at this time too that the credit unions, consumer co-ops and agricultural marketing co-operatives took root in the United States, English Canada and Quebec.

In most countries, the consumer co-op remained the most influential form of the model, followed by agricultural co-ops, credit unions and worker co-ops. As the co-operative movements grew, however, and the co-op form became more and more adapted to the market realities of specific industries, the original vision of a co-operative community and the creation of a co-operative commonwealth became marginalized by the main currents of co-operative development. Co-op success in practical terms seemed to come with the sacrifice of the unifying and comprehensive vision of co-operation as a medium for a just economy on a societal scale. In many places, co-operative culture and practice reflected more and more the conventional attitudes and practices of firms in the industries where co-operatives operated. Instead of challenging and changing mainstream practice, many co-ops ended up borrowing from it. The regeneration of co-operative culture inside these organizations was stifled by the termination of co-op education programs, a mainstay of co-operative principles. In many industrialized nations, the co-operative movement entered a phase of conservatism.

Thousands of co-operatives were also created in countries like the Ukraine, Poland and Hungary before state socialism extinguished their autonomy and usurped the co-op model for state purposes. With the rise of centralized socialism in the USSR, Eastern Europe, Asia and parts of Africa, co-operatives became the instrument of choice to implement state policies for production and economic development. Voluntary co-operation was replaced by mandated co-operation. And so it came about that centralized socialism became far more damaging to the integrity of the co-op idea and the realization of its potential than capitalism itself. To this day co-operatives in many of these countries signify little more in the minds of the populace than instruments of state coercion. It is a tragedy of economic and human misuse whose negative effects are still being felt.

During the 1960s and after, the dominance of the consumer co-operatives was challenged by the ascendance of new co-op forms such as producer co-ops, and the vision of a new world order of a co-operative commonwealth gradually receded. In Canada a new openness to social intervention on the part of the state resulted in the creation of a co-op housing movement through skillful and determined lobbying on the part of Canadian co-ops and their allies in the labor and social justice movements. The co-operative movement experienced a new wave of growth as popular attitudes in the West become more open to alternative ways of viewing and being in the world. The rise of the New Left rejected orthodox socialist ideas and pushed for the creation of more democratic and inclusive alternatives in politics, economics, culture and social life. National co-operative movements became more diverse. In Canada and the US co-ops sprung up like mushrooms to open the way to whole new industries in health food, organics and housing, and the original ideal of the co-operative community was recast in the form of communes, co-operative farms and the rise of the environmental movement. It was an era of experimentation and new divides opened up within the traditional co-operative movement that were both generational and attitudinal. At an institutional level, the lack of attention to new and emerging forms of the co-operative model slowed the development of co-operative theory and its relevance to changing times.

Beginning in the eighties a new stage emerged for the co-operative movement. It builds on the visionary roots of its founders, while moving beyond the industrial and retail models that had conditioned the growth of co-operatives as an alternative for the organization of enterprises. In the West, with the retreat of many governments from the support of public services that followed in the cost-cutting and privatization decades of the eighties and nineties, co-operatives arose to fill the gaps in human and social services. The provision of social care emerged as one of the fastest growing areas for new co-op development all across industrialized societies.

But the most significant feature of the current stage of the co-op movement's evolution is the rediscovery and reinvention of co-operatives in developing countries, often as a direct response to the destabilizing effects of globalization. Today, the co-operative vision is contending at a global level with factors that in many ways mirror the conditions of the early co-operatives of newly industrialized England. Like then, a single worldview in the form of the free market doctrine has come to dominate both the theory and practice of economics and public policy. Like then, individuals, communities and entire nations are subjected to the narrow interests of tiny elites with catastrophic consequences to individual lives, the environment and the well-being of societies. And like then, the effects of globalization are forcing communities and nations to seek alternatives that can make the market work for the many, not just the few. With the global economy in crisis and the old financial order in disarray, with the free market idea in disrepute and with the corruption bred by the absence of democratic institutions in the political and the economic arenas, viable alternatives to the free market myth have never been more urgently needed than now.

CHAPTER 3

Co-operation Italian Style

Bologna is the red city. The stone-set streets, radiating out from the city center like a web, are lined with ancient arcades that end in a long, graceful row of arches that flows out past the medieval gate of Porta Saragossa to the hilltop church of San Luca which keeps watch over the town below. From here, at sunset, one can watch the city glow like embers as the distinctive rust red of the walls and walkways and terra cotta tiles take in the setting rays of the sun.

The deep red of its walls is one reason for the city's nickname. Its politics is the other. Bologna comprises the buckle of what has come to be called Italy's Red Belt (*la zona rossa*) — the territory that stretches across the middle span of the country from Ravenna in the east to Genoa in the west. Bologna is the capital of the region of Emilia Romagna, which, along with the regions of Tuscany, Umbria and Le Marche to the south, constitutes this singular geography of socialist history, political thought and culture in Italy.

For the millions of visitors that arrive here annually, its food, fashion and art, along with its stunning landscapes, conjure a beauty and quality of life that is the envy of the world. And so it should be. Few regions have blended economic prosperity, natural and architectural beauty and rich cultural endowment with such enchanting effect. But the blessings that seem so much a part of this place have been hard won through a bitter and protracted struggle for political power that sixty years ago had severed the region, and Italy itself, in two. Divided by the political fault lines of left and right, socialism and fascism, Italy was in the grip of a national schism whose repercussions are still being played out. Nowhere did this struggle have a more lasting, and surprising, outcome than Bologna and Emilia Romagna.

With a population of four million, Emilia Romagna is one of Italy's 20 administrative regions. The River Po, the region's lifeblood, runs east from the central spine of the Apennine range and deposits the rich alluvial silt that has made Emilia Romagna the breadbasket of Italy. South of the river and transversing the region from east to west runs the Emilian Way. This ancient Roman road is now a major thoroughfare with the region's key towns and cities spaced tidily along its length at 30-kilometer intervals.[1] Bologna is situated midway and is today a major commercial and transportation hub, its train station a linchpin linking rail lines to destination points across the country.

Emilia Romagna is Italy's most prosperous region and Bologna among its wealthiest and best governed cities. The per capita income of the region's residents is the country's highest, unemployment is the nation's lowest, the distribution of wealth the most egalitarian, and its products — among the world's most coveted brands — account for the second highest proportion of Italy's total exports. This is the home of Ferrari cars and Ducati motorcycles, of Parmesan cheese and Parma ham, and of the 400,000 small, bustling firms that flourish in this economic hothouse. The intensity of the region's entrepreneurial activity is staggering. There is one enterprise for every ten inhabitants. The continuing success of these enterprises have made Emilia Romagna a classic case study for understanding the mechanics of a successful small-firm economy. At the foundation of this economic powerhouse and a key reason for its success, is the world's most successful and sophisticated co-operative economy. It represents one of the very rare examples, perhaps unique in the world, of the co-operative model migrating out of the co-operative movement to shape the organization and operating mechanics of the surrounding capitalist economy. The result is an economic model that includes co-operative and capitalist firms alike in a system that allows small and medium firms to compete globally through the use of co-operation as an industrial strategy. The Emilian Model as it has come to be known, is the antithesis of large-scale corporate capitalism and its most compelling small-firm alternative.

The formal co-operative economy in Emilia Romagna is extensive and highly diversified. Here I am using the term "co-operative economy" to denote co-operative enterprises and the relationships and institutions that link them together as a sector within the broader economy.[2] Collectively, 8,000 co-operative enterprises account for 40 percent of the region's gross domestic product (GDP). Most of these are small or medium in size, like the capitalist firms of the region. However, some are sizable and are among the region's largest enterprises. These typically belong to the Lega di Cooperative e Mutue (the Federation of Co-operatives and Mutual Societies) or "Lega" as it is best known. The Lega is one of the three main co-operative federations which, like most everything else in Italy, are historically associated with one or another of Italy's political parties.

The Lega was the first federation to be formed and the biggest, with its roots in the socialist movement and in particular the former Communist Party of Italy (PCI). The second largest, ConfCooperative, is associated with the Christian Democratic Party and the Catholic Church. AGCI (Associazione Gruppe di Cooperative Imprese) is aligned with the liberal and republican political tradition. The trade unions too, trace their allegiances to the individual political currents of the country and their federations are historically associated with one or another political movement. In recent years, following a protracted political upheaval in the mid 1990s in which the old political parties were disbanded and new configurations came into being, Italy's co-operatives formally severed their political party ties. But the historical antecedents of left and right, socialism, Catholicism and republicanism have left a fading imprint on each of the movement's federations and their members.

Although co-operatives are present in nearly all the key sectors, they predominate in construction, agriculture, food processing, wine making, transport, retail, machine production, housing and social services. Sixty percent of the region's inhabitants are members of at least one co-op and fully ten percent of Bologna's residents work for a co-operative. In other cities that rate is even higher. In Imola, located just a half-hour southeast of Bologna, most of the main enterprises, both commercial and social, are co-operatives. In this region of 100,000 inhabitants, 54,988, or 50 percent are stockholders in the area's 115 co-operatives.[3] Over 60 percent of the town's GDP comes from its co-operatives.[4]

The role of co-operatives in Emilia Romagna has not been restricted to the commercial economy. Italian co-operatives have led a paradigm shifting reform in the production and delivery of social care. In Chapter Five we will explore more fully the significance of this movement for the future of public services, the state and the social economy. In Emilia

Romagna, and Bologna in particular, the rise of social care co-operatives marks a major advance in the theory and practice of co-operative enterprise. Social co-ops hold the keys to a fundamental rethinking of public services, to the reform of state paternalism with respect to civil society and to a seminal new role for the social economy.

As in so many other places, Italy's first co-operative was a consumer co-operative founded in Torino in 1854, just ten years after the inception of the co-op store in Rochdale. In 1856, a glass production co-op was established in Altire and in 1861 the first credit co-op was established in Lodi. From this point on, the co-op model flourished and by 1886 there were enough co-operative societies to warrant the establishment of the Lega Nazionale, Italy's first co-operative federation.

The precursors of the co-operative societies were the friendly societies which, as in Britain, preceded the creation of formal co-operative enterprises. These societies had already taken root in Piemonte, the region just north of Emilia Romagna where the political culture and regional constitution were proto-democratic and allowed for the creation of mutual associations. Elsewhere in Italy in the early 1800s governments were absolutist and prohibited the free association of citizens. The south of Italy, for example, was under the control of the Bourbon monarchy until the late 1800s. This diverse political culture was characteristic of a fragmented land that was not united as a country until 1861. Political diversity played a decisive role in how the co-operative movement was to evolve, and how very different social conditions influenced regional patterns of industrial and economic development. The differences are most evident between the north and the south of the country and will be obvious to anyone traveling across Italy today.[5]

In Emilia Romagna, the organization of agriculture along the Po valley and the struggle over control of the land was central in the evolution of co-operation in the region. One factor in the spread of a co-operative culture was the inescapable necessity of water management along the Po valley. The building of canals and dykes, the drainage of swamp areas, the reclamation of land — all these works established relationships of mutual aid and collective action that extended across classes and regions. The region's agricultural economy and its system of shared land use and management was the material basis of the light manufacturing economy that arose there; its social and production relationships evolved into a pattern of co-operative industrial organization.[6]

Throughout much of central Italy agriculture was based on share-cropping, a farming system in which the landowner provided the land while tenant farmers provided the labor under agricultural contracts that were renewed annually. Sharecropping was an additional source of rural co-operative traditions that formed a basis for the extension and evolution of co-operative economic practices throughout the economy.

In Emilia Romagna, sharecropping was used in combination with contract and day labor. Unlike absentee landlords, landowners in the sharecropping system were actively involved in the affairs of the farm and shared expenses with the tenants. Farmers were required to submit 50 percent of their crop as rent along with other favors and services, in-cluding subjection to the landlord. In return, the landlord was bound to the care and protection of his sharecroppers. The relationship between landlord and sharecropper was direct, mutually dependent and paternal-istic. Among much of the aristocracy the attitude toward the peasantry was one of benevolent dictatorship. Landowners exercised considerable power over their tenants' lives, including the approval of marriages and control over whether a tenant could work off the estate, while sharecrop-pers enjoyed a security of tenure that gave them the status of a privileged caste in contrast to those peasants, contract and day laborers, with no security on the land.[7]

In addition to the mutual dependence of landlord and tenant, there was an extensive network of co-operation and mutual aid among sharecropping families. One example was the *auitarella*, the traditional exchange of labor between families at crucial moments of the agricul-tural calendar. Another was the *fattoria*, the group of buildings that constituted the center of production at the heart of the estate. Estates were subdivided into a number of sharecropper farms and the *fattoria* was where farmers shared use of large agricultural equipment, the olive presses, the wine vats. Here too, was where the overall plans for the es-tate were drawn up.

Despite its paternalism and exploitative elements, the old sharecrop-ping system in Emilia Romagna established a pattern for work and so-cial relations that was highly mutualistic and sustained a social harmony extending across classes that was widely acknowledged and admired. It established a pattern of co-operation, especially among the working class, that was to survive and flourish. But rural class harmony was not to last. It came to a bitter and brutal end with the rise of commercial and industrial agriculture at the beginning of the 1900s and the destruction of the old social and economic relations that this entailed.[8] Foremost among these changes was the gradual replacement of sharecropping with untenanted wage labor and the shift of power from landowning nobles to commercial leaseholders who had little interest in preserving the patriarchal patterns of co-operation and accommodation with the peasantry. For the peasantry, this change entailed dispossession and conflict with a new breed of industrial farmer. It also opened deep divisions among the property owners themselves as a new commercial ethic displaced the aristocratic values of land as a cultural and social patrimony. As early as 1881, the agronomist Marchese Luigi Tanari complained that alongside traditional landowners like himself who maintained "the old patriarchal spirit," there intruded the presence of a new breed of farmers "characterized by a greedy industrial spirit which they are injecting into the management of the farms," men whose "principal infatuations are experimental adventures, rents, and profits."[9] It was an epochal transition away from social and cultural values deeply embedded in the land that ultimately required the destruction of land as the repository of cultural values and the foundation of an ancient form of social life and its transformation into a commodity.[10]

By the first decade of the 1900s, unemployment, landless labor, growing militancy and an uncompromisingly hostile attitude on the part of commercial farmers combined to turn the farmlands of Emilia Romagna and Tuscany into battlefields of a rural class war. Socialist organizers and propagandists skillfully exploited the volatile conditions to extend their membership among rural laborers with the result that by the fall of 1919, the Provincial Socialist Federation claimed a membership of 70,000 in the countryside and 16,000 in Bologna, including 40,000 agricultural workers and 9,000 sharecropping families.[11] On their side, the property owners countered with increasing violence and intimidation culminating in the fascist squads of Mussolini. The co-operatives that were formed in this era were instruments of social and political revolution, but also a means of pooling labor and securing scarce employment for landless workers.

Politics are woven deeply into the co-operative fabric of the region. The co-operatives of northern Italy are more than just commercial enterprises. They are social and cultural institutions that grew out of revolutionary ferment. A large number of these co-operatives arose as a response to economic hardship in a way that the capitalist firms did not. Some of the largest and most influential trace their beginnings to the early 1900s when the region was still poor and before the onset of the "economic miracle" that accompanied Italy's industrial development in the 1950s and '60s. After the devastation of the World War II, the co-operatives were a central part of the larger political struggle to re-build Italy along socialist lines. The Communist and Social Democratic parties spearheaded this effort throughout Italy and land reform was an essential part of it.

During the war, Italy's peasants were promised land. When the war ended and the promised reforms failed to materialize, landless peasants throughout Italy became militant. In the south, between 1944 and 1949, the peasant movement created 1,187 co-operatives with a quarter mil-lion members. The co-ops took over more than 165,000 hectares of land in Sicily, Calabria and Lazio.[12] In Emilia Romagna and throughout the Red Belt, tenant farmers finally severed their traditional subservience to the landowning elite and demanded radical changes to the relationship between landlord and tenant. They were joined by a growing army of the landless poor that now constituted the majority of agricultural workers. Throughout this struggle, the PCI led the action to organize farmers along with the CGIL, the region's largest trade union. Activists worked tirelessly organizing meetings in the evenings, going from farmhouse to farmhouse, and building up the region's peasant and co-operative associ-ations. The lasting association of the Communist Party and the region's co-operatives date from this time.

And so the significance of the region's co-operatives resonates with deep political and social overtones. During World War II, many of their members were on the front lines in the resistance movement. Bologna was at the heart of the fight against fascism. The faces of the partisans that perished in this struggle still look out from the grainy images that are mounted on the wall of the municipal hall facing Bologna's main plaza, the Piazza Maggiore. Some died in action. Many were simply ex-ecuted. But it was in Bologna where the first major overthrow of Nazi forces by the partisans took place on April 27, 1943. The images of the city's liberation from fascist control also form part of the tableau on the same municipal wall.

Yet Emilia Romagna, like Italy itself, was a region divided. Forli, the birthplace of Mussolini, is just a short drive southeast of Bologna. Italian fascism was born here. The mechanistic, modernist lines of fascist era monuments still stand as a not-too-distant echo from that time. And throughout Italy, if one visits the flea markets and antique fairs, there is an abundance of fascist memorabilia for sale in a way that would be quite unthinkable in Germany. This is one sign of Italy's continuing ambivalence about its fascist past. The fact that Mussolini is still respected here in some quarters, that he never became the demonic figure that Hitler was to become, is another.[13] (On a slightly more bizarre, if characteristic note, the Italians also have a penchant for labeling wines with dictators' portraits. You can find souvenir vintages with the figures of Mussolini, Hitler and Stalin glaring out from the labels of assorted special blends. One can express one's finer culinary sensibilities right along with one's authoritarian proclivities whether they run to Stalinism on the left, or Nazism on the right.) But to return to the main point, just as Emilia Romagna served as the founding home of the fascist movement so was it the center of the most passionate opposition. And with the rising tide of totalitarianism, the region's co-operatives remained a defiant thorn in the side of fascist power.

The Fascist Repression

Mussolini's fascist squads unleashed a persecution campaign against the co-operatives and trade unions from the earliest days of the fascist movement. Emilia Romagna's co-operatives were torched by the blackshirts, their leaders jailed, beaten up or assassinated, their organizations destroyed in the protracted night of fascist rule in Italy. The following excerpt from a telegram sent to the Prime Minister by a local Deputy in Bologna vividly captures the stark violence of this time:

> Must report to your Excellency the very grave situation which has been created in the town of Budrio. Terrorized by an unpunished fascist squad using clubs, revolvers, etc. Union organizers and municipal administrators forced to leave for fear of death. Workers forced to lock themselves at home because of beatings and threats of beatings. Unions and socialist club ordered to dissolve themselves within 48 hours or face physical destruction. Life of the town is paralyzed, authorities impotent. Mass of the workers request energetic measures to protect their freedom of association and personal safety.[14]

Still, the co-operatives managed to survive. Sensing that he could not neutralize the co-operatives through intimidation alone, in 1926 Mussolini established the Co-operative Board of Control and annulled the autonomy of the co-operatives forcing them to accept fascist overseers and to join ENTE, his own fascist co-operative association. Fascist unions were also set up by local bosses who recruited landless laborers and sharecroppers by rewarding them with a job or even a piece of land which the leaders of the fascist squads had little difficulty in extracting from their patrons, the local landowners.[15] It is also true that Mussolini, despite the fearsome reputation of fascism as a ruthlessly efficient repression machine, had a difficult time consolidating power over his own movement; it took at least seven years from the time he seized power.[16] It was a typical Italian recalcitrance and a constant source of frustration for Il Duce, who was given to complaining that he was the least obeyed dictator in Europe.[17]

Hundreds of co-operatives lost their best leaders in the battle they waged to protect their freedom. Their survival today is not merely an economic success story. It is a triumph of immense political and social significance for the people of this region. When the war finally ended and Italy was picking up the pieces of a shattered nation, the signal importance of the co-operative movement to the democratic idea was written into the founding principles of the constitution of the new republic. It was a remarkably radical document. Article 45 recognizes the right of co-operative associations to exist, to remain free and independent democratic organizations and to receive the recognition and support of the state. (Article 46 recognizes the right of workers to collaborate in the running of their workplaces while Article 4 recognizes the "right to work" for all Italians.)

It is not easy to overstate the magnitude of this accomplishment. When Mussolini came to power the co-operative movement was a source of resistance not just in the political arena but also in the structures of the economy itself, where co-operatives flourished in the numberless towns and villages of the region. Their power and influence was not merely ideological. They were a source of employment and pride, producing goods and services that were essential to their communities and conveying to their members a solidarity of purpose that was woven into their day-to-day lives in tangible, visible ways.

In Ravenna, on the Adriatic coast, there is a worker co-operative called CMC (*Co-operative Muratore e Cemintiste*) — the Co-operative of Masons and Builders. It was established in 1901 by 35 workers as a small association of manual laborers working in construction. It is today a leading international engineering firm engaged in major construction projects around the globe. The new subway in Milan and the massive tunneling drills that are being used in the word's largest construction project, the Three Gorges Dam in China, were designed by CMC.

One year I was invited as a guest to the co-operative's annual general meeting. The original stone building is still at the heart of the complex, the former factory site now turned into a cathedral-like open gallery rising up 50 or 60 feet to a vaulted ceiling. A photo display commemorating the co-op's history, its leaders and members, runs round the perimeter of this space. Down the center of this gallery, some 200 feet in length, ran 2 rows of tables laid end to end with enough seating to accommodate 400 or 500 people. The actual meeting took place in an anteroom attached to the hall. The tone was sober and ceremonial, and commenced with a reading of the co-operative's founding charter. This was followed by a call for the formal approval and consent of the membership to the articles of the charter. The social bond that commits the membership to the mission of the co-op is thus brought to mind and renewed every year as it has for one hundred and seven years.

Following the business meeting the assembled group moved to the hall where scores of people had already been gathering. This is where the real meaning of the co-operative became manifest. Coursing in through the doors and finding their way to friends and fellow workers was a microcosm of Ravenna itself. Young and old, professionals, laborers, men, women, children, entire families came in such a spirit of camaraderie and celebration that it was clear the co-operative was an institution whose connections among its members and the community delved far deeper and broader than its operations as an enterprise. As wine flowed and food was shared out and the simple joy of fellowship filled the gallery, the gathering evoked a sense of something very grand — and far bigger than itself. It was history, community and a pride of purpose that had lasted over generations. The co-operative no longer belonged just to the members. It was a patrimony of the whole community. Seated there along the tables were all the generations that had been part of this story: the current membership, their sons and daughters — many of whom would also join the co-op — and most poignantly the elders, the old men and women now in their eighties and nineties, who were still voting members. Their connection to this co-op was now as much a part of their inmost identity as their church or their family. This same astonishing scene has been replicated, year in and year out, in thousands of co-operatives large and small, across the length and breadth of Italy.

The co-operative movement in Emilia Romagna has earned a commanding presence in the economy and culture of the region. Co-operatives in Emilia Romagna are no longer marginal alternatives to the mainstream economy. They have become a determining force in the mainstream. In every key industry, co-operatives play a central role. And while some have retained their strictly regional presence, many have now vaulted to the international stage with operations in countries around the world. Emilia Romagna is home to some of the world's most successful international co-ops. Their experience is a key reference for understanding the unique challenges of running a successful co-operative on a global scale.

Like CMC in Ravenna, SACMI is a worker co-op whose origins began just after the First World War. Imola, where the co-op was founded, is a veritable hive of co-operative activity. Walking along the clean, lively streets of this medieval town one is struck by the congruence of the ancient and the new. The artisan food shops bulging with hanging prosciutto hams and jars of spiced honey and thick wheels of parmesan thrive among the palazzos and piazzas of the historic center, which in turn blend gradually into the light industrial districts of the periphery. The prosperity of the town is palpable. But its major industries, much of the housing, the roads and public infrastructure, the financial services, the social services, the schools, all owe their existence in one way or another to the co-ops that built or operate them. SACMI is among the town's most venerated institutions.

The co-op was established in December 1919 by a group of nine young unemployed mechanics, all veterans, who founded a mechanical workshop to deal in general construction and repair. Its first administrator was the former mayor of Imola and its headquarters were in premises donated by the town council. Throughout the 1920s the Blackshirts regarded it, quite correctly, as a "dangerous nest of anti-Fascists" and torched it. When the Germans occupied Imola on September 8, 1943, the company dismantled its machinery and hid it in the surrounding countryside to prevent it being taken to Germany. This was a common practice in occupied territory where not only a region's factories were dismantled and sent back to the fatherland but, even more monstrously, a country's topsoil could be stripped and shipped away.[18]

The co-op started up again after 1945 when its mechanics were asked by Cooperative Ceramica, a neighboring ceramics co-op, to repair the tile-making presses that had been destroyed by air raids. SACMI then realized it could produce the pressing machines that the ceramics co-op purchased from Germany. It marked a turning point for the co-op. SACMI tapped into the quickening pace of machine production and industrialization that came with Italy's reconstruction in the fifties and sixties. The co-op soon became Italy's most important designer and exporter of specialized ceramics presses and furnaces as well as a major research center for new ceramic materials. By the 1980s SACMI was designing and building whole ceramics factories to the specifications of clients around the world. Today, SACMI is a new species of global co-op — a hybrid organization that is still owned and directed by its 390 members in Imola, but whose operations include control of 60 capitalist firms, 37 of them abroad, and sales in 100 countries.

Globalization has been good to SACMI and to Imola. The co-op has been able to internationalize its reach while maintaining its local identity. But it has also meant that the co-op idea originally held by its founders has had to evolve to survive. It has meant that the imperatives of global reach have had to be reconciled with the realities of co-op dynamics in a democratic organization. How do mutuality and solidarity among 390 member-owners square against a holding of 60 companies with a work force of 3,000 non-member employees? What kind of co-op is it that operates an international network of companies whose connections with the co-op is one based on strict commercial profit, not reciprocity? How big is too big for a co-op to remain a co-op? These are the questions that co-op visitors to SACMI invariably ask. The answers are not always the comfortable ones that visitors might like to hear. The scale of SACMI's operations and its success as a co-operative enterprise operating on a global scale has meant that the ideals that might be taken for granted for a small, local co-op can't always be applied at this level.

The tension between global scale and co-op identity is perhaps the most difficult of all challenges that the co-op model has to contend with in an era of global markets and it is a question we will return to over the course of this book. For if co-operation is to offer a realistic alternative to corporate capitalism it has to provide a means by which this tension between large scale and localized reciprocity can be resolved. In SACMI, there is a clear-cut distinction between the co-op in Imola and its international operations. The co-op remains an intensely social institution with its sense of place and community remaining paramount in its allegiances. As is the case with CMC and Ravenna, SACMI embodies much of what Imola sees about itself as a flourishing community with a distinct history and a promising future. SACMI's members are quite unsentimental about what it means to survive as an enterprise in a global economy. What matters most is the survival of the enterprise as a co-op. This is one reason why membership is not automatically offered to the 5,000 employees that work in the firms owned by the co-op.[19] What makes SACMI a success as a co-operative enterprise is the quality of the social relations and the solidarity that exists among members. Everything else is based on this, just as it is in other co-ops.

The preconditions to membership in SACMI are stringent. Employees must have worked there for at least five years before they can be nominated for membership. The nominee will then be assessed on the basis of their work ethic, their level of skill and most importantly how they relate to other workers and their capacity for being a committed, contributing, co-operator in a democratic organization. These are traits that can only be observed first hand, from daily contacts with co-workers. They are crucial to the maintenance of the member solidarity that sustains the co-op through tough times. Membership is earned, it is not a right. For the SACMI members the inclusion of unknown individuals as members would mean the end of the co-op, a corrosion of the social bonds that make the co-op what it is. Once, when asked about this distinction between co-op members and the majority of non-member employees, the past president, an old-school partisan warrior, remarked without hesitation that it is better to have a narrow door to membership and have the co-op survive, than to have an open door and have the co-op fail. It is hard to argue the logic of his point. What it raises is how, or whether, to extend this same logic to those workers who could also benefit from the co-op idea in their own faraway places and circumstances. As it is, SACMI is very cognizant of its social and economic role in the communities where it operates. The co-op spends substantial sums in community and social development projects both in Imola and in its locations abroad. One example is its spending $380,000 to build a vocational school for the *meninhos da rua*, the street children of the favela of Sao Bernardo do Campo, a suburb of Sao Paulo in Brazil experiencing an extreme degree of social degradation.

If the conditions of SACMI membership are daunting, so is the cost. The price of membership in SACMI is about $300,000[20] with about half this amount underwriting SACMI capital shares. This is not paid all at once by the member but as a loan by the co-op that is paid back over a 15-year period through salary deductions. If a member leaves before this time the paid amount is returned to him. If the member stays in the co-op this entire amount is returned on retirement along with interest. So a member's investment generates a very substantial retirement package on top of what the employee would earn from the government pension. During the course of his employment the member receives a share in the co-op's surplus on top of his salary. SACMI is unionized and has the highest wage rates and benefits in the industry. In these days of "flexible" work forces, outsourcing and convenience dismissals, a job at SACMI is often a job for life. Unsurprisingly, there is a long waiting list of applicants both for employment and for membership.

Meanwhile, the combination of memberships and the placement of the lion's share of the co-op's annual surpluses in an "indivisible reserve" has allowed the co-op to self capitalize its growth. Italian law requires commercial co-operatives to invest 80 percent of their surplus in a reserve that may not be divided among members. It is a collective and intergenerational patrimony. This cap on the amount of a co-op's surplus that may be distributed among members is the quid pro quo that allows co-ops to be exempted from having to pay income tax on this undivided capital. It was the growth of this capital reserve that prompted the co-op to pursue its acquisition strategy. SACMI, like many other industrial co-operatives that accumulated large indivisible reserves, was able to finance its growth with little or no recourse to outside loans. This type of co-operative capital accumulation, reinforced by legislation, has returned enormous benefits not only to co-op members, but also to the broader community. The indivisible reserve stabilizes the enterprise, encourages ongoing investment in the business, and secures the co-op's future. It is a collective asset that passes down between generations of members and so becomes a social patrimony. The indivisible reserve acts as a major disincentive for hostile takeovers of co-ops by other firms, even if members are prepared to sell, as the reserve reverts to the state if it is not allocated within the co-op sector. Finally, it helps keep the co-op financially autonomous and solvent, especially in hard times. In times of crisis like the present, when access to credit is the primary threat to conventional capitalist firms, the accumulated indivisible reserve is a lifeboat.

The question of scale and co-op identity is sooner or later faced by every co-op that becomes a success, as so presciently noted by Bernstein in the late 1800s. This is especially the case in production co-ops where social relations among workers determines whether and how the decision-making culture of a democratic organization will meet the demands for growth emerging from the marketplace. SACMI has attempted to address this issue by carefully distinguishing the co-op membership in Imola from the commercial operations and relations that are entailed by its foreign acquisitions. The co-op's strategy entails the deployment of capital to serve co-operative — and social — ends, a strategy that has been taken up by other large co-operatives, as we will see below.

SACMI is only one example of an Italian co-operative that has crossed a threshold to an entirely new economic scale, encompassing local, regional and international dimensions. What is most distinctive about the Italian co-operative movement, however, is the degree to which co-operatives in the last 30 years have emerged as dominant players not only in the regional economies of places like Emilia Romagna, Tuscany and Trentino, where they have a tradition of success, but at the national level also. As a group, co-operatives have exceeded capitalist firms in the rate of employees hired, in the scale of operations and in market share of key sectors.[21]

Renaissance of the Italian Co-operatives

Until 1971 Italian co-operatives, although numerous, were of a limited size. But the 1970s marked a turning point for the movement. The model began to take off, accelerating rapidly during the 1990s when co-operatives seem to have capitalized on an accumulation of experience, managerial and strategic skill, the formation of co-operative networks and the skillful deployment of co-operative capital to fuel growth.[22] In 1971 co-operatives with more than 500 employees represented 2.3 percent of all Italian companies of this size. By 2001 this figure had risen to 8.1 percent. This growth among the largest co-operatives is exactly the opposite of the prevailing trend among capitalist firms that shrank in size while co-ops grew.

During the 1990s, the number of people employed by co-operatives in Italy rose by 60 percent against an average of 9 percent for capitalist firms. Co-operatives accounted for one quarter of the total rise in employment in the decade between 1991 and 2001. In particular, the 1991 census gave the number of workers employed by social co-operatives (co-ops providing social care) as 27,510; by the 2001 census, this figure had risen more than fivefold, to 149,147. The overall size of co-operatives also increased in this period, especially among larger co-operatives. For those co-operatives employing between 50 and 1,000 workers, the share of the labor force increased to over 9 percent. This phenomenal growth at the level of the largest enterprises signaled the arrival of the co-operative form as a major force in Italy's business world.[23]

Special mention needs to be made of large-scale retailing, where co-ops are market leaders in Italy. Consumers' co-operatives control 19 per cent of the market while retailer co-ops control an equivalent amount. Together, this means that co-ops control 38 per cent of retailing in Italy, increasing sector integration and market penetration while the rest of the Italian economic system experienced a fragmentation during the same period.[24]

The significance of this evolution of the largest co-operatives for Italy's co-op movement as a whole is crucial. The 105 largest co-operatives represent only 0.15 percent of the total number of co-operatives, but they account for 57 percent of all co-operative members, 34 percent of co-operative turnover, and 22 percent of all co-op employees. Italy's co-operative movement has become larger, more concentrated, more complex and far more powerful within key sectors of the national economy.

How has this happened? How was it that at a time when many Italian enterprises were reducing in size, co-ops flourished and began to dominate in key sectors? And what does this have to say to the conventional notion that co-ops are a marginal form destined to remain small and ineffectual as an economic force?

The answer seems to lie within the ethic and social capital relations among co-operatives themselves once a critical mass of enterprises has been reached. Italian co-operatives mastered the art of mobilizing common interests. In addition, the presence of co-ordinating umbrella institutions capable of forging new partnerships, discerning long-term strategic opportunities at industry levels and mediating the establishment and mobilization of sector-wide resources has been a key factor in the Italian case.

Co-operatives, always given to the creation of mutually supportive networks amongst themselves, raised this strategy to new levels at the end of the 70s and the 80s. They consolidated operations, merged smaller co-ops within larger organizations and forged complex networks that linked co-ops and non co-ops alike around common goals. In key sectors, networked co-operation aggregated smaller enterprises into industry-wide consortia that operated at regional and later national and international levels. One instance that illustrates this networking capacity is the integration and scaling up of the co-op construction sector.

In the early 1900s, agricultural workers created co-operatives to find work and pool the labor of the unemployed, especially in the rural regions as we have already seen. They had already begun to form consortia of smaller construction and labor co-ops at a regional level. But in 1978, the co-ops took a critical step with the merger of the powerful consortia from Bologna (founded in 1912), Modena (1914), and Ferrara (1945) into the *Consorzio Cooperative Costruzione* (CCC). The new organization provided a wide range of business services and supports that were previously beyond the capacity of the smaller co-ops that were its members. It negotiated larger building contracts for which it could co-ordinate labor and specialized services, it handled administrative, financial and legal issues, and it monitored legislative and environmental issues for the sector. It also expanded to cover an operational range far beyond the original area.

A project was then drawn up with the assistance of Legacoop to unite all the existing construction consortia throughout Italy's regions with the CCC in order to co-ordinate Legacoop's development strategy within the construction industry. This was achieved in 1990 with the incorporation of *Consorzio Nazionale Cooperative Approviggionamenti* (ACAM), the National Consortium of Building Supplies Co-operatives. The CCC now has 230 member co-operatives employing 20,000 workers and with a turnover of 230 million euros it is Italy's leading construction enterprise.[25] This co-operative networking strategy has been applied in the co-operative retail sector, in the services sectors, in co-op financial services, in the growing social care sector and more recently in agriculture and food production.

Essential to the expansion of the co-operative model to include the creation of second and third tier co-operative networks and consortia, is the legislative environment that has enabled Italy's co-operatives to grow in this way. The co-op legislation that was drafted in the early 1900s explicitly granted co-operatives the right to create consortia. This is a power that is often denied to co-operatives in other countries. Secondly, as mentioned earlier in the case of SACMI, legislation passed in 1977 granted complete tax exemption to co-op profits designated for indivisible reserves.[26] This power to accumulate untaxed capital greatly aided co-operatives in their ability to capitalize growth. The third factor that played a key role in this process was the passage of legislation in 1983 that allowed co-ops not only to hold shares in joint-stock companies, but also to control them. The measure allowed the formation of co-op-controlled groups as well as the power to raise capital in markets.

The sectoral and regional networking strategy that was pioneered by Italy's co-operatives to such effect was not limited to the co-op sector. It was to play a seminal role in the phenomenal success of the capitalist small-firm economy of Emilia Romagna as well.

But what has emerged in the course of this remarkable story is the challenge posed to the co-op model not by the familiar problems of marginality and lack of power but rather the opposite. Italian co-operatives have shown conclusively that the vaunted efficiency of capitalist firms can be matched — and exceeded — by co-operatives. Provided with the legislative and market tools that enable them to utilize their natural strengths, co-operatives can outperform their capitalist competitors in sectors that were formerly thought to be natural capitalist strongholds such as large-scale construction and engineering, retailing and financial services. As will be outlined in the following chapter, Italy's co-operatives have shown not only that the co-op model is effective at national and even international scales of operation, but also that co-operation is a lifesaving strategy for the survival of small and medium capitalist enterprises as well. But how does the co-op model deal with the challenges of size, the consolidation and concentration of economic power and the unique demands of performing in markets dominated by corporate — and capitalist — rules of the game? This is the unprecedented dilemma faced by the world's most successful co-operative movement and we begin to examine some of the answers in the following chapter.

CHAPTER 4

The Emilian Model and
the Socialization of Capital

It isn't the size of the firms or the particular industrial structures
of the region that make the Emilian Model work. This is just the hardware.
Co-operation is the software that makes the system run.

— OSCAR MARCHISIO —

The co-op system in Emilia Romagna has achieved an internal coherence and integration that is unique. Whether through the power of personal relationships and a shared history, or the pursuit of strategic partnerships among co-operatives, or the creation of sector-wide systems for co-op development, the co-operatives of Emilia Romagna have succeeded in building a powerful, autonomous co-operative economy alongside an advanced capitalist economy. The systems and ideas that sustain this co-op economy are a result of carefully pursued legal, constitutional and political choices. They represent the culmination of a century of struggle. The creation and preservation of the co-operative enterprises that have helped sustain the region represents one aspect of this struggle. The other was the role of the regional government and the regionalization of political power in the 1946 Italian constitution. Even then, it took 30 years before political conditions in Emilia Romagna were to allow the nascent possibilities of the co-op system to blend with the power of regional government to create a co-operative economic model that extended beyond the co-operatives themselves to the economy as a whole.

The first thing that must be evident to anyone traveling across this region is how intensively developed it is. The rich, rolling fields of agriculture are everywhere interspersed with industrial buildings and plants, the landscape a dense matrix of urban and rural patterns in which orchards and vineyards vie for space with the towns and factory buildings that blend seamlessly with each other. Unlike the languid, romantic vistas of Tuscany and Umbria, Emilia Romagna presents the no-nonsense landscape of a region built for work.

The most distinguishing feature of Emilia Romagna's industrial paradigm is the emergence of what has since become a key strategy for the successful development of a small-firm economy — the clustering of small firms in industrial districts. Industrial clusters were perfected in this region and an extensive literature has been devoted to what has come to be known as the Emilian Model. And although the model has undergone significant changes since its inception in the early '70s[1] the pattern of industrial development that it represents remains a unique instance of successful co-operation in a capitalist framework. Here, I wish to concentrate on the connections between this model and the patterns of co-operation, both formal and informal, that are a central aspect of the social and political history of the region.

The co-operation of small firms in industrial clusters is the reason why the firms of the region have continued to thrive despite all expectation to the contrary and in the face of received theories concerning industrial development in a global economy. The Emilian Model proved that firms can remain small and still compete in a global marketplace. The clustering phenomenon of small firms in industrial districts also arose in other regions such as the Rhine in Germany, the Ruhr valley in France and even areas like Silicon Valley and the industrial clusters of Boston and Seattle in the United States. But Emilia Romagna's success became the foremost example of a modern, complex, highly sophisticated small-firm economy that posed an alternative to the gargantuan corporate development epitomized in the industrial models of the United States, the UK and much of Europe. Indeed, the Fordist and Taylorist industrial models from the early 1900s that relied on heavy capital investment, large industrial plants and the regimentation of labor tasks by large work forces never took hold in this region.[2] The traditional artisan production models that had long before been eclipsed by the onset of industrial development in England and elsewhere were maintained in Emilia Romagna. Industrialization here followed a different course, a gradualist path that incorporated and adapted the existing forms and relationships of small-scale production.

Initially, the region's agricultural economy gave rise to the specialized industries that emerged as an extension of its needs. The processing and packaging of food products gave rise to the design of specialized machinery that is still the singular expertise of the area. As early as the first decades of the 1900s, Emilia Romagna led Italy in the application of machine production for food processing and agriculture. Machine production for agriculture then evolved to respond to the unique requirements of a whole host of industries, from ceramics and textiles to surgical equipment and high performance cars.

For example, Bologna is today the world's leader in packaging; its machines package everything from condoms to cigarettes. And as Bologna evolved into a center of packaging, so other areas became specialized in the design and manufacture of products that had a historical connection to those regions. Sassuolo had always been a center of pottery and ceramics production. Photos from the turn of the century depict a cottage industry centered on the farm household. With increasing specialization, the area emerged as the center of a ceramics industry. The small ceramics firms that flourished in this district became manufacturers of the world's finest ceramic tiles. The town of Carpi became a center for the design and manufacture of hosiery and knitwear. Its beginnings were in the production of the region's traditional woven baskets. The machinery that was later applied to weaving baskets from straw was then redesigned for weaving cloth. The small firms of Prato designed and supplied high-quality cloth to Italy's most prestigious fashion houses including Armani, Zegna, Prada and many others. Italy's finest footwear is produced in the region surrounding Ascoli Piceno. Piacenza became famous for its buttons. Parma and Modena became centers of food production and exporters of Italy's most famous food products.

Eventually, over a hundred industrial districts bloomed in Emilia Romagna, each one composed of highly specialized firms clustered around a town or region and producing a characteristic product for export to the rest of Italy and abroad. This is Italy's largest exporting region, accounting for 13 percent of the country's total.[3] The firms have traditionally been small — between 5 and 50 employees — the quality of the products are among world's finest and the target markets are global. How then, given the challenges of diseconomies of scale, fierce global competition, market intelligence and access, capitalization, co-ordination product distribution, could small firms such as these survive, even thrive, in a global market? The answer was co-operation.

The production model of the industrial districts depended on the willingness of local entrepreneurs to co-operate while remaining competitors. It rested also on the involvement of the regional government in understanding the strengths and weaknesses of this system and devising strategies, in partnership with the stakeholders, to allow the system to adapt to internal and external threats. A key to this approach was in understanding that industrial districts are organic economic forms. They are not static, they evolve, and their strength lies in their ability to adapt to the changing needs of their constituent enterprises and to the shifting dynamics of markets and economic forces beyond their control. How this comes about is a combination of political vision, the skillful management of competing interests and the possibilities that are latent in the social relations fostered by a culture of co-operation — the region's social capital.

The role of the regional government in this story is central. It is impossible to understand the evolution of the region's unique economy without reference to the establishment of regional governments by the Italian state in 1975. Regional governments had already been mandated by the republican constitution of 1946. They were to function as a median level of governance between the commune, or municipal level of government at one level, and the federal government in Rome at the other. But the Christian Democratic governments that succeeded each other after the war resisted introducing them. They feared, with good reason, that regional governments would open the doors to a level of government that would be under the control of leftist parties. This was especially true in Italy's Red Belt where the Christian Democrats were perceived as guardians of an economic and political order that was corrupt, clientelistic and devoted to the preservation of privilege, especially for the large industrial concerns that provided the party's economic base. All this changed with the elections of 1976.

The Rise of Regions

The years leading up to the 1976 national vote were Italy's most tumultuous since the end of the war. Everywhere, student uprisings were spilling into the streets, supported by the trade unions and growing public sympathy. Facing fierce, unprecedented political opposition and dropping steadily in their percentage of the popular vote, Christian Democrats agreed to establish the regional government system in Italy as part of the 1976 federal election. In addition to the federal government Italians would vote for regional government representatives in each of Italy's 20 regions. The results of this historic election changed the power map of Italy and installed leftist administrations in Emilia Romagna, Tuscany, Umbria and Le Marche. At the municipal level, all of Italy's major cities were in the hands of leftist administrations, a reprise at a much broader level of the revolutionary results of the 1919 elections. It was a watershed election and Emilia Romagna has been ruled either by a Communist administration or some combination of Social Democratic-Communist coalition since that time. This was the first time that the political left in Italy had the power to enact an economic and social program of its own making at a practical level. It was to find its most powerful expression in the changes that then took place in Emilia Romagna with the Communist Party acting as the central organizing and mediating political force in the region. What ensued provides a blueprint for how governments can play a catalytic role in analyzing, mediating and mobilizing strategic interests in the building of a regional small-firm economy.

One of the first tasks of the new regional administration was to create a mechanism through which the regional economy as a whole could be understood, its strengths and weaknesses diagnosed and a program of development established. It created an economic planning and development agency, ERVET, that has had a lasting impact on the development of the region's strategic sectors. ERVET was a public-private agency funded and directed by a partnership between the regional government and its key allies among business, labor and academic institutions. It undertook a careful analysis of the regions' key economic sectors, diagnosed the particular strengths and weaknesses of the firms comprising these sectors and established a series of service centers to provide strategic assistance to the firms and the industrial districts of which they were a part. While the particular services provided by each service center were tailored to the needs of the sector in which they operated — ceramics, agricultural machinery, footwear, clothing, etc. — the overall strategy was the same: to increase the productive capacity and competence of individual firms and to ensure that the linkages between firms in the industrial districts remained strong and were further mobilized to strengthen the system as a whole. Some of these service centers (ASTER, Democentre) were engaged exclusively in research, training and technology transfer.

Most importantly, the service centers were structured on a co-operative model. They were funded through a mix of ERVET funds and member fees and directed by elected representatives of the firms that used their services. This ensured that the centers' services would correspond to the real needs of the firms.

The programs and services of ERVET and the centers reinforced the co-operative bonds between firms and within the industrial districts. Research funds for product development or the development of new technology were granted only to groups of firms that had agreed to work together. In Carpi, the service center CITER developed an online database for its members that contained thousands of fashion designs, color combinations and textile patterns that cut to a fraction the time involved in assembling a design prototype. The center sent agents to the world's top fashion shows and twice a year produced a compendium of upcoming styles so that the Carpi firms could prepare and design their products accordingly. These were services that exceeded the capacity of any one firm in the region. With CITER's aid they were able to compete on a global field. Over the course of the next 20 years, ERVET and the service centers became a major institutional force behind the rapid rise in the region's economic performance.[4]

The use of ERVET as a think tank and diagnostic development agency epitomized the willingness of the regional government to act as a mediating and mobilizing force among the various interests in the region. The pre-existence of political alliances between the co-operative movement, the small artisan firms and the trade unions with the PCI, along with the extensive co-operative economy already operating on the ground, meant that an entirely new form of co-operative economy could be fostered. For unlike the Communist leadership in Rome (much less the rest of Europe), the leadership in Emilia Romagna was not averse to incorporating capitalist enterprises and the market system into its economic vision for the region. The co-operatives were a central influence in the acceptance of market forces as a key element in humanizing the economy. Moreover, the Communist party was coming to terms with the fact that the traditional rural base of the region's economy was rapidly changing with the rise of the small firms in and around the towns and cities. It was determined to devise a strategy that incorporated a broad cross section of the region's class structure that extended beyond the traditional working-class base of the party. The PCI in Rome was more statist and conventionally communist than its Emilian cousins who had been deeply influenced by the co-operatives of which nearly all were members. Their political experiences and their personal relationships were deeply interwoven with those of the co-operative movement. When the PCI in Rome pressed them for a more centralized and statist model of economic development that sidelined the co-operatives, they replied that if it came to choosing between their co-op and the Communist Party, it was the party card they would tear up.[5] The traditional command and control model of statist economics was left behind and what emerged was a unique blend of co-operative ideas and systems applied to the small firm capitalism of the region. The Emilian Model was the result.

The Emilian Model

In its essence, the Emilian Model is a co-operative production system that requires the collaboration of many small firms in the manufacture of a finished product. Each of these firms is highly specialized and exists as part of a network, or more usually a group of networks, that produce an item for export. This interconnection of discrete firms in a commodity chain has also come to be known as a *filiére*, a term denoting a connecting filament among technologically related activities.[6] In the past, at the time when the Emilian Model achieved its characteristic form, most of these networks functioned as a satellite system in which a lead firm would be responsible for the design and co-ordination of the production cycle for a specific client. The various elements of this process would be contracted out to satellite firms that specialized in a particular aspect of the production cycle. For the production of a line of sweaters, for example, the lead firm would be the one in contact with the market, the firm that had designed the sweater and secured the contract from a buyer. In turn, the actual manufacture of the product — dying the yarn, twisting, weaving, finishing, ironing, quality control and packaging — each of these distinct steps in the production process would be the responsibility of a separate firm that specialized in this function and participated in this particular manufacturing network.

In the first phase of this model, during the seventies and eighties, the lead firm in one product line might at other times serve as a satellite to another firm for a different line. The leadership was thus in constant flux as individual firms sought to secure contracts of their own and then subcontract the production to other feeder firms. A firm would typically be active in a number of networks that were simultaneously producing different products. And so despite the high degree of co-operation, there was also intense competition, both within the clusters among networked firms and among those firms in the district who were not in a network but were vying for acceptance into one.

Cooperation and Competition

It was a system that seemed to draw on the best attributes of co-operation on the one hand and competition on the other. Co-operation enabled small firms to take on large contracts and, through networking, achieve economies of scale and scope that were ordinarily available only to large corporations. The constant interplay of commercial and personal relations among these firms was reinforced by their geographic proximity. Many of these entrepreneurs grew up and went to school together. In many cases, satellite firms were spinoffs established by former employees of a lead firm. This was encouraged. The co-operative element embodied in the cluster model was a natural extension of pre-existing social relations within the local community. And this was a key reason why commercial contracts among firms were largely informal. They were based on trust. Almost all these complex commercial relations were conducted on a handshake. In a setting where established patterns of co-operation and trust are weak the transaction costs entailed in such a system, assuming it were ever to get off the ground, would be astronomical. Here, they were nearly nonexistent.

The patterns of co-operation extended far beyond industrial production to address basic issues such as capital investment, applied research and product development, the gathering of market intelligence, export support and technology transfer. On the question of capital investment, for example, firms would organize credit co-operatives. These groups, or *consorzi*, would then take responsibility for the loans taken out by their members, operating much as a loan circle for small firms. The fascinating antecedents of this model extend back to the early Middle Ages when any merchant in a foreign land could be held responsible for the debts of a defaulting fellow citizen. The whole merchant community was jointly responsible for its members and had a common interest in their honesty.[7] Adapted to the credit needs of Emilian firms, *consortio* loans are provided at very low rates by co-operative banks, many of which were first established as a source of credit for farmers. So successful are these consortia, and the default rates so low, that the large national banks have been trying to break into this market for years, with little success. The smaller regional banks provide for almost all of the region's capital needs.

The nature of the competition within the industrial districts is equally a factor in the success of the system. Unlike the positional competition of Anglo-American capitalism where the object of competition is to drive one's opponent out of the market or to ruin them, competition in the industrial districts focuses on performance and product excellence. The logic of this competition is to raise the standard of economic performance not only at the level of the firm, but of the industrial district as a production system and of the region as a whole. These traits, along with a scale of enterprise that allows owners to be directly engaged in the production process, are embedded in the region's artisan culture. And true to this culture, product quality and firm performance became the measures of success and the keys that gained a firm entry into a production network. A reputation for quality, reliability and flexibility were indispensable if a firm hoped to survive in the cluster system, for if one link in a production chain fails, the entire system is affected. This same reputation and a consistent capacity for innovation is all that ensures that leading brands will continue to do business with the region's firms despite the fact that wage rates here are among the highest in the world.

Since its emergence in the seventies and eighties, this system has undergone important structural changes and these have taken place within a greatly changed political environment. The old hegemony of the PCI has disappeared. So too has its distinctive role as the driving force behind a region-wide planning vision that centered on broad development goals and the cementing of social and communal bonds as well as economic and systemic supports to individual firms. These regional goals were complemented by the work of municipal governments that promoted social integration and a wide network of social services such as public transportation, gymnasiums, cultural activities, health care, infant care and low-cost housing.

With the demise of the PCI following the upheavals in the Italian political system in the late 1980s and early 1990s, the vision of the left in Emilia Romagna lost its socialist focus. The PCI splintered into competing factions and the PDS (Democratic Party of the Left), which inherited the lion's share of the old allegiances, adopted a posture of closer collaboration with the larger business interests of the region. The party's orientation became liberal and social democratic. This in turn was accompanied by a sharp fall in political militancy. The party's members in the region more than halved (dropping from 373,437 in 1989 before the fall of the Berlin Wall, to 162,861 in 2000) and its chapters were cut by three quarters.[8]

Business interests were not slow to exploit the moment. Led by Confindustria, the leading association of conservative business interests in Italy, large business groups pushed for the adoption of neo-liberal policies that emphasized a minimal role for government with respect to long-term planning and development of the region's economic systems. The first casualties were ERVET and the service centers and, by extension, the regional government's lead role in fashioning policies that pursued broad strategic goals that extended beyond the narrow interests of specific business groups or individual firms. Instead of acting as an intermediary and catalyst focusing on strategic sectoral and geographic questions bridging a wide range of interests, ERVET was channeled into project-driven tasks that could show commercial legitimacy. Budget cuts meant that public money that was previously used to break new ground in high-risk areas came to an end. Now, the kind of information sharing and system building that was once considered a public good became hostage to narrow commercial aims consistent with a new, neo-liberal view of the world. As one observer put it:

> A narrow concern with cost-effective delivery of client-determined projects seems to be emerging, in keeping with a general neo-liberal trend worldwide towards lean and task-specific institutions. Such specialization, in terms of efficiency of delivery of services to clients, can be seen as a move towards more effective organizations. But, precisely at a time when a broader, goal-driven agenda needs to be considered…such a "slimming down" risks eroding strategic capacity [and that] for path-shaping or goal-setting policy formulation.[9]

These changes in the region's political orientation meant change in the way interests were mediated. The reconstituted ruling party embraced a model of governance similar to the business-dominated systems of Northern Europe. At the same time, in addition to playing a more pronounced political role, business associations increasingly pre-empted the roles of ERVET and the service centers by turning into service providers, rather than simply industry representatives. This was the case with services aimed at providing firms with information about new production and quality standards and certification processes, adapting their managerial structure to new market trends or having access to targeted research funds managed by the EU or the Italian State. As a consequence the local governments in the region increasingly deferred to business associations in formulating and managing economic policy rather than seizing the initiative.

In 1999, Emilia Romagna was the first region to implement new regional administrative and financial powers made possible by the passage of new federal legislation in 1998.[10] A three-year economic planning process called the Regional Three-Year Plan (RTYP) combined these powers to forge a new direction for economic development consistent with the new, neo-liberal dispensation. The results were predictable.

Along with the reorientation of ERVET in 1993, most of the service centers were ultimately closed or privatized in keeping with the neo-liberal view that if the private sector is providing, or wants to provide market services, the government should stay out.[11] The report from the first year of implementation of the RTYP indicates that the largest share of public funding that was earmarked for regional economic development was channeled to individual firms, not broad sectoral initiatives that could benefit a range of firms or industrial districts as a whole.[12] This accounted for a staggering 80 percent of total funding (73,840,000 out of 92,800,000 euro).

According to the perceptive analysis carried out by Alberto Rinaldi, the change in the region's industrial policy could not be clearer. Sixty-five percent of regional resources went to individual companies, while only a minor share was assigned to actors operating as "integrators" of the local production systems: consortia, business associations, chambers of commerce, local governments and research centers, or to foster the implementation of area-wide programs. Tellingly, almost nothing went to ERVET's real service centers.

Depressingly, even a region like Emilia Romagna with its vibrant and highly innovative approach to blending co-operative values with astute market-oriented policies was also drawn into the vortex of neo-liberal thought during the 1990s. A more detailed study of how this came about would, I am certain, reveal a great deal about the state of political ideology and its relation to social, economic and political realities at the high tide mark of the free market era. Nonetheless, it remains to be seen what the effects of this change in political and economic outlook will mean for the region. And in the current economic and political climate, so different from the heady days of neo-liberal dominance of the 1990s, it will be interesting to see whether the political leadership will remember the region's remarkable past achievements and recover its collective sensibility.

Despite these changes, it seems clear that at the operational level of the industrial districts and the firms that comprise them, the vital sense of co-operation as a winning strategy remains, and in some ways has grown even stronger. The fundamental elements of a shared production system distributed among clusters of firms continues. At the same time the internal structure of the industrial districts has undergone changes prompted not so much by government policy as by the logic of competition, changing global markets and the evolving demands of production.

Lead firms have now attained a clear dominance within many industrial districts. They have grown larger, their design and logistical expertise has expanded and improved, and they have taken on a leadership role by investing directly in the production process. They have become centers of product research and development. In this role, their global contacts and their presence in the changing markets allow them to transfer knowledge back through their regional networks. And unlike the earlier, reactive tendency of small firms to adapt to the changing demands of markets and clients, lead firms and their network partners now use their knowledge to forecast change and to consciously mould the economic environment, not just react to it. This has been a signal evolution in the sophistication and capacity of the modern industrial district.

A greater interaction among networks has also evolved, often cutting across industrial districts to combine production elements on a regional scale. Fears that the industrial networks might fail to adapt to the escalating pressures of globalization have so far failed to materialize. And while many of the smaller firms in some of the districts have disappeared, especially those firms that were vulnerable to the rise of cheaper competing products, they have been replaced by others. And in those cases where buyers or lead firms had outsourced production to lower wage areas, particularly in Eastern Europe, production has once again been relocalized in the region. Low wage rates were simply no substitute for the level of skill and innovation, the capacity of firms to collaborate and problem solve and, most of all, the social and professional linkages that made the industrial district system so effective. Most importantly, the need for firms in production networks to be able to share knowledge, to innovate and to became more active partners with lead firms in locating and solving problems has led to an even greater reliance on co-operative relationships.

However, challenges to the small firm co-operativism of the districts remain. Succession is an endemic problem. Many small firms are still family owned and the old patterns of familial succession are breaking down as children pursue other life goals. There are problems of management. Old managing styles that may have been appropriate in the fifties or sixties when many of these firms were established can no longer meet the complexities of changing expectations, heterogeneous work forces, technological change and global markets. Finally, the ever-present need for product innovation, research and technological advancement is a continuing challenge to the small firms. Despite this, efforts by the regional government to address this by linking the region's universities with the industrial districts has been paying off. In the space of the last five years, Emilia Romagna has become Italy's most intensive user of research and development facilities and now leads the country in the number of new patents registered.[13] Moreover, the survival rate of the region's small firms remains the highest of all Italy's economic regions.[14] There is no question that the social, entrepreneurial and institutional co-operation that is the basis of the region's industrial model is at the heart of this survival at a time when globalization and the ongoing economic crisis is playing havoc with economies elsewhere.

In many ways, the Emilian Model represents a socialization of capitalism. Saying so is not meant to disguise the very real problems that are intrinsic to any capitalist system. One of these was the problem of exploitation that existed within the small firms themselves. Many of these had relied on the low-paid labor and long working hours of extended family members or workers that weren't covered by the collective agreements that applied to large firms. But beyond the challenges of small-firm production, the ingrained, pathological compulsion to produce at environmentally ruinous levels is not redeemable by any pattern of industrial production so long as capitalism remains a system based on unending consumption. No amount of co-operation within a capitalist framework will solve this. But what co-operation can do is humanize a capitalist economy. It can foster and sustain economies of small enterprises that are rooted in community and yet can survive in a global marketplace. It can mitigate the catastrophic effects of large-scale, nomadic production systems and their impacts on the environment, the community and the character of work. Co-operation can provide a viable alternative to delocalization and the dehumanizing effects of work devoid of skill. It can cultivate a sense of shared purpose, a collective concern for the success of all enterprises, including one's competitors, and an understanding that the success of one firm may be intimately connected to the success of all. The success of one enterprise does not require the failure of another.

Although in absolute size the co-op economy is smaller than the capitalist system, its influence on that system has been profound. The success of the small-firm economy of Emilia Romagna is based on the modes of mutual aid that are a natural part of the co-op system. The co-operatives of the region have benefited in turn. The close interaction between co-op and non-co-op systems has allowed the strengths of each to transfer over and influence the other. If the art of co-operation through industrial networks has allowed small capitalist firms to survive in a global era, the entrepreneurial drive and innovation of the capitalist firms have proven a spur to the growth and competitive competence of the co-operatives. They have become better and more sustainable enterprises for it.

In the end, it may be that the success of the Emilian Model in this most difficult of times will not rest on the policies or political orientation of the party in power. It will ultimately rest on the resilience and durability of the patterns of mutual support and the perceptions of collective interest that have grown up in the area over the last 50 years while the modern Emilian economy was being established. The co-operative entrepreneurialism that served as the Emilian Model's template has laid down an economic and social paradigm that raised the region's economy and quality of life to the forefront of Italy and Europe. The final verdict on the resilience and survival value of this approach is being passed as this is being written. The global economic recession is taking the true measure of economic models everywhere. Time will soon tell if the conjoining of economic and social goals through the practice of co-operation will serve as a lifeboat for small-firm regional economies.

CHAPTER 5

Social Co-ops
and Social Care

In the small town of Trail in the BC interior, Annie Albo, at the age of 91, lay dying with congestive heart failure in the Kootenay Boundary Region Hospital. Her husband Al, aged 96, was also in the hospital, sick and exhausted from the worry and strain of caring for his wife. They had been married for 70 years.

One day Annie was wheeled into her husband's room and told to say goodbye. She was being transferred to a nursing home in Grand Forks 100 miles away. Hospital staff had already strapped Annie to a gurney so she was not able to embrace her husband in the few moments before they took her away. They said their goodbyes. Annie Albo died alone two days later on February 19, 2008. Al died 13 days after that.

When the newspapers broke the story a wave of outrage swept the province. Angry letters to the editor, withering television coverage and uproar in the BC Legislature wrung an apology from the Minister of Health and a promise to examine how such a heartless decision could have been made. Nurses working at the hospital organized a petition calling for a public inquiry. According to Margaret Kempston, a registered nurse who worked at the hospital, the Albos' treatment was "horrible and disgusting" but she added that spousal separation "happens all the time." The final injury came to light when a government official confirmed that Trail's single palliative bed was in fact available when Annie Albo was separated from her husband and forced out of the hospital despite the frantic objections of her family. During the course of the inquiry into the conditions leading to the decision, senior managers at the Regional Health Authority refused to answer any questions, saying flatly that proper procedures had been followed. In the end, no one was found at fault, no accountability was forthcoming, no disciplinary action was taken. Nothing changed.

This heartbreaking story illustrates perfectly the tragic consequences and needless suffering caused by a dysfunctional system. Countless stories could be told of other seniors and their families who have endured similar distress and indignity in communities across Canada, across the United States, indeed everywhere patients are powerless to influence bureaucracies that serve institutional interests instead of the patients. The story of Annie and Al Albo touched a raw nerve across the province. It was not only empathy and fellow feeling that prompted the outpouring of anger. It was also the unsettling question the story raised in the minds of many readers: "Could this happen to me?"

Stories documenting the neglect and abuse of seniors have been a staple element in Canada's headlines and news hours for many years. They are depressingly familiar and just as shocking today as they were 30 years ago. What receives less attention is the pervasive anxiety and silent struggle that millions of seniors face daily as they contend with the challenges of aging with few supports at home, in their communities or from government. These fears of isolation, maltreatment and neglect have remained a constant presence in the lives of the vulnerable, whether they be people living with disabilities or those whose life's fortunes have left them stranded at society's margins. They have reason to worry. Social care systems have been unraveling steadily over the last 20 years. The economic crisis that descended like a pall across national economies in 2009 only deepened the worry.

In developing countries things are much, much worse. Social policy remains at the bottom of national priorities, taking a far back seat to commercial and industrial development. The "restructuring" programs that accompanied IMF and World Bank loans for economic development throughout the eighties and nineties often dovetailed with home-grown corruption to ensure that what little social care existed would remain at rudimentary levels, if not collapse altogether. Social policy was always the first area to suffer as governments were forced to reduce public spending in return for loans. The prospects for quick profits lay with the misuse of massive expenditures on economic development and industrial growth, not health, education or relief of poverty.[1] Lacking the organized political base and the civic mechanisms for reform that are present in the industrialized north, social policy in many of these countries reflects the deep-seated corruption and incompetence that seems a permanent feature of state systems in developing countries.[2] The lack of social care remains the great open sore in the body politic of poor nations, and the very institutions that were created to aid in the relief of global poverty are largely responsible.[3]

But in the industrialized north, social care systems that have taken a century to build up have been deeply damaged by three decades of government retrenchment, neglect, and the catastrophic effects of free market ideas on public services. These systems constitute the complex fabric of publicly-funded safety nets, from universal health care to unemployment insurance and services for the handicapped that have been needed to offset the market failures in human services that are endemic to a capitalist system. How civil society in general, and the co-op movement in particular, have responded to the effects of these free market ideas is the focus of this chapter.

Historically, the rise of social care in the advanced capitalist societies is inseparable from the advent of democracy, which in turn became possible only with the rise of an organized working class.[4] This is understandable. The struggle for democracy in the West was waged, in large part, to establish a political system capable of distributing to the majority a share of the material security and prosperity that was the privilege of elites. This only comes with a commensurate distribution of political power. So social policy — the broad distribution of material security through public means — is one factor of democracy. What I want to show here is how democracy is essential for the protection of the human and social dimension of social care itself. The character of social care — the nature of its content, its manner of operation and the distribution of its benefits — has remained relatively unchanged since the great wave of social reform was enacted after the end of the second world war. It was at this time that universal systems of social security, health insurance, family benefits and public welfare were established.[5] And while it is true that the nature and extent of these social care systems varied greatly from one country to the next, and especially between Northern Europe and America, they shared essential common features, in particular the rising importance of government as the provider of social care. But almost all the social policy reforms in Europe and North America since then have been centered on matters of redistribution — extending the coverage of social welfare systems to larger segments of the population.[6] The way these services were delivered — the fundamental character of the relation between the state and the citizen — remained relatively unchanged until the introduction of free market ideas in public policy in the 1980s. Until then, publicly funded social programs were delivered almost exclusively by the state through centralized bureaucracies.

To be sure, these vast delivery systems succeeded in distributing benefits to unprecedented numbers of people. The quality of life for the vast majority of people improved more than in any previous period of history. Centralized bureaucracies were deemed essential for systems in which universal coverage required regulation, standardization of services and equality of access. Their moral foundation however, was based on notions of charity — the social responsibility of the state to care for its members. But it was a profoundly paternalistic system in which the state provided and the citizen received. This is the nature of charity. The essential character of this disempowering, and ultimately belittling system was not to be altered until the 1980s when, ironically, the state monopoly over social care was called into question by the adoption of free market principles in the public services by Margaret Thatcher. This shift in the presumptive role of the state by the embrace of the free market cracked a centuries-old mould that had fixed the citizen as a powerless dependent of the state in matters of social care. The fact that citizens contributed to the cost of these services through their taxes had little effect on the powerlessness they often experienced when actually using these services, particularly welfare which carried with it the additional indignity of social stigma. It was a model whose antecedents extend back to the Poor Laws that stripped the poor and the weak of their autonomy and social identity. Just as the adoption of utilitarian, free market ideas dissolved the relations between the commercial economy and society at the dawn of the industrial age, so too has the adoption of these same ideas threatened to destroy the social content of care in the public economy.

Social care is being commodified. The desocializing dynamics of the industrial revolution that were, at least in theory, contained within the market economy have now reached deep into the public systems that were once the preserve of the state. The colonization of the public domain by commercial interests in the late 20th century is in some ways analogous to the enclosure of the commons in the 18th century. As a result, a number of uncomfortable questions arise. Will civil society find the means to reclaim the social and collective foundations of the public systems that are being abandoned by government and annexed by capital? In an era where free market ideas and the influence of capital reign supreme within government, can the state be trusted with public welfare? If not, what is the alternative? And finally, can social care be humanized?

In Canada, as in much of the industrialized West, most of the debate on the changing role of government has centered on its retreat from the provision of public services, largely as a response to the deficits of the '80s and '90s and the rise of the view that the private sector can do better. But changes in social policy and the delivery of social care have also been fuelled by widespread public discontent with traditional delivery systems. People were fed up with the paternalism, inflexibility and dehumanizing attributes of state bureaucracies. The story of Annie and Al Albo recounted at the beginning of this chapter had become a pattern all too familiar for far too many people. Combined with burgeoning public deficits this provided a fertile context for the rethinking of public services.

When universal social care systems were first established at the beginning of the last century, first in Western and Northern Europe and then later in North America, social, cultural and economic conditions were far different from what was to evolve in the wake of the unprecedented material prosperity generated by capitalism. Throughout most of the 1900s, large numbers of people of Western society were still an accident or a sickness away from total ruin. Programs like basic social security, health care and worker compensation were designed to provide a basic standard of care for large classes of people. It was an era marked by a mechanistic industrial paradigm, an age of assembly line automation that paved the way for the service-based consumer society that has since come to replace it.

But this transition to a post-scarcity society has brought its own attitudes and expectations along with it. Chief among these is the accelerating individuation of society — the strange rise of the individual as someone who is defined solely by what he or she buys and the construction of personal identity as an extension of market forces. Fuelled by the relentless message of the free market, this has made choice in the marketplace a criterion of personal freedom and a symbol for consumer culture as a whole. Previously, in the mass industrial age, basic health care and universal social security reflected a model of social care that was geared to large classes of people who lacked these necessities. Social needs were generalized. In the post-scarcity era, in the fantasy age of unlimited personal consumption, needs have become *specific* and *concrete*, reflecting the precise needs and preferences of individuals, not classes. With society awash in material goods, people now expect that social goods and services will also recognize and respond to them as individuals. Their growing failure to do so provides one means of understanding a possible new future for civil society generally and co-operatives in particular.

The very notion of standardized systems of care that can be applied to all, regardless of personal preferences, has become something of an anachronism. And although the reaction against universalism is rooted in the dubious belief that basic needs have now been addressed, a belief that is willing to overlook the dire conditions of many that still struggle in poverty or barely survive on social assistance,[7] yet it is a point of view that has become characteristic of the consumer age (or at least that segment of society that has the money to pay for alternatives, and is not prepared to wait in line). This is especially true for those public goods that are amenable to personal preferences, and most especially to their improvement in quality by the expenditure of disposable income, for example, health care, home care, services to the disabled and public education. This shift in social attitudes, combined with the inability — or unwillingness — of the state to respond to the change in public expectations, has been a key factor in opening the way for the commercialization of social care. There is a growing market for it. Another factor is the failure of those forces that believe in universal public care to understand this change, to acknowledge its meaning and implications and to provide progressive responses that are capable of addressing it.

What has eventually arisen is a twin movement. A push for more pluralistic and private models of care on the one hand — a continuation of the free market logic — and a contrary movement toward noncommercial, social economy solutions on the other. Both approaches call for more pluralism in how care is delivered and more choice on the part of the individual. They differ radically on how this should be achieved and this in turn comes from profound differences in the perception of what social care is.

The privatization of social care is the familiar route of the free market approach. The *socialization* of care, on the other hand, is less well known and less documented. The fact that it is also less *lucrative* for private interests goes a long way to explain why so little attention has been paid to it. The other reason is that for two decades a relentless campaign to discredit government and the very notion of public services has been conducted through all the available channels of the media and the academy by the think tanks and private sector promoters that champion the privatization of public services. The clamor for privatization, particularly in health care, has not subsided. There is simply too much money to be made. Despite this, and despite the growing demand for individualized care, public opposition to the privatization of universal systems has remained strong. But something is changing nevertheless. A new interest has arisen in the role of civil society with respect to public welfare and social care.

The rise of social co-ops and other forms of social enterprise has gained considerable attention since the glow of privatized care lost some of its original luster. In Canada, for example, the failures of privatization in areas such as home care and long-term care were widely reported throughout the 1990s. The current crisis of the free market model has also undermined calls for its extension in the public sector. (With the recent collapse of the financial and stock markets for example, how many would listen now to proposals for the privatization of social security?) The rise of social enterprise as a new, hybrid form of social care has been met with growing interest. In the co-operative sector, the emergence of social co-ops has been the most significant change to occur in the movement in 30 years. These are co-operatives whose primary purpose is the provision of social care, not only to their members but also to the community as a whole. Their primary areas of activity have focused on services to marginalized populations, and to society's most vulnerable groups. These developments signal a change in attitudes toward the market on the one hand and the role of government and the public sector on the other. Privatization is not the only way the market can be used to reform social care. There is a social alternative that reflects a shifting perception of how civil society must now relate to changing times.

On Civil Society and the Social Economy

The term "civil society" has now entered, or more accurately re-entered, the vocabulary of common political discourse. It is a very ancient idea with roots in the political and moral philosophy of the ancient Greeks and the democratic society in which it was first conceived. The stress on the moral life that was a central part of Greek philosophy was always bound up in the concept of civic duty and the pursuit of the just society.[8] For Plato, the ideal state was one in which people dedicate themselves to the common good, practice civic virtues of wisdom, courage, moderation and justice, and perform the social and occupational role to which they are best suited. Aristotle in turn, held that the "polis" — the city state — was an "association of associations" and the social reality that made political life possible.[9] For these thinkers, there was no distinction between state and society. Their idea of civil society as a political concept was profoundly influenced by the democratic institutions of Athens. It was made possible by the fact that individuals were not mere subjects of an absolute power. They were independent actors with the freedom to form horizontal bonds of mutual interest with others and to act in pursuit of this common interest. This was the essence of citizenship. Politics in the modern sense became possible. This link between civil society and democracy was to remain a defining feature of the term.

As the fortunes of democracy rose and fell in Europe over the ages, so too did the idea of civil society as a conceptual tool to explain the operations of society and, ultimately, to change them. In the Middle Ages, with the rise of church and state absolutism, the classical notion of society as a civic body was suppressed, as was political freedom. It was replaced by the authoritarian notion of society as the temporal extension of a sacred order that was eternal and unchangeable. Social relations were fixed. Politics was once again the exclusive prerogative of the powerful. The notion of citizenship was not to revive until the rise of civic humanism in the fifteenth and sixteenth centuries when the idea of civil society was resurrected and absolutism was once again challenged. The rebirth of civil society accompanied the rise of republican cities like Florence and Sienna that in turn became centers of the Italian Renaissance. The idea then found its modern expression during the Enlightenment when philosophers and political reformers sought once again to limit the powers of state and church, in large part by defining civil society as the source of political legitimacy. It is no accident that the recent interest in civil society is also linked to resistance against authoritarianism — most dramatically in Eastern Europe before the fall of the Soviet bloc[10] — and, within the global justice movement, against the rise of corporate power and the co-optation of the state by corporate interests.

In its narrowest modern sense, civil society refers to social organizations involved in the political process, for example, political parties. But in its broadest and most accepted sense, civil society is the social impulse to engage in free and democratic association, to create community and to engage in the operations of social life, which include politics. This is the sense of civil society that is used by writers such as Vaclav Havel.[11] Unlike ancient times however, civil society is now distinct from the workings of the state as well as from the operations of the private sector. Some writers also stress a distinction from the family as well.

For Havel and a long line of writers extending back to Aristotle, civil society remains the elementary fact of human existence. It is what makes human life possible. For Aristotle it was both the means and the end of human association as the pursuit of the good life, which is in essence a social life. In this sense, the institutions that arise from civil society (the schools, the voluntary associations, the trade unions, the courts, the political parties, etc.) provide the individual with the means to realize their own humanity and by so doing to perfect the whole of society in the process. The state is an outgrowth of this impulse. It is fascinating to read Thomas Paine in this connection, particularly with reference to the raging debate surrounding the proper role of the state and the growing demands on the social economy to fulfill social and public services:

> The great part of that order which reigns among mankind is not the effect of government. It has its origins in the principles of society and the natural constitution of man. It existed prior to government, and would exist if the formality of government was abolished. The mutual dependence and reciprocal interest which man has upon man, and all the parts of civilized community upon each other, create that great chain of connection which holds it together. In fine, society performs for itself almost everything which is ascribed to government.[12]

Alex de Tocqueville, visiting America in the late seventeen hundreds, famously attributed the vitality of the young democracy to the richness and diversity of its associational life.[13]

Within civil society, a huge portion of civic activities are carried out by organizations created to provide goods and services through collaboration, by people acting together to realize mutual interests. They constitute that sector which is composed of non-profit and voluntary organizations, service groups, cultural organizations such as choral societies, charities, trade unions and co-operatives. This economic aspect within civil society has also been described as the third sector or the social economy. The value of the economic activity generated by the social economy in the Western democracies is huge — and growing. As a percentage of total economic force, for example, Canada's non-profit workforce is the world's second largest. With an estimated economic turnover of $75.8 billion, Canadian non-profits account for 8.5 percent of the country's GDP (including the economic value of volunteer effort). Canadian non-profits account for 2,073,000 full-time-equivalent employees, nearly matching the total of 2,294,000 employees reported in Canada's manufacturing sector.[14] If we include the economic value of co-operatives, credit unions and social enterprises, the economic value is even higher.

For both civil society and the social economy, the notion of reciprocity is fundamental. It is also essential for understanding the means by which a new view of social care, a civil view, might be developed as a more humane alternative to current systems.

On Reciprocity

Reciprocity is the social mechanism that makes associational life possible. It is the foundation of social life. Reciprocity is a system of voluntary exchange between individuals based on the understanding that the giving of a favor by one will in future be reciprocated either to the giver or to someone else. A simple example is the loan of a lawn mower by one neighbor, call him Frank, to another, say, Fred. Frank makes the loan on the assumption that at some later date Fred will return the favor. If Fred does not, the basis of reciprocity falls apart. No more loaning of the lawnmower to Fred. Moreover, Fred's non-reciprocity, if it continues, affects his reputation. Other neighbors will also stop extending favors to Fred. Willingness to reciprocate is a basic signal of the *sociability* of an individual. Taken to an extreme, the complete unwillingness of an individual to reciprocate is tantamount to severing the bonds between themselves and other people. Reciprocity is thus a social relation that contains within itself potent emotional and even spiritual dimensions. These elements account for an entirely different set of motivations than behavior in the classical economic sense of "maximizing one's utility" as a consumer — that is to say, maximizing one's pleasure as a self-interested pursuit, as taught by Bentham's version of utililtarianism.

Contrary to this, reciprocity animates a vast range of economic activities that rest on the sharing and reinforcement of attitudes and values that are interpersonal and constitute essential bonds between the individual and the human community. What is exchanged in reciprocal transactions are not merely particular goods, services and favors, but more fundamentally the expression of good will and the assurance that one is prepared to help others. It is the foundation of trust. Consequently, the practice of reciprocity has profound social ramifications and entails a clear moral element. Reciprocity is a key for understanding how the institutions of society work. But it is also an economic principle with wholly distinct characteristics that embody social as opposed to merely commercial attributes. When reciprocity finds economic expression in the exchange of goods and services to people and communities it is the social economy that results. Examples range from the provision of burial services through the creation of friendly societies in the 1800s to the promotion of neighborhood safety through organizations like Neighborhood Watch today.

Finally, reciprocity is egalitarian. It presupposes a direct relationship of equality between the individuals involved. It is very different from altruism or charity, where the giver may have no relation to the receiver and where there is a clear asymmetry of power. In the matter of social care this has profound implications.

The concept of social economy, like the term "civil society," has only recently come back into prominence after a long period of neglect. Originally, social economy referred to the theoretical approach first developed by the utopian socialists, especially the early founders of the co-operative tradition — Owen, Fourier, Saint Simon and Proudhon.[15] The term was first applied to the early co-operatives that arose from their work by economists like Charles Gide and Léon Walrus and sociologists like Frédéric le Play.

Like their co-operative antecedents, social economy organizations pursue their goals, whether economic or social, on the basis that individuals' contributions will be reciprocated and the benefits shared. Reciprocity is the economic principle that defines both the activities and the aims of these organizations, whether they are co-operatives, voluntary associations or conventional non-profits. Their primary purpose is the promotion of collective benefit. Their social product is not just the particular goods or services that they produce, but human solidarity — the predisposition of people in a society to work together around mutual goals. Another name for this is social capital.[16] As opposed to the capitalist principle of capital control over labor, reciprocity is the means by which a social interest — whether labor, citizen groups or consumers — can exercise control over capital. As a subdivision of civil society, its use of reciprocity for economic purposes is what distinguishes the social economy from the private and public sectors.[17]

With the rise of interest in civil society and the social economy, the market view of society as composed of two separate sectors — the private and the public — is once again being challenged. From the start, the notion of social economy was a reaction against economists' narrow reading of the economy as a dimension divorced from society. The social economy entailed an enlargement of classical economics to include the social relations that accompany and underlie the creation and distribution of wealth and to situate economic behavior within the wider compass of social reality. This is the larger frame in which social economy has its original meaning. Current efforts to highlight civil society and the social economy as countervailing forces to the market view are a continuation of the historical struggle to reclaim the social dimension of economics. What this means and how it is being realized in the context of social care and the changing role of the state is where we now turn our attention.

Social Co-operatives

Sasso Marconi is a small town located 17 kilometers south of Bologna. It takes its name from the high cliff that dominates the area, and from the inventor Gugliemo Marconi whose palatial home still stands in aristocratic splendour just outside the town. Tucked in the green hills overlooking the winding traffic of the valley below stands a white farmhouse, the center of an old farming estate. In the kitchen, the piquant smell of simmering tomato sauce fills the room. Working away at the long wood table is a rotund young man with a rolling pin. He is intent on his task, delicately kneading and forming the small potato gnocchi that will be on today's lunch menu. Outside others are bustling about, working the garden, setting tables on the sunlit terrace, cleaning vegetables. This is CopAps,[18] a social co-operative that operates a weekend trattoria here, catering mostly to families with children that take the day trip up from Bologna. During the week the co-op runs a program for people with psychological handicaps. The fellow expertly working the pin at the table has Down syndrome. He is one of the twenty or so individuals who take part in the life-skills training, employment preparation, landscaping and environmental awareness programs run by the co-op. The co-op also runs a horticultural business. In the gardens surrounding the house, medicinal herbs grow in carefully tended rows. These are sold commercially, as are the 120,000 plants grown annually in the co-op's greenhouses located just outside Bologna. It is a flourishing operation.

The revenue to operate CopAps comes primarily from three sources: one third from fees paid by the families of the participants, one third from commercial revenue earned from the sale of the co-op's products, and the balance from operating landscaping services for the surrounding towns. The co-op maintains public parks, refits them to make them more accessible to people with disabilities and maintains a number of the region's cemeteries. After costs, the co-op reinvests its surplus in the development of its program.

Founded in 1979, the co-op had its beginning in the deepening frustration and dissatisfaction of caregivers and families with the poor standards provided by government programs to disabled family members receiving care. Throughout the 1970s a parent movement had been growing, with families demanding more control over the ways in which family members with disabilities were being treated. Caregivers, too, were a driving force of this movement. At CopAps, parents and caregivers felt certain that with more control over the content and delivery of the care, they could do better. Starting as a worker co-op of care professionals, the organization evolved into a new model, a social co-op in which both caregivers and families shared control as members. Those most responsible for the welfare of the residents determined all major decisions, from program content and design to the development of commercial activities. After much lobbying and government resistance, the upstart co-op was recognized by the municipality of Bologna and granted a contract to run the program. CopAps became one of the earliest social co-ops in Italy. The model spread, transmitted by the innumerable networks of the region's co-operative organizations, professional associations and parent groups and finding ready ground in the continuing dysfunction of state programs and government cutbacks. During the 1980s the activity of these new co-operatives, along with sustained political pressure, resulted in their formal recognition in Italian legislation in 1991. Today, social co-ops are a central aspect of Italy's social services system. In the city of Bologna, 87 percent of the city's social services are provided through municipal contracts with social co-ops.

The rise of social co-operatives represents a new frontier in the shifting boundaries between public, private and commercial spheres. Social co-ops embody the collectivist and co-operative traditions of the past along with a new focus on individual choice and the use of market forces that till now have been hallmarks of neo-liberal approaches to social policy. The combination of these elements make social co-ops a kind of social experiment that places civil society at the forefront of social service reform. These co-ops are inventing models of care that embody the strengths and values of civil society as an alternative to both state and market systems. In the process, they are forging new roles for civil society and government. And while the debate in Italy concerning the role of the state has raged as it has in all the Western democracies, the practical outcomes within Italy have been far more interesting as indicators of where the future of social policy reform may ultimately lie.

According to the 2005 census there were over 7,000 social co-operatives in Italy providing social services throughout the country. Social co-ops employed 280,000 individuals, of whom 30,000 were disadvantaged workers. This represents fully 23 percent of the non-profit sector's total paid labour force, even though they represent only two percent of non-profit organizations. More recent figures put their number at between 12 and 14,000.

As described in the legislation, social co-ops have as their purpose "to pursue the general community interest in promoting human concerns and the integration of citizens." In this sense, social co-operatives are recognized as having goals that promote benefits to the community and its citizens, rather than maximizing benefits solely to co-op members. Italian legislation also acknowledges the common interest public bodies such as municipalities and health boards have with social co-ops in promoting public welfare and emphasizes the possibility of collaboration between them. In consequence, an important symbiotic relationship has developed between these co-ops and the municipal bodies that are primarily responsible for contracting their services.

Since their establishment, social co-ops in Italy have resulted in improved access and a net increase in the variety and quality of social care. This increase has not been at the expense of civil service jobs, which was a major concern of the public sector unions. Instead, the public services have concentrated on areas where state regulation, oversight and centralized information and distribution can benefit the system. Social co-ops focus on the front lines of care where service design and relationships between caregivers and users are paramount in determining the quality of care that is received. Personal care to the elderly and the treatment of people with addictions are two examples. In addition, the relative cost of care in areas where social co-ops have been operating has declined while the quality of care has improved. Job satisfaction among employees working in social co-ops is also higher than that reported in either the public or private sectors, despite the fact that wage rates are generally lower.[19] Why is this so?

The reasons flow from the nature of social care itself and the ways in which co-op models require caregivers and users to make explicit and reinforce the human relations that underlie care. The principles of reciprocity, equality and accountability are inalienable qualities of humane care. They are also organizational attributes of co-operative organizations. They are not attributes of either state or private for-profit systems.

The Case for a Co-op Approach to Social Care

There are three compelling reasons for the promotion of co-operative models for the delivery of social care. The first has to do with the nature of social care and the kind of models that are best suited to deliver it. This concerns the question of relational goods. The second reason concerns the relation of organizational structure to service design, delivery and efficiency. The third reason is the need to humanize care through the socialization of its content and its manner of operation. The democratization of care is essential to this.

Relational Goods

The "discovery" of relational goods is one of the truly paradigm-shifting developments in recent economic analysis. Unlike conventional goods relational goods cannot be enjoyed by an individual alone but only jointly with others. They are like a specific kind of public good, in that their nature *requires* that they be shared. As a consequence, participation in their consumption actually creates an additional benefit to others and increases the value of the good itself. Examples include the collective joy of an audience experiencing a musical performance, the generalized laughter at a comic film or the surge of energy that explodes when one's team scores a goal in a stadium. The more people enjoy a relational good the greater its utility. When Canadians gathered in their thousands in bars and living rooms and on street corners to watch Canada win Olympic gold in men's hockey in 2010, the electricity that flowed right across the nation was relational joy on an epic level. On a more intimate level, relational goods acquire value through sincerity, or *genuineness* — they cannot be bought or sold. Friendship and caring are relational goods and they are their own reward. They are things whose sale would immediately destroy their worth.

In social care, relational goods are those services to persons that are characterized by the exchange of human relations. Because in relational goods the quality of the personal relationship lies at the core of what is exchanged, in social care they can be optimally produced only by the provider and recipient acting *together*. Beyond this, relational goods have also been defined as the value of the relationship itself, over and above the particular goods or services that are produced.[20] These qualities apply to the unique nature of social care. Reciprocity — entering into a relationship of mutual benefit on the basis of equality — is the basis for a type of care where both caregiver and recipient share in the generation of care as a human relation, not as a purchased commodity or a charitable offering. Reciprocity in social care entails sharing among equals of information, responsibility and power. It is the source of dignity for the user, of vocational gratification for the caregiver and of mutual accountability for both. Without the democratization of care through the sharing of power and the reordering of relationships on the basis of equality none of this is possible. Co-operative structures in which power is shared between provider and user make this possible.

Consider, for example, care for a person with a disability. A reciprocal relation would provide the recipient the means to determine how his or her care would be provided: they would have a say in determining when the service would be offered, who their care-giver would be, what the content of the care would be and how their personal preferences and needs could best be served.

Services such as education, health care and care for people with disabilities are social because they are not merely commercial commodities. They refer to social relations that are wholly different from the exchange of commodities for profit that characterize commercial transactions. This is why the reference to such services as "products" or the recipients of social care as "clients" is so profoundly false. It is the unthinking urge in a market society to commodify human and social relations. Neither state bureaucracies, which *depersonalize* social service recipients, nor private sector firms, which *instrumentalize* recipients as a source of profit, can ever be suited to the provision of relational goods.

To be clear, I am not claiming that private sector firms are incapable of attending to the caring aspect of a social service. I am saying that the cultivation of the relational aspect of care, what is in essence its human factor, is not generally in their interest since it means investment in time and therefore money and their objective function is to maximize profits. The same problem of conflicting priorities also serves to undermine private firms' incentive to invest in employee training and professional development, resulting in additional reductions in service quality, employment standards and staff morale. In both cases — state and for profit delivery — what suffers is the quality of the caring and reciprocal relationship which is at the heart of the service being offered. This shortcoming of conventional delivery systems has little to do with the *intentions* that lie behind these models of social care. What is at issue is the faulty *physiology* of the structures and the *economic principles* used to provide care to people. As will be explored in more detail below, neither the redistributive economic logic of government nor the commercial exchange logic of the private sector can do justice to the reciprocity principle of social and relational goods.

On Form and Function

It has often been argued (although recently this argument has taken a battering) that the private sector is more efficient than the state in the delivery of public and social services, including health care. Government delivery of theses services is criticized as inefficient, not cost-effective and incapable of responding to the real needs and preferences of "consumers." Conversely, it is argued that contracting out public services allows governments to cut expenditures while increasing access and choice through the introduction of competition by the private sector.

In Canada this argument continues to be made, particularly in the provision of health care, through its promotion by such powerful interests as the Canadian Medical Association (CMA), which has lobbied hard for the use of private clinics for testing, lab services, CT scans and surgical procedures while doctors continue to work in the public system. At its 2008 annual general meeting, the CMA approved a motion calling on the organization to "develop a blueprint and timeline for transformational change in Canadian health care to bring about patient-focused care by February, 2009." "Patient-focused care" is a euphemism for privatization, and the rationale for this shift toward private care is "better access and patient choice." In a similar vein, former CMA president Brian Day, a strong proponent of privatized health care, said, "Competition, consumer choice and market principles barely exist in our health care system...without competition we cannot expect improvement, let alone excellence."

The use of commercial market analogies like competition and consumer choice to bolster the case for private delivery of health and other types of care are groundless, both theoretically and empirically. The reasons why are clear and well known and it continues to astonish how this case is still being made and still taken seriously. The principles which apply to the production and distribution of public goods are wholly different than those that drive the production of commodities in the private market for the simple reason that public goods are meant to be accessible by everyone, irrespective of their ability to pay. The application of commercial principles such as the "right to choose" and "competitive excellence" can apply to public services only if those services remain universally accessible. This is the non-exclusionary principle that defines a public good. The moment an individual is excluded from accessing a health service because they cannot afford to pay for it, that service ceases to be a public good. This would be the immediate consequence of user fees for health services that are not available in the publicly funded system.

If, on the other hand, a health service is provided to all regardless of the cost incurred by the requirement for profit, the entire system becomes far more costly and even less sustainable. The American model of market-based health care is a case study in this folly. Additionally, the private provision of essential services like health care generates market failures because private markets take no account of the external benefits of health care to the broader society. Because a private market is controlled by the need to generate a profit, private firms will produce only those amounts or types of a good, whether health care or housing, or anything else, that will guarantee a profit. This is regardless of the need for that good or the benefit that would accrue to the community as a whole by its provision. When it comes to providing public goods, market failure — the inability of a production system to satisfy a market need — is built into the DNA of a private market model.

The production of public goods by the state is also subject to market failures, although for different reasons. Direct provision of services by government creates inefficiencies that stem from the nature of bureaucracies to generate costs without a commensurate contribution of value to production. And while governments can correct for market failures to ensure that an optimal quantity of services is produced, this comes at a cost that becomes unsustainable when an unlimited growth in service demand is coupled with the inherent costs of bureaucracy.

Organizational form is fundamental to the relationship between the content of social care and the systems that provide it. In state-delivered systems, social care is properly perceived as a civic right that should be available to all citizens equally. But equality in service delivery rarely translates into social care that is fair or appropriate or responsive to the unique needs of individuals. What is fair for all is often grossly unfair for individuals. Universal access through state systems requires that services be designed for application to large classes of users, not individualized cases. Inflexibility, remoteness and regimentation of care are a necessary consequence. This is the inevitable dehumanizing and impersonalizing effect of bureaucracy.

All this is well known, both academically and in the lived experience of countless individuals who have had to endure the inefficiencies and indignities of bureaucratic systems. An alternative to both private care and traditional government delivery is essential if the public nature of health and social care is to be protected and yet made responsive to people's actual needs and preferences.

Co-op models for providing health and social services have shown a remarkable capacity to provide new types of care at a cost, and in a manner, that blends the benefits of a public good with the choice and responsiveness usually associated with a private sector service. For example, social co-ops have played a major role in improving both the quality of home care and the working conditions, wages and professional competence of home-care givers. (One outstanding instance is Home Care Associates, located in the South Bronx.) Another example is the provision of life-skills training and employment to people with intellectual disabilities. In Langston Ontario, worker co-ops have been established whose members are intellectually handicapped adults who were once "clients" of sheltered workshops. In the co-ops, they not only find meaningful employment, they sit on the board of directors and have a say in how the enterprises are run. The reasons for these kinds of improvements stem from the structure of co-operatives as user-owned and -operated organizations. Like public services, co-operatives have a mutualistic function: to serve the collective needs of member-owners. In the case of social co-ops, these aims are extended to the community as a whole. But the scale of delivery is much smaller — community based — and unlike government systems the design and delivery of these services rest in the hands of co-op members, providing them the choice that is characteristic of the private market.

In the case of health services, co-operatives have pioneered a patient-focused approach to health care that is a direct consequence of user control over the design and delivery of these services. Similarly, in the provision of social care, social co-ops and other forms of social enterprise have increased the range of services available to citizens while simultaneously containing the costs for the provision of these services by the state. In both cases, the co-op model has been most effective when it is developed as a complement to, not a substitute for, public services. In those places where social co-ops are most advanced, their proponents advocate strongly for government to continue playing a central role in the funding and regulation of public services.

The case of social co-ops in Italy shows that their multi-stakeholder structure is a key factor in the role they play in lowering costs, increasing service innovation, addressing market failures and responding to the changing needs of individual users. The involvement of stakeholder groups in the production and delivery of services confers advantages that differentiate these co-ops from conventional non-profits, private firms and government agencies.[21]

Since social co-ops are controlled by a variety of stakeholders, costs are contained because they are not controlled solely by those who receive monetary benefits from the organization — employees in the case of non-profits or investors in the case of private firms. The control rights exercised by consumers and volunteers moderate the distribution of profit and the rise of costs so social co-ops can provide services more efficiently. The involvement of consumers and volunteers in the delivery of services also lowers the cost of production.

The involvement of multiple stakeholders also reduces the traditional asymmetries of information that compromise the efficient delivery of services in non-profits, welfare service models and private firms. Consumer involvement, in particular, increases access to information, spurs innovation in service design and raises the levels of transparency and accountability in the organization.

Social co-ops are better able to cope with insufficient budgets, which is a key market failure of government services. Capitalizing services through a combination of public and private funds is a key strategy for distributing costs in a way that subsidizes those who are less able to afford the services. The involvement of multiple stakeholders also limits the monopoly market control of government services and the attendant problems in the ability of users to access services that actually reflect their preferences.

Finally, since social co-ops are not as limited in the distribution of profits as conventional non-profits, they are better equipped to raise capital from members, funders and other stakeholders. They are also able to provide a limited return on capital to investors and funders. These capital advantages make social co-ops more entrepreneurial and more able to finance innovation in service delivery or the development of new projects.

Democratizing Care

Social co-ops, like all co-operatives, are defined by the fact that they grant control rights to stakeholders and members. In this sense, they are distinct from other non-profits which are defined essentially by the constraint on distribution of profits. In a co-operative structure, it is the element of member control and ownership of the co-operative that defines both the culture and the operations of the organization. In those social co-ops where the service users are also members, the operation of control rights has the capacity to transform the user from being merely a passive recipient of care, an *object* of care systems, to being a protagonist in the design and delivery of the care, an active *subject* in the care relationship. Social care becomes a shared outcome between caregiver and care receiver. This element of personal control is fundamental to the reform of social care systems, particularly for those who are most dependent — people with disabilities, the poor and the marginalized. The reform of social care, its transformation into a humane system of social relationships, requires at minimum its democratization.

Beyond Defensiveness

Despite the role that social co-ops in Italy have played in social care reform, for the most part organizations within civil society as a whole have been very reluctant to engage government around the question of remaking social care. For two decades, any reform has been controlled by private sector groups in the advancement of their own commercial interests, and, perhaps, as part of a genuinely held belief in the superiority of free market models. This has meant that civil society, and the political left generally, have been placed in the position of defending a dysfunctional status quo. Organized labor, in particular, has been unwilling to countenance any move that can be construed as weakening the state's role in public services and, by extension, compromising further the jobs of civil servants. In Canada, as elsewhere, the ripping up of collective agreements and the downsizing and loss of thousands of public sector jobs have taken their painful toll. Among the crippling effects is a fortress mentality on the part of organized labor. But the uncomfortable question must still be asked: If labor's interests, in Canada at least, are driven solely by the fact that the bulk of their members and dues-payers are in the public sector, how can they be a force for a reform of social care that questions the received role of the state?

On the whole, the posture of the political left and those segments of civil society that have become active in this issue is defensive — a conservative force in opposition to change. Given the damage done to public services in the name of "reform" over the last two decades this is understandable. But the continuing defense of the state monopoly model is untenable, shortsighted, and reveals serious weaknesses. The short-term interest of labor is one issue. A second is the dependence of many civil society institutions on government. Civil society, despite its formal distinctions from the state, remains a dependent sector, in many ways a client sector of the state. Too many non-profits, NGOs and the leadership they employ are kept in operation solely by government funding. For example, more than 50 percent of the cost for services provided by voluntary non-profit social welfare agencies in the United States is funded through government purchase-of-service arrangements. Government funds account for 65 percent of the Catholic Charities budget, over 60 percent of Save the Children and 96 percent of the funding for Volunteers of America.[22] The same is generally true in Canada. This absence of autonomy has undermined these organizations' capacity to represent, and fight for, the interests of civil society as a sector with its own interests apart from those of the state. At a time when government has all but erased the distinctions between private and public interests, its dependency on the state also threatens civil society's capacity to demand reform of public institutions in accordance with values appropriate to those institutions and the public interest. Failure to take full measure of the issues at play and to show leadership on what is perhaps the defining question of public policy at the dawn of the 21st century has left the field precisely to those forces least concerned with the public interest.

For those who advocate a more humane alternative to the status quo, it is not enough to demand that civil society play a larger role in the protection of existing social services. New models of social care are needed that embody the attributes of reciprocity, accessibility and accountability. This point has been made by many groups who provide care to people in need and their communities. It has been a key element in the promotion of the concept of "blended care" which seeks to reform the health system by incorporating the principles of prevention, community involvement and user control into the provision of primary health care. Similarly, the push by the disability community for individualized funding, whereby an individual directly receives the funds to purchase his or her care, has been an attempt to introduce the principle of autonomy and personal choice for individuals dependent on personal care services. But what is lacking is the blend of organizational form and public policy that can combine empowering and socializing delivery models on the one hand with new economic and power-sharing relations with the state on the other. What is needed is a new conception of market forces with respect to social care and relational goods.

Civil society finally has to reflect upon and articulate civic solutions to the challenges of social care in a new era. This entails the liberation of civil society from its subsidiary status to the state, the maturation of the sector as an independent social force, and the creation of a true civil economy for social and relational goods — a social market suited to the unique operations of the social economy. Only in this way will the overwhelming power and influence of the capitalist market be brought into balance with civic values. An autonomous civil economy based on reciprocity and civic values makes possible the political power necessary to negotiate a new social contract for a new age.

Creating a Social Market

A recent experiment in Bologna may hold the key to establishing a social market without compromising the obligations and prerogatives of government while at the same time tapping into the social economics of reciprocity.

In 2002, a foundation called the Fondazione del Monte di Bologna e Ravenna started to experiment with new ways of funding social care to seniors. Previously, like most foundations, it had provided grants to a variety of social service groups that then delivered care to seniors and their families across the city. The service organizations retained full control of the funds while the users of these services had little or no role in influencing the content or quality of the care they received. Nor was it easy for consumers to seek more appropriate care elsewhere if they were unhappy. The funded groups were established organizations, secure in their funding, and had little incentive to change so long as power remained exclusively in their hands. Accountability flowed to their funders, not to the people they were meant to serve. Moreover, the model incorporated one of the worst attributes of privatized services in the public sector, the isolation of third-party contractors from the funder on the one hand and users on the other. Under third-party contracts, the buyer (in this case a private foundation) does not use the services acquired, the consumer does not pay for the services received and the contractor stands in the highly advantageous position of dealing with a buyer who rarely sees what is purchased and a consumer who never bears the expense. This is a recipe for low accountability, which affects service quality, and for the absence of consumer influence on prices, which provides no controls over cost.

This is the classic charity model of care that has now become universal among non-profits. The problem in Bologna was that in many cases seniors and their families were unhappy with the care they received. But having no control rights in the organizations nor any say over the funds that paid for the services, they were powerless to do anything without jeopardizing the care they depended on. As with government delivery models, these non-profits, despite their best intentions, shared the common faults of paternalism, inflexibility and lack of transparency that flowed from the absence of accountability to users. All this changed when the foundation decided to bypass the organizations and to provide funding directly to seniors in the form of social vouchers. Instead of funding the supply side of social care, they would fund the demand side. Three hundred and seventy-six seniors and their families were involved in the program.

Each voucher covered the costs for a specified package of services. There were different packages depending on the type of services that individuals needed and on their respective ability to pay a portion of the costs. Those who were less able to cover the full costs were subsidized by the foundation and the contributions of those users who could pay more. Finally, the social vouchers could be redeemed at any of a group of pre-authorized service organizations, whether co-op, state-operated or privately run. Overnight, the balance of power between service provider and service user was reversed. Now, seniors or their families could select those service organizations that best provided for their needs. The social vouchers were the universal currency for services, they looked identical and the portion of private contribution to social subsidy was known only to the foundation, so there was no stigma or discrimination attached to their use. Nor was it possible for providers to compete on the basis of cost since the vouchers covered all costs equally. Competition arose solely on the basis of quality. In the course of three years, the quality of senior care improved, costs dropped and the organizations that flourished were those that focused on service quality, innovation and flexibility. Social co-ops that included seniors and their families in their membership did best.

What are the lessons from this experience? First, it indicates that supply side funding for social care can have a direct bearing on the quality of care received. This should come as no surprise. Competition will inevitably arise, not in the familiar manner of government contracts where low cost is often the deciding factor, but rather in a manner favorable to service users. Nor should it be surprising if the organizations that received charitable and government funding should resist such a change. Ultimately, however, social care isn't about the providers; it's about those who depend on their services.

The second lesson is that the limited social market for senior care that was created in this example is replicable on a much larger scale. A social market can be created that involves a different set of relationships and incentives among service users, service providers and funders, whether public or private. The use of vouchers is just one mechanism for empowering citizens. The deeper issue concerns the distribution of economic and political leverage to those who are meant to be served.

There is no reason why vouchers, or other means of placing market power in the hands of citizens, should be associated exclusively with the political right as is currently the case. The use of market power for social care is just as amenable to socially progressive purposes if the market in question is structured around civic principles. All markets are not commercial or capitalist, and the sooner social reformers and progressives understand this, the sooner we can start resolving the contradiction between social goods and antisocial delivery systems. Civil society must grapple with how economics can be made to work for civic purposes — as a social market.

Six factors seem essential. The first requires shifting the production of many social care services from government to democratically structured civil institutions. Government would retain its role as a prime funder for these services. The first portion of this equation is already well underway. Governments have been unloading social services to private and non-profit providers for two decades. It is the second aspect, the need for user control and service accountability that is lacking (as too, is the funding). Social services that receive public funding and are not under the direct control of the state should be conveyed only to those organizations that give users control rights over the design and delivery of those services to users. This applies equally to non-profit and for-profit services. Examples include organizations that provide elder care, family services or day care. Moreover, those services that remain under state control, and there are many (social security, public pensions, public auto insurance, health care services, etc.), should be democratized as far as possible. Everyone with a health card, a social security number or a driver's license should be entitled to membership rights in the institutions that control these services and to representation on the boards that direct these organizations.

Consider health care. In most jurisdictions, Regional Health Authorities are wholly funded by government. Yet they are run like private corporations with their CEOs and boards appointed by Health Ministers. The single most important measure that could be taken to improve their responsiveness to the needs of the communities they are meant to serve is to enable direct community representation on these boards through democratically structured organizations at a local level. And while a case can be made that services like employment insurance, that are highly centralized and nationally administered would make such democratization unworkable, a large portion of state-controlled services are regionally based. The basic principle of subsidiarity, whereby services are controlled by those levels of the state that are closest to the user, would be immeasurably enhanced if it were combined with democratic governance. As we will see in the case of Japan's health co-ops in the following chapter, it is precisely the presence of democratic control by community members that has generated one of the world's leading examples of preventive care.

Second, government funding should, at least in part, flow directly to social care recipients who would then select the services they need from accredited organizations of their choice. To qualify for receipt of public funds, these organizations must have provisions for user control over their operations. In addition, funds must be made available for the organization of independent consumer co-operatives to assist users and their families in the identification, evaluation and contracting of care services to their members. This is crucial, especially in the case of users who haven't the means or the capacity to adequately select and contract services on their own.

Third, social care organizations must have the legal ability to raise capital from among users and from civil society more generally on the basis of social investing. Within a social care co-op, both users and community members would be able to purchase capital shares for the purpose of capitalizing the co-op. These shares would yield a limited return to investors and investor control within the co-op would also be limited to ensure democratic control by co-op members. As social investments these capital assets would not be taxed as income. Social capitalization also requires the creation of a social market exchange based on the principle of reciprocity. Individual investors would purchase shares yielding a limited return, with the capital being used to provide credit and investment capital to social economy organizations. Shares would also be eligible for tax credits on the basis that such investments have a clear and direct social benefit.[23]

Fourth, any surpluses generated by these organizations should be considered, at least in part, as social assets. All social care organizations using public funds would establish an indivisible reserve for the expansion and development of that organization and its services. A portion of operational surplus would also have to be used for the partial capitalization of the social market exchange through the purchase of shares.

Fifth, the primary role of government would be to continue to provide public funds for social care services and to establish the rules of the game. In partnership with service deliverers, caregivers and users, the state would regulate and monitor service delivery, establish service standards, license service providers and enforce legal and regulatory provisions.

Finally, service design and the designation of service needs would take place, as much as possible, at the community and regional level of delivery. This requires the creation of civil and municipal associations of public and community stakeholders to ensure the accountability of services and the flow of information necessary for effective budgeting, service design and delivery. Most importantly, this decentralization of service delivery must include the democratization of decision making through the sharing of control rights with service users and caregivers.

These provisions are obviously not exhaustive. They do, however, outline a direction for the considered development of a market structure that is focused on the social and economic realities of the goods and services it is meant to facilitate. There is nothing here that is indefensible on theoretical, political or pragmatic grounds. What is really at issue is whether key actors and organizations within civil society and the social economy can establish a consensus on the changed reality and the need for civil society to play a new role — to, in effect, grow up and take its place as an autonomous sector of society in proper balance with the state and the commercial market. Until this happens, the progressive colonization of social and public space by capital will continue.

The argument for promoting a renewed role for civil society in the production of social services does not mean abandoning the fundamental principle of collective responsibility for these services. Nor does it mean abrogating state responsibility in favor of private market solutions. It does mean the delinking of public goods from exclusive government control. Public funds would still flow to these services and they would remain universally accessible. But the organizational structures that provide them would become progressively civic. Civil society is the repository of those values and social relations that are best suited to the provision of care in a manner that is humane, responsive and founded on those principles of reciprocity and mutuality that are the hallmarks of caring relationships. What is lacking is the development of civil society institutions that are capable of applying these values on a scale, and in the context, of a modern mixed economy.

In many ways, the struggles over public services that have gripped civil society are part of a necessary maturation process that in the end will give birth to new forms of social care. The spotlight that has been thrown on the role of civil society with respect to social care is not one that it sought. It arose as a consequence of the changes that were thrust upon the state as a result of financial, organizational and ideological pressures. In the developing countries in particular, the pressures — some would say coercions — attending globalization have been especially damaging to the idea of social goods as a civic obligation. As a result, social care is in danger of losing its social meaning.

To date, the posture of the leadership that has arisen in civil society to respond to these changes has been defensive and wholly inadequate to meet the changes that are sweeping away cherished notions of the role of government, the individual citizen, the private sector and the meaning and content of social care. What is urgently needed is a clear and courageous understanding of the immense forces at play and the vision to guide the emergence of a wholly new role for civil society as the wellspring and ultimate guardian of those social and civic values that humanize our relations as citizens. This is true whether we speak of caring for each other in our times of need or ensuring that the blind interests of capital don't replace the bonds and obligations of a caring community with the dehumanizing mechanisms of commerce. This is not just a question of lost jobs or the declining quality of care, critically important as these questions are. What is at stake is the idea of social care as a community's obligation to care for its members on the basis of a common humanity as expressed through relationships of mutual responsibility. It is for this reason that the expansion of reciprocity through the democritization of social care is essential.

Co-operative institutions play a unique role in this process both as a source of ideas and historical experience and as models for the realization of these values in actual social relationships. As the social co-ops in Italy show, and as we will soon see in the experience of the health co-ops of Japan, co-operatives can offer the means to move beyond the conventional framework of this debate to advance a new vision of care that places in better balance the values of civil society with the resources and redistributive powers of the state. Such a project is central to the reclamation of social value in the political and economic institutions of our new century.

CHAPTER 6

Japan

Nothing really prepares a visitor for their first encounter with Tokyo. The entry from the highway leading from Narita International Airport is a descent along twining ribbons of concrete and steel suspended 10 and 20 storeys above the teeming city. At night, the effect is like drifting through canyons of glass and light. A walk along the glittering commercial districts of Shibuya or Shinjuku is an excursion into the heart of some colossal, pulsating virtual reality panorama. It is impossible to believe that such a world, fitting only to some future time, should exist now, erected in a scant 50 years from the ashes of the old city consumed in the fire bombs of World War Two. The ancient wood and paper homes, the narrow streets and secluded gardens—almost nothing of that past remains, save in the memories and customs that still bind this uncommon people together. These have survived and have remained the foundation upon which the new city and the new Japan have been built. They catch one by surprise, like the delicate kimono-clad figure of a woman appearing like some exotic flower on a crowded platform, cellphone to her ear, as the sleek, serpentine form of the world's fastest train flows into the station. Perhaps in no other place do tradition and hypermodernity coexist in such precarious balance.

When Japan emerged from the inferno of World War Two, she was a nation prostrate. All of her cities save Kyoto and four others were incinerated in a calculated war of terror waged by the Unites States on unprotected civilians. In Tokyo, 100,000 people perished in the firestorm that engulfed the city during a single six-hour bombing raid on the night of March 9–10, 1945.[1] Two hundred and eighty-seven thousand buildings and homes were destroyed and the heat generated by the fierce winds that whipped the densely packed city brought rivers to the boiling point.

Probably more persons lost their lives by fire during this six-hour period than at any previous time in history.[2] The destruction of Dresden and the atomic bombings of Hiroshima and Nagasaki are engraved as indelible symbols of atrocity in Western consciousness. Yet the incineration by fire bombing of Japan's cities, that resulted in far greater suffering and loss of life, has all but disappeared from historical memory.[3]

Given this horrific background, the reconstruction of Tokyo and the re-emergence of Japan as a global economic power within a mere twenty years after the war are among the true miracles of the twentieth century. They are testaments to the regenerative power of the human spirit when the social ties that bind a people are harnessed to the achievement of humane and peaceful ends. Perhaps this is the light that emerged from the dark tunnel of fascism that led Japan blindly to catastrophic imperial war. During this time, when militarism and fanatical nationalism had spread deep roots among the Japanese population, Japan's co-operatives were already an outspoken voice for peace. And, despite the government's efforts to destroy them during the war,[4] the co-operatives re-emerged in the post-war years with the promotion of peace work as a central part of their mission.[5] When it was founded in 1951, Japan's Consumer Co-operative Union, the largest consumer organization in the country, adopted "For Peace and a Better Life" as its motto.

Today, Japan's consumer co-operatives have nearly 17 million members, making them the largest organized consumer movement in the world. One third of Japan's citizens are members of a consumer co-op. In the year ending March 2007, Japanese consumer co-operatives had a total turnover of $22 billion, making the consumer co-operatives the third-largest retailers in Japan.[6] In addition to consumer co-ops, agricultural and worker co-ops comprise an additional six million members. Co-operatives are the mainstay of Japan's rural economy providing essential production, processing, transport, distribution and marketing systems in fishing, forestry, and agriculture. Norinchukin, Japan's agricultural co-operative bank, is the 31st largest bank in the world with assets of $530 billion and is the national backbone of those three industries. Every rural village has a co-op store and access to co-op financing and co-op insurance. Almost every farmer, fisherman or forest worker is a member of a co-op.[7] This widespread presence in Japanese society, coupled with a clear social mission, has made the co-operative movement a unique force for change in contemporary Japan. Co-operatives are working at the frontline of consumer issues, food safety and security issues, environmental reform, social care reform and the provision of health care.

The rise of co-ops in Japan is closely interwoven with the interplay of Western ideas and revolutionary historical changes that, together, moulded the transformation of Japan into a modern state commencing in the mid-1800s.[8] The Samurai revolution that opened Japan to the modern era in 1868 followed two centuries of self-imposed seclusion in which foreign influences were resolutely resisted by the Shoguns that had ruled the country since the 1600s. They feared (quite rightly as it turned out) that Christian missionaries and other Western influences would undermine Japan's independence and the Shogunate hold on power. But, as the Borg say, resistance was futile.[9] This was a time of industrial revolution in Europe, imperial expansion and the rise of global trade and the colonial economies. By the time Commodore Matthew Perry of the United States steamed into Tokyo Bay in July 1853, Japan's rulers were realizing that for good or ill, Japan had to enter the global economic game. The immediate consequence was the economic and political subjugation of Japan through exploitative trade treaties imposed by the Western powers. Japan became a semi-dependent colony subjected to the global colonial system. It was a traumatic historical passage that prompted the collapse of the old world Shogunate, the unification of the country under Samurai power and the embrace of Western ideals.

By the start of the 1900s, Japan was enthusiastically adopting and interpreting Western ideas and institutions that were believed to hold the keys to imperial power. These included ideas about the state, the military and industrial development. Their assimilation into Japanese political and cultural realities was a central strategy in the drive to liberate Japan from Western dependence. So single-minded was this pursuit by Japan's new leaders that at the opening of the 20th century, Japan was the only constitutional nation-state outside the West and the only instance of an industrial revolution outside Europe and the Americas.[10] By 1905 Japan had the capacity, as well as the ambition, to be a colonial power on a par to challenge the West.[11] She soon embarked on an aggressive imperial policy throughout Asia.

The first co-operatives appeared in 1897. Japan's embrace of Western models included the adoption of co-operatives as instruments of economic development. Its Industrial Implantation Policy included passage of the Industrial Co-operatives Act in 1900, modeled on German credit unions and agricultural co-operatives.[12] With a legal framework in place, and the support of a labor movement growing in tandem with a new industrial system, consumer co-operatives based on Rochdale principles began to be organized in urban districts. Kobe Co-op and Nada Co-op were among the first and most active of the co-ops in this era and they played a key role in the expansion of the co-op movement throughout Japan. However it was after World War II, with the rise of "livelihood co-operatives" that the co-op movement started to become a significant force in Japanese society and to take on a distinctive Japanese coloration.

Livelihood co-operatives focused on quality of life. They blended market, social, environmental and cultural values in a manner that set Japanese co-operatives apart. This definition of "consumer livelihood co-operatives" as holistic organizations that aim at improving the overall quality of life was adopted by the Consumers Co-operatives Act of 1948 and reflected the unique character of this movement. Unlike consumer co-ops in other countries, these co-operatives were based on the organization of *Han*, literally meaning "a small group" or "unit" of five to ten families, to make up the organizational and operational backbone of this system. Japanese Han illustrate how the co-op model evolved to encompass not only the traditional economic and social concerns of co-op members, but also the broader questions of economic, social and cultural change that have profoundly affected Japanese society as a whole.

The cultural and social roots of this characteristic Japanese phenomenon extend back to the Middle Ages and the operation of mutual aid groups called *Yui* during Japan's feudal period. These groups established the social template for the extraordinary rise of the co-op movement in Japan in the years following World War II. A second, and much less recognized influence, was the Shinto religion with its stress on ritual purity, cleanliness and the sacred unity of humans and the natural world. These religious and cultural qualities were to reappear, transformed and politicized, in the post-war consumer co-op movement.

Yui were features of a collectivist tradition that was a central aspect of agricultural production in Japan, as it was in so many other societies. Embedded in village life for generations, Yui were used as work brigades for the recurrent cycles of seeding, weeding, harvesting, irrigation and pest control that were all elements of rice cultivation.[13] These contributions of village members to the work of cultivation were further reinforced by *Murahachibu*, or ostracism, which acted as a powerful sanction against those who contravened village rules. Freeloaders were excluded from any communication or transaction with villagers. Yui were also to be found in Korea and Taiwan. Similar models were used throughout Indonesia and Bali where water societies known as *subak* had been using co-operation to manage irrigation and pest control in the rice terraces of the Indonesian archipelago for a millennium.[14] Another form of mutual help group was the *Koh* — a rotating credit union that was used throughout Japan in the Middle Ages. The spirit of collectivization that runs so powerfully through Japanese society is clearly visible in these precursors to co-operatives.

In the modern era, this collective tradition was manipulated by the state and blended with nationalist ideology as an instrument of social and ideological coercion. As in Europe at this same time, collectivism showed its dark element in unprecedented depth and scale. European fascism embodied what most appealed to Japan's militarist leaders. Japan's military government forced villages and traditional *Chonaikai* (neighborhood associations) to act as agents of government control rather than autonomous bodies. The war regime during World War II imposed the creation of *Tonarigumi* throughout Japan. These were groups consisting of 10 to 15 families in each neighborhood, ostensibly for purposes of mutual assistance, but also for purposes of civil defense, the transmission of propaganda and political surveillance. Neighborhood informants with links to the police infested these organizations.[15] Each unit was also responsible for the allocation of rationed goods, public health, civilian order and organizing patriotic rallies. Participation was mandatory.[16] These groups were abolished in 1947 by the American occupying authorities but in one of those wonderful ironies of history, the co-operative movement built on this militarist legacy to advance a wholly different movement for social and economic reform. General MacArthur's administration supported this movement, seeing in co-operatives a means for advancing the democratic values it was trying to inculcate in post war Japan.[17] Other democratizing political institutions were also supported, including trade unions, women's organizations, political parties and professional interest groups. In 1952, when the Japanese were granted the rights and privileges of citizenship, many flocked to these organizations, sparking a renewal in civil society that was central in the ongoing reform of Japanese society and political culture and that continues to this day. Passage of the Consumers Co-operatives Act of 1948 was part of this process of democratization and post-war reconstruction.

The years immediately following the war were a time of extreme privation. Food shortages demanded rationing to avert famine. And just as Tonarigumi distributed rationed goods during the war, co-operatives quickly emerged to distribute rationed food and other basic goods in the hard years that followed. This connection between co-operatives and food security remained a constant in the evolution of Japan's consumer movement even after commodities once again became available. When the Japanese Consumer Co-operative Union (JCCU) was established in 1951, it consolidated Japan's consumer co-operatives and established a nationwide foundation for the extraordinary growth of the movement after the war. Access to reliable, quality food products remained a priority, as did a more general commitment to improving standards for the quality of life. But it was the incorporation of Han as the basic unit of member organizations and democratic governance that was to drive the growth and extend the reach of co-operatives throughout Japanese society.

Modern Han were first used as an organizing tool for member participation by the Tsuruoka Co-op in Yamagata Prefecture located in the northeast of Honshu, Japan's largest island, in 1956. This came about when a co-op employee suggested that a group of members meet at one of their houses to learn how to use the co-op's self-service shop. Finding the idea an effective means for promoting communication among members, the co-op developed Han as its primary organizational unit seeing in the small groups an ideal form to balance centralized co-ordination of co-op operations with decentralized distribution of co-op products and the strengthening of member relations. Like the earlier Tonarigumi neighborhood associations, Han were ideally composed of seven to ten members, each representing a household. Membership in a local Han was, however, voluntary. Today, there are about 1,000 Han with over 11 million members throughout Japan, most of them belonging to co-ops associated with the JCCU.[18]

The Japanese Consumer Co-operative Union is the largest and most powerful of Japan's co-operative institutions. But for a broader understanding of how Japan's consumer co-ops are pursuing a transformative social mission, Seikatsu Club offers a compelling example. The name *seikatsu* means "life," as in "the lives of people." In this context, "living people" signifies people who are not only consuming, but are consciously addressing the deeper values of life by how they conduct their daily activities.[19]

Seikatsu Club Consumer's Co-operative Union is an association of 30 consumer co-ops with 300,000 members active in 19 prefectures across Japan. Over 90 percent of its members are women, making it one of Japan's most powerful women's organizations. The association's co-operatives are further organized into 200 branches, which have independent management and carry out autonomous activities at a local level. Seikatsu Club is funded by its members who make monthly contributions of 1,000 yen (about US$11), and who also invest substantial sums in the association. The accumulated contributions of members has grown to $296 million, an average investment of approximately $1,000 per member. Seikatsu Club's head office has a total of 106 full-time staff, and combined with the staff working at the co-op and branch levels and the co-op companies, the total employed are about 1,300.[20]

Seikatsu Club began in 1965 when a group of housewives organized a collective buying club to purchase quality milk at affordable prices. They believed that the milk companies that dominated the market at the time were offering an inferior product and manipulating prices.[21] But this concern about food quality, although essential, was not restricted to food as such. Seikatsu Club members looked beyond food itself to the systems and values in which it was embedded. The poor quality milk sold at monopoly prices was the product of a specific, and corrupted, economic system. Members opposed the economic and cultural underpinnings of consumer culture that gave rise to unsafe food and unhealthy lifestyles, and the reduction of individual and social identity to patterns of consumption. They opposed the very idea of the "consumer" as a definition of people.

By the 1960s, Japan's food economy had been transformed by a headlong flight into consumer culture. The basis of Japan's agricultural economy was (and remains) small farm holdings, unlike the giant corporate farms of Europe and North America. But the traditional food system, based on local production for local consumption, was being industrialized along Western lines. The production of food for mass markets entailed introducing food additives, chemicals, preservatives, antibiotics — in short, the whole soup of chemical and biological "enhancements" that are inseparable from industrial food production. One of the world's healthiest food systems was wrecked overnight. Increasingly, Japan's food was imported from abroad. These changes yielded the predictable results: an epidemic of obesity, increased diabetes and heart disease and rising alarm on the part of consumers, particularly housewives, over the safety of their food. Food became a flashpoint and symbol of the waste, environmental destruction, and cultural degradation of consumer culture itself. It was through the element of food that Japan's consumer co-ops sought to reclaim a holistic communal and environmental ethic. For Seikatsu Club this entailed a radically different approach to the question of consumption, food production and economic organization. In this, Seikatsu Club placed itself at the heart of an issue that, perhaps more than any other, has come to personify the underlying forces at play between global industrial and economic trends on the one hand and their effects at the level of personal consumption and health on the other.

From the start, the neighborhood Han groups were convinced that the only way to fully ensure the quality of the food they were consuming was to establish a direct relationship with food producers. Starting with milk, and then expanding to include other staples such as rice, soy, eggs and vegetables, local co-operatives created a dense web of mutual support relationships in which consumers dealt directly with producers to access safe, quality products. This became a distinguishing feature of the food co-ops and it remains the world's outstanding example of consumer-producer collaboration for food security.

A rigorous quality control system was established for food purchase contracts with producers. (*Teikei*, or contract, means "partnership," but philosophically it means "food with the farmer's face on it."[22]) Farmers contracted for a specified amount of produce based on pre-orders by co-op members. Produce was then delivered to co-op distribution centers where delivery trucks brought the pre-ordered products to the neighborhoods. Local Han would then coordinate the neighborhood distribution. The system was efficient, cheap to operate and subject to careful supervision by co-op members. It cut out the middleman, ending profiteering; it allowed farmers to plan and produce for a confirmed buyer, thereby avoiding the waste and risk associated with mass production for uncertain markets; direct distribution from farm to household eliminated the need for stores, warehousing and expensive packaging, thus cutting capital and overhead costs; and the system facilitated direct communication and collaboration between consumers and producers on how to improve the system and the products. Soon, with the support of producers, Seikatsu Club had established a milk company and its own production of miso according to strict quality controls. It now owns nine companies that produce products for its members.

Over the last 30 years, this partnership with producers has brought 3,000 consumer goods to the market in accordance with Seikatsu specifications. Sixty percent of these are food items. And in contrast to supermarkets that stock up to 300,000 items, Seikatsu Club offers only one brand of each product it sells. This brand is usually superior to the rest, and the practice reduces unnecessary competition between brands and eliminates advertising costs that are passed on to the consumer. In the co-op's view this reduces the manipulation of consumers, especially since co-op members test products before they are brought to market. The prices of the main consumer items are determined according to a producer cost guarantee system, in which all producer costs from production to distribution are made public. In this way, the producer's livelihood and business are secured. Finally, the restricted stock of basic goods means that the co-ops can place large bulk orders for a single product, often reducing costs to below what even large retailers can offer.

Throughout its operations, Seikatsu Club enforces safety, health and environmental principles that guide its operations. Producers ratify these principles and work closely with the association in order to participate in the system and work with members to improve standards. Producers make product information public based on the independent standards Seikatsu has set in agriculture, fishery, stock raising and processed food. An Independent Control Committee, consisting of Seikatsu Club members and producers, examines the degree to which standards are met and revises standards to a higher level. This is done purposely to force national standards upwards. Under the supervision of the Independent Auditing Committee, Seikatsu Club members carry out "mass independent auditing" of production sites. This auditing of product standards by members is one of the characteristic activities of the association and, along with product testing, is one of the most popular activities of co-op members. Seikatsu Club also ensures that the products are environmentally safe. For example, in 1979 the SCCU developed its own natural soap to replace synthetic detergents. This was part of a national campaign to totally ban synthetic detergents.

These efforts to ensure access to high quality, unadulterated food and to protect the environment have deep roots in Japanese culture. It is not

surprising that Seikatsu Club and its allies have so committed themselves to this issue. Aversion to contamination and to despoliation of
nature's systems are deeply embedded in Japanese culture and religion.
The virtue of cleanliness is nearly obsessive. It is evident in the complete
absence of litter on the streets and in the sparkling cabs in which uni-
formed drivers wear white cotton gloves. There are spotless white doilies
on the car seat headrests!

In Japan, Shinto notions of ritual purity are an extension of seeing
nature as a sacred domain. The contamination of food and the desecra-
tion of the environment through industrial production and mass consumer culture are violations of the deepest order. Given this context, the
triumph of consumer culture in Japan in so short a span of time, without
the gradual rise of mercantile values that accompanied this transition in
Europe, is even more astonishing than it first appears. It speaks to the
overwhelming, seductive power of consumer culture as well as the near
heroic efforts of Seikatsu Club members to resist it.

Product Labeling and Advocacy

In January 1997, Seikatsu Club, in co-operation with producers, in-
spected every consumer item in the market and adopted its own labeling
system, which excluded genetically modified (GM) food, feed and additives. It then conducted a national campaign to force local governments
in Japan to have GM food labeled as such, presenting a petition signed
by 680,000 people to the National Assembly.[23] This effort expanded to
include participation of other co-operative groups to stop the genetic
modification of rice and concluded with a national survey on GM food.
Seikatsu Club's efforts to prevent the cultivation and consumption of
GM organisms in Japan has had its effects. The campaign has succeeded
in halting the development of GM rice conducted by the Ministry of Agriculture, Forestry and Fisheries (MAFF), local governments and private
companies. Especially successful was the campaign to halt Monsanto's
GM rice development, which the company intended to use to promote
its GM rice in the Asian market.

This campaign continues at an international level. Seikatsu Club
fought to establish traceability, fully compulsory labeling, full implementation of the precautionary principle and safety inspections by third parties as a basic principle of international food inspection standards for
genetically modified food. The recent outbreaks of BSE ("mad cow dis-

ease") and highly pathogenic avian influenza have added even greater urgency to these efforts. Seikatsu Club and other consumer organizations are engaged in a front-line battle against unsafe food practices whose lethal effects are spread worldwide through a combination of global agribusiness systems, lax regulations and weak government oversight. These threats will only escalate with the ongoing drive on the part of both agribusiness and governments to liberalize agricultural trade in discussions of the World Trade Organization's Agreement on Agriculture. One outcome will be to open Japan's markets even more to foreign suppliers.

It is not hard to see in this scenario a sobering analogy with the current global economic crisis. The same lack of industry oversight combined with global reach and high-risk practices that sowed the world economic crisis could easily translate into a far more lethal outcome through the contamination of global food systems. Greater consumer control over food production has never been more urgent.

Within Japan's co-op movement, Seikatsu Club has moved furthest in linking its co-operative social mission with an overtly political strategy. This is unusual, insofar as many national co-operative movements, including Japan's, adopt a strictly neutral stance with respect to political affiliations. This is true also in Seikatsu Club's case. Rather than ally itself with a political party, Seikatsu Club has embarked on a long-term effort to reform and influence Japan's political system by running its own candidates for municipal office. The aim has been multi-pronged: to institutionalize policies that promote healthy living and protect the environment, to improve social welfare and to strengthen local communities.

In a way that is similar in philosophy to the Han model, Seikatsu Club has organized co-op members to gather together at a regional level to form independent political organizations. This was the genesis of the SeikatsUSHA Network (*seikatsUSHA* meaning people who live, i.e., "inhabitants," as opposed to "consumers"). The Network has succeeded in electing over 140 representatives to municipal councils across Japan, with the majority being women. In a land where politics remains a man's game, this in itself is a major accomplishment with respect to women's rights. The Network movement has emerged as a vibrant grass-roots political force, driven by consumers in a bid to reverse the usual trend of politics in our times. That is, instead of corporate interests co-opting politics to advance market interests, consumers are reclaiming politics to assert social interests over markets.

Workers' Collective Movement

Closely aligned with its political work and food operations is Seikatsu Club's effort to promote co-operative workplaces in local communities. Its Workers' Collective Movement organizes local co-ops where workers own, manage and run their own enterprises, often closely linked to the operations of the consumer co-ops. About 400 worker co-ops have sprung from this movement. They employ 15,000 people in enterprises such as box lunch preparation, baking and food processing activities, care for the aged and handicapped, recycling, editing, advertising, design and the sorting and distribution of consumer materials.[24] Certainly, the Worker's Collective Movement has an economic objective and it has generated work, often employing women whose first work experience is with these co-ops. But what underlies the initiative is the conviction that communities are sustained by institutions that are locally controlled and embody the social values and economic forms that reinforce community life — cooperation, a shared identity and the social capital that enables people to work together toward common aims. Its collective food buying and distribution, political work, consumer education and environmental work, support for the aged and the handicapped — all these initiatives are linked in Seikatsu Club's effort to build community and healthy living as antidotes to the destructive effects of consumerism.

Seikatsu Club is an important model at many levels. It unites consumer and small producer interests in a food production system that combines local production with local consumption and environmental protection as one alternative to industrial food systems. But at the foundation of this system is a profound communal sensibility. Seikatsu Club, and the Japanese consumer co-ops as a whole, rest on a foundation of neighborhood associations whose members share a social as well as an economic bond. And while food safety and healthy living remain at the heart of their work, the changing nature of Japanese society is having an impact on Han and the involvement of members in the work of the co-ops. Japan's consumer co-ops are contending with aging memberships and a base of volunteers that grew up in a very different age. The sense of communal purpose is waning in Japan. Young people are not joining the co-ops. The changing role of women means that the traditional housewives who stayed at home and were the backbone of Seikatsu Club are now entering the labor market and have less time for co-op activities in the neighborhood and within the household. As with other consumer cultures, these factors have contributed to a growing individualization within the membership of Seikatsu Club as well as the other consumer co-ops. Communal distribution of food has declined sharply and has been replaced with home delivery.[25] Increasingly, Seikatsu Club is seeing its mission as one of community building and the provision of specialized services to members whose needs are both social and personal. Senior care, health care, recreational services and a range of other social services are now central aspects of Seikatsu Club's mission, as they are with the Japanese Consumer Co-operative Union and its members.

How Japan's co-operatives deal with the growing individualism and declining sense of community in Japanese society will surely determine the future of its co-op movement. But this seems a universal problem that equally affects the co-operative idea in countries around the globe. Japan's experience holds important lessons for co-operatives and other social movements that are also trying to address the underlying social dynamics that drive, or deter, the formation of healthy communities.

Health and Happiness

On a quiet street in the suburbs of Nagano a group of about 20 have gathered. They are talking animatedly, sitting in clusters on the tatami mats that cover the floor of this quintessential Japanese space — clean, simple lines, wooden beams framing the cream-colored walls, translucent paper screens dividing one room from the next. A woman is quietly padding around the room, serving tea to the guests. Arranged on the floor in front of them are illustrations, notebooks, charts, markers, plastic containers holding various items. This is a meeting of a local Han whose members are learning how to take urine samples. They are associated with the Nagano Co-operative Health Clinic and a nurse is here to train them.

Over the last 30 years, Japan's consumer co-operatives have established 120 health co-operatives representing nearly 3 million members. These co-ops operate more than 13,000 beds and employ 1,635 doctors and an additional 21,000 staff. Their nurses, social workers, doctors, physiotherapists and other health professionals work hand in hand with community members to operate a unique community approach to health care. As with the consumer co-ops, Han are the basis of this system. And similar to their role in building community through the reform of Japan's food systems, Han view personal health as an extension of healthy communities. The symbiosis of professional health care with community activism in these co-ops is the foundation of a preventative approach to health care.

As in the West, Japan's health system is in a state of flux, incorporating experimental blends of public and private systems. Since the 1960s, the country has adopted several programs associated with the welfare state. Japan's national, municipal and employer insurance plans provide universal coverage for health and residential care to its citizens, and its fee-for-service system falls somewhere between Canada and the United States with respect to the state's role in health funding. About 70 percent of health expenditures originate in the public system. But Japan also allows substantial leeway for the private sector. This balance between public and private care has been tilting increasingly toward private systems, as in the West. It is a trend that has been fostered in the last 20 years by reduced public investment in health care, occasioned in turn by tax cuts for corporations and the wealthy at the expense of the middle class and the poor. In this, as in many other things, Japan has followed the neoliberal playbook with a particular zeal. Combined with the world's most aged population, this has resulted in rising health costs that have been met in large measure by direct payments by Japanese citizens. The trend is continuing, with private contributions to public health plans due to increase in 2009. As always, the burden of the change will fall most heavily on those least able to afford it. That such a policy will result in cost savings to Japan's health system is doubtful. Similar policies in the West have deprived those who most need them of vital services (it's the poor who get sick the most), and led the sick to avoid using health services in order to avoid costs, leading to undetected illness and delayed intervention. All this increases costs to the health system. The additional stresses that will surely follow in the wake of Japan's current economic downturn will make matters even worse.

In this context, new solutions have to be found and Japan's health co-ops have created a vital alternative. Combining aspects of public and private models, but rooted firmly in a disease prevention and healthy living philosophy, Japan's health co-ops go far beyond the reactive treatment of symptoms that has become endemic in both public and private systems. Understanding health as primarily a personal responsibility, the co-op system has carefully linked healthy living and food security with the cultivation of social bonds that are an essential determinant of health. Just as the partnership between food producers and consumers has generated a new paradigm for a localized food economy, so has a partnership between health professionals and citizens created an alternative approach to health care. Han are central to this strategy.

The role of Han in Japan's health co-ops is to anchor professional health care in the systems and values of social life. This entails a two-way flow: the transfer of technical and medical expertise to health volunteers, and the flow of health intelligence from the community to health professionals. The partnership of each co-op health hospital or clinic with a specific community through the work of the Han has made Japan's health co-ops the most effective practitioners of preventive health in the world.

Han perform a number of functions for the co-ops they are associated with. First, they act as early warning systems for the emergence of health problems. Han members are trained to conduct a variety of health checks at regular intervals within the community. Like the group in Nagano described above, they analyze urine and stool samples, measure weight and muscle mass, take blood pressure and conduct tests for diabetes. The results are then sent to a professional at the health co-operative where prompt action can be taken if the data indicate a problem. The savings in health dollars, let alone in health outcomes for individuals, are immense. Han also distribute information and conduct seminars on such matters as cold prevention and healthy diets and provide a social network through which community members can take part in group exercise, food preparation and cooking classes and group excursions. The entrances and lobbies of many health co-ops are often a focal point for Han activity. Here, volunteers set up booths offering fresh fruit and vegetables, dietary and cooking instructions and information on the Han's many social and cultural activities. All this is part of a community approach to health in which social bonds and healthy life choices form the context within which health practice, in the sense of professional health intervention, has the most beneficial effects.

Finally, Han do fundraising. The co-op hospitals and clinics are financed through a combination of state health plans for health services, community bonds to cover capital expenditures such as new buildings and equipment purchases and, to a smaller extent, member fees. However, unlike other health facilities, particularly private ones, the health co-ops make a determined effort not to restrict their services on the basis of whether members can pay for them. The increase in user fees for health services is absorbed by the co-op for those who are not able to afford the rise in costs.

This extremely specialized approach to health care has demanded a wholly different mode of training for health professionals. Health co-ops play a central and highly respected role as a training system for doctors, nurses, and other health care workers.

Elder Care

The vast majority of patients in hospitals are seniors. In many cases, one would have difficulty in discerning a regular hospital from a senior's facility. Nearly one in five Japanese are now over the age of sixty. It is no surprise therefore that Japan's co-ops have focused so squarely on senior care as an issue.

A large portion of the health co-op system is devoted to rehabilitation centers for the elderly. In many of these centers, the average resident is 85 years of age or older. But what is most astonishing is that over 45 percent of the residents in these facilities return home after a short stay, usually less than six or seven months. The primary goal of the centers is to enable seniors to return to their homes and their communities where, if necessary, they can be tended by home care workers that are associated with the worker and consumer co-ops operating in the neighborhood. The preservation of social relationships within the individual's own community is the cornerstone of this approach, greatly contributing to seniors' autonomy, health and well-being, as well as combating the isolation and loneliness that is so often a feature of conventional senior care facilities in North America.[26] The pain and suffering of spousal separation as described in the chapter on social co-ops would be unthinkable in one of these co-ops.

The other aspect of the co-ops' work with seniors that is worth mentioning is the creation of worker co-operatives that offer both services and meaningful employment to seniors. Much of this work is taken up directly by the two worker co-op federations in Japan, the Japan Worker Co-operative Union (JWCU), associated with the trade union movement, and the Women's Worker Collectives (WWC), that were set up by Seikatsu Club.[27]

Unlike in Canada and the US, Japan has no mass organization representing the elderly. The co-op movement aims to fill this gap by recruiting seniors into worker co-ops that offer them the chance to remain active and to retain their connections to community. The first Senior Co-operative (Koreikyo) chapter was founded in 1995. By 2000, 27,000 seniors had joined chapters across Japan. Today, Koreikyo has over

100,000 members and a chapter in each of Japan's 47 prefectures. Its goal is one million members. Koreikyo's central mission is to find ways to help seniors remain in their own homes as long as they possibly can. It approaches the problem from two angles: to get frail seniors the help they need to stay independent; and to help able seniors find paid work so they can stay active by providing service to others.[28] For many seniors, this link to community service adds a profound sense of value and meaning to their lives and it has become the primary motivation for joining these co-ops. Everyone knows that to feel needed, to be useful, is deeply important to our sense of self-worth and mental health. Japan's co-op movement is responding to a fundamental human need in its connection to seniors.

What makes Koreikyo unusual is the way it combines features of consumer co-operatives, which are common in Japan, and worker co-operatives, which are not. These two different kinds of co-operatives are combined by the simple method of a "pay-as-you-go" ticket system. The different prices of the co-op's services are published, and generally kept slightly below market prices. Members buy books of tickets and as they use co-op services they turn over the appropriate number of tickets to the co-op member providing the service.

In addition to home-helpers and transportation for medical appointments, Koreikyo provides a wide range of other services to its members. These include nursing home care (feeding, changing bed linens), alterations for clothing and home repair and renovation. Koreikyo also links its members to the community and social services provided by local Han as well as the services offered by its own co-op members — touring and hobby groups like knitting and doll-making, social service volunteer opportunities, fundraising for Koreikyo and other charitable institutions, reading and discussion circles and newsletter publishing. Chapters in different parts of the country provide cooked lunches and dinners, home delivery, day-care centers for seniors and even three assisted living centers.

In Japan, until quite recently, daughters-in-law and daughters were the primary care givers at home for the elderly who were fortunate enough to have families to care for them. During World War II, Japan lost nearly 3.3 million men. More than two million women lost the opportunity to marry and raise a family. This group of women cared for elderly parents in extended households. Today, they are in need of long-term care themselves but do not have families to care for them. While recent statistics show that about half of Japan's aged continue to live with their families, extended family living will likely decline. More and more of Japan's seniors are finding that with or without families of their own, co-operatives like Koreikyo are becoming an irreplaceable part of the solution to many of the problems that aging presents.

A preventive approach to health is, of course, well known in the West. It has become part of the mantra for progressive health policy, along with such practices as team-based approaches to health delivery, expanding health care beyond the brotherhood of doctors, for example, to nurse practitioners. But much has conspired to prevent their realization in practice. This is not the place to delve into detail, but one thing that surely prevents this approach from becoming a reality in Canada and elsewhere is the isolation of the health establishment from the broader community. More particularly, this means the absence of an organized, local community structure — similar to the Han concept — that could partner with health institutions to put such a model in place.

Health co-ops do operate in Canada and the United States. In Canada they were established in the 1960s during the bitter battle and a strike by doctors who were determined to prevent the introduction of universal health care. Many of the best practices associated with preventive health care were pioneered by these co-operatives. In the United States as well, some of the finest examples of community-based care are health co-operatives established as alternatives to the privatized for-profit system that plagues health delivery in that country. The Seattle-based Group Health Cooperative, which was founded in 1947 by a coalition of consumer co-operatives, labor unions, and idealistic doctors and nurses, operates one of the largest, and highest-rated, health management organizations (HMOs) in the Midwest. This too was established only after a protracted battle with the medical establishment, including the American Medical Association, which tried to crush the co-op by blacklisting its doctors.[29] Vested interests die hard, and nowhere is change more difficult to achieve than in the challenge to professional castes that continue to dominate the health field. But change is coming all the same. It may be delayed, and it may be compromised, but the demand for reform remains constant and once it aligns with a model that empowers people and mobilizes their communities, it is irreversible. The visionary linkage of food, health, social care and community by Japan's consumer co-ops is but one example of what is possible.

CHAPTER 7

The Daughters of Kali

Kali reigns over Calcutta.[1] She is the Dark Goddess. Emblematic of destructive rage and triumphal power, four-armed, red-tongued, swinging a severed head and wearing a garland of human skulls, she dances in ecstatic fury over the body of her consort, Siva. A tribal deity that draws forth fear and frenetic faith in equal measure, Kali is complex, contradictory and mystical, blending chaos and wisdom in a manner that makes the Terrible Mother the perfect symbol for Calcutta, the city named in her honour.

Kalighat temple remains one of Hinduism's holiest shrines and the origin of the city that has grown around it. For centuries pilgrims have flocked to the temple near the banks of the Hooghly River, a branch of the Ganges that empties into the Bay of Bengal. Today, as before, pilgrims, and the vast economy of religiosity that accompanies them, continue to flow here. With its strange fusion of superstition and spirituality, purity and putrescence, Kalighat gave rise to both the swarming city and Calcutta's oldest red-light district. Where pilgrims came, so too did the discarded women. Some — the widows, the outcast — sought mere shelter and sustenance; others came to service both pilgrim and priest. In both cases desperation drove many inevitably to prostitution.[2] And through the ages there stood Kali — primal, powerful, a source of strength and solace to the most forgotten of India's faithful and Hinduism's most potent symbol of feminine power. Kali was, and remains, the protectress of the outcast, the despised and the powerless — none more so than the women who trade sex for a living.

I had come to Calcutta to learn about Asia's first, and largest, sexworker's co-operative. I had first found out about USHA Multipurpose Co-operative when I was looking for models that could be applied to a bold project that my association in Vancouver was supporting in the city's notorious Downtown East Side. It was here that nearly sixty women from the sex trade had disappeared in what was to become Canada's most horrific case of serial murder against women. Sex workers in Vancouver were fearful. They had seen their friends vanish without a trace and were determined to establish a safe haven for their trade. The BC Co-operative Association had helped them incorporate a co-operative as a means of taking control over their work and providing themselves some modicum of safety. It was in Calcutta that women in the sex trade had first developed the social and political organization that was to become a model for empowering sex workers the world over.

A visit to Calcutta is a test of endurance. For both residents and visitors, it is a city to be suffered. Infamously dysfunctional, it took the particular lunacy of the British to establish the seat of their empire here. Predictably, it was a strictly commercial logic that persuaded them to do so. Before this, the area was a forgotten collection of small, fly-blown villages centered round the Kali temple and located on the malarious marshes and mud flats of the Bengal delta.

Calcutta is a new city, just over 300 hundred years old, and a British creation. It was founded in 1690 by Job Charnock, a British merchantman and an agent for the English East India Company.[3] When Charnock was appointed company agent for Bengal in 1686, the company was headquartered at Hooghly, 40 kilometers upstream from the present city. But hostilities between the British and the locals forced the company to seek a new base. Moving up and down the muddy banks of the river, Charnock finally settled on the tiny hamlet of Kalikat as the future site of the company. It seemed a good idea at the time. Situated around the elbow of the Hooghly, it was protected by the sweep of the river on the west and by the jungles and marshes on the east. The river was deep enough for easy navigation and the curve at this spot offered a spacious harbour. From a trading and military standpoint, it was ideal. For people having to actually live here, it was a purgatory. Calcutta's searing dampness saps the will and discourages all but the most necessary effort. From mid-March till the beginning of the monsoon, the temperature climbs to 43 or 44 Celsius and stays there. The effects on the city today are unbearable. The tar liquefies on the roads. The Howrah bridge, a cat's cradle of steel girders that stretches 705 meters across the Hooghly, is habitually a meter longer by day than by night. The heat and humidity alone should have forewarned what lay in store for the city.

But with that blithe self-assurance that has always stamped British disregard for the common sense that confounds mere mortals, the East India Company won the right to occupy the site in 1696. Calcutta came into being. As it grew, a confusion of Indian and Western influences, a commercial melting pot and a court for empire, there also arose an army of the poor and the destitute that were to become a lasting symbol of the city. In swelling numbers, the city absorbed the fortune seekers and those whom fortune forgot. Calcutta became the capital of India and the second city of the British Empire. Surrounding the cloistered precincts of the commercial elites, beyond the protective walls of the colonial palaces, wave upon wave of humanity poured into the city. Succeeding cycles of war, famine and unrest deposited a desperate underclass seeking refuge from death, disease and every affliction of a people struggling through the violence and turbulence of new nationhood, partition and religious and communal conflict. Their huts, ramshackle confections of scrap and rusting tin, clung against the city walls like the detritus of a departed tide.

The intermingling of these opposing fortunes, of the poor and powerless with the mandarins of empire, British and Bengali alike, offered fertile ground for the city's blooming sex trade. Sonagachi, Calcutta's largest and most notorious red-light district, arose as an adjunct to the dispensation of British power — secular, commercial and just as needful of the pleasures of the flesh as every age that preceded it. Along with the endless throng of lorrie drivers, migrant laborers, soldiers, sailors, rickshaw pullers and roving husbands, the quarter thrived by serving the officials of the East India Company and the burgeoning civil administration.

Sonagachi

Sonagachi is situated at the north end of Calcutta, leading off from the long, smog-filled canyon of decaying buildings and snarled traffic that crawls up Chittaranjan Avenue along the city's central spine. The name Sonagachi derives from a Sufi holy man called Sora Gazzi who ministered to the people living in this quarter. A temple consecrated in his memory can still be seen at the western end of the neighborhood where the main entrance used to be. Now, most people access the district from the thoroughfare along Chittaranjan or emerge from the subway that runs beneath the avenue. The setting is one of decrepit three- and four-storey buildings lining close, congested lanes crowded along a noisy and chaotic marketplace. Sewage and garbage disposal in the district are medieval. Rats are a plague. Ravens are everywhere. An estimated 4,000 sex workers live and work in the 370 brothels that operate here. During festival periods, this number jumps as women join the trade to pay for the added expenses of the holy days. The buildings that are used for the sex trade house several brothels that range in size from 5 to 25 rooms. Living space is cramped and dark, with toilet and washing facilities used in common. It is not unusual for four to six women to share a single room, partitioned by curtains. I visited a room where three generations of a family share space with itinerant sex workers bringing the number of inhabitants to ten.

The sex trade in Sonagachi relies on the 20,000 or so men who visit the district regularly. They are mostly migrant workers living away from their families and eking out a living doing physical labor, often in the construction industry. Some are regulars, visiting their chosen partners exclusively and developing long-term relationships with them. They are known as *babus* and occupy a recognized place in the ecology of the community.

Sex workers operate within a strictly recognized hierarchy that is organized around the amount of money they earn. The top group belongs to the upper class or "A" category, also called *Agrawalis* as this group originally came from Agra. These women are attractive, experienced and command prices ranging from 1,000 to 5,000 rupees per week (about 22 to 110 US dollars). The next group is the mass of young, inexperienced workers who occupy the "B" category and earn from between 500 to 1,000 rupees per week. The lowest tier is composed of older women who earn less than 500 rupees per week. When they are too old to trade for a living, one can see these women begging in the streets. Except for the few, poverty here is endemic.

Sex workers operate independently or under the control of madams (*malkin*) or pimps (*mastaan*). The pimps can be seen congregating in clusters on the street and are recognizable by their attire; they wear a white sleeveless undershirt over a sarong. Mastaan collect one-quarter of the earnings while madams take an even 50 percent. Rooms are rented on a daily, weekly or monthly basis. If a sex worker does well, in time she may come to own her own room, subletting it to other sex workers, or even acquire other rooms that she then rents as a madam in her own right.

At first sight, Sonagachi appears the same as most other neighborhoods in Calcutta. It is cluttered with the usual mix of cars, carts, rickshaws and trucks that compete with the pedestrians for possession of the narrow streets. An endless assortment of shops, stalls and workshops line the roads and alleys, offering every conceivable type of good and service. Most of the shops are tiny, some no larger than a cupboard, with the shopkeeper sitting on a ledge like a yogi and dispensing spice, rice, paan, fruit, cloth, sweets, cigarettes, to the bustle of people that flows through the warren of streets. In the deeper alleys, one sees tanners, bakers, tailors and metalsmiths sweating over forges and beating out iron on the blackened anvils. Sonagachi, like every other neighborhood in Calcutta, resembles a densely packed village. The age-old habits that its residents have carried with them from rural life are being created anew, using the familiar patterns of village life to make life possible in this most unforgiving of cities. The intimacy of the village within the noise[4] and chaos is one of the city's most memorable features.

In some ways, it is misleading to call Sonagachi a red-light district. The phrase reduces what is in fact a complex, thriving neighborhood to a single aspect. The sex trade here, although very old and a major source of income for the area, is only part of a larger social fabric, a rich tapestry of trades, occupations, lifestyles and relations that blend together to create a wholly unique and compelling society in miniature. Prostitution here is not marginal. It is mingled deeply into the lifeblood of the community.

Historically, prostitution in India has had a far more accepted presence in mainstream society than in the West. Some of India's first sex workers, the *Devadasis*, operated from temples. In the Yogimara Cave located in the Ramargh hills of Andhra Pradesh, inscriptions dating from the 3rd century BC make reference to temple prostitutes and are among the earliest archeological evidence for sex workers in India.[5] Prostitutes and courtesans in ancient India seemed to have a more respected status than was to be the case in modern times, particularly in Bengal where Tantric practices and the cult of Kali were cultivated.

Many sutras celebrate human sexuality, with Vatsyayana's *Kama Sutra* being best known for its frank exploration of sexual love. But on the question of sex workers or courtesans the *Kama Sutra* is extraordinary in its frankness. The sutra contains an entire book of six chapters dealing exclusively with courtesans and addressing such questions as deciding on a friend; what constitutes an eligible and ineligible lover; acquiring a lover; how to get rid of him; giving the beloved what he wants;

signs indicating he's losing interest; how to get money from him; weighing different types of profits and losses; how to get back together with an ex-lover; and the different types of courtesans. More than 1,500 years ago Vatsayana pointed out the reality of, and the need to take care of, the female orgasm, long before the dawning of this theme in Western literature.[6] He also noted the existence of male and female homoeroticism and of transgender sexuality in the India of his time.[7]

For any observer of the sexual culture of contemporary India, the relative tolerance of sex and sex work in ancient India presents a stark contrast to the suppression of sexuality that coincided with the imposition of Victorian values during English rule and the rise of a Puritan strain of Hinduism. And while Western culture has undergone a revolution in sexuality (one with its own dark side to be sure), sexual culture in India remains deeply problematic and steeped in patriarchy, hypocrisy, superstition and a continuing infantilization of sex. One need only consider the degree to which Bollywood films are soaked with that peculiar mix of rampant desire and chasteness to see how stunted and socially frustrated sexuality has become in India. But aside from the tortured gyrations of Bollywood actors, which are admittedly hilarious, there is little to laugh at. The consequences of this sexual repression, combined with a patriarchal culture, are truly catastrophic for women. The tragic evidence of this will become plain in the stories of the women that follow. Meanwhile, the average pious Indian male experiences sexuality as a shame-ridden affair hemmed in by religious prohibitions, social condemnations and cultural traditions such as arranged and child marriages (an astounding 70 percent) that, taken together, pre-empt the fruition of a healthy sexual life.

At the time Calcutta was founded in the 1690s by the English East India Company, sex workers as a community were not looked down upon by other sections of society. Some of the early colonial administrators recognized this. They saw that the life of a prostitute in India was very different from that of her counterpart in England. Prostitutes in Calcutta had a recognized domain and terms of exchange recognized by the colonial courts. Until the 1850s they issued summonses against customers that defaulted on payment. All this changed with the Crimean War and the rise of Victorian values within the imperial bureaucracy. The combination changed the world of the Indian sex worker forever.

Horrified by the numbers of British soldiers suffering from venereal diseases following the Crimean War, the British Parliament passed the Contagious Diseases Act in 1854, which was subsequently enforced throughout the Empire. On 1 April 1869, the Indian Contagious Diseases Act of 1868 came into effect. Its primary element was the compulsory registration and medical examination of the city's sex workers, especially those whose clients were British soldiers. What followed was a brutal assault on the sensibilities and self-respect of sex workers and their communities. Ignoring the powerful sensitivities against nudity in Indian culture women were often forced to disrobe in public while undergoing medical examination with the use of metal instruments. Those who fled or were reported as absentees from the examinations had warrants issued for their arrest. Others who were unable to bear the shame committed suicide. Beset by the colonial police and chased down in the service of a "beneficial law" sex workers were criminalized, driven underground and subjected to indiscriminate arrest and punishment.

The abuses that accompanied the enforcement of such a law might have been predicted. The sordid details began to come out when the sex workers themselves rebelled and petitioned the courts against the Act and its enforcement after police had arrested 1,400 of them. Charges of abuse of power, graft, violence and molestation were later proven in court. Policemen were sacked. Once the abuses became public, demands for the suspension of the Act began to draw support in England. Following a sustained campaign, the Act was suspended in Calcutta in 1883 and finally scrapped in 1888. But the views it embodied crystallized in the attitudes and subsequent practices of civil and police authorities and continue to this day, as do the abuses. However, the lesson of rebellion and resistance was not lost. Now, after two centuries of living in the shadows, the more than 16,000 women that work in Calcutta's sex trade are once again claiming their place in the light of day.

In February 1992, the World Health Organization approached the All India Institute of Hygiene and Public Health Calcutta to conduct a baseline survey to assess the incidence of sexually transmitted diseases and the prevalence of HIV among sex workers. Also active in the project was India's National Aids Control Organization (NACO), set up inside the Ministry of Health to help fight the AIDS epidemic at a time when the Indian government was still in denial. Four cities were selected: Calcutta, New Delhi, Mumbai and Chennai (Madras). This question of health gave rise to a movement that combines female empowerment, social justice and economic freedom to challenge the patterns of power and discrimination that have kept sex workers suffering and silent for too long.

At that time, Dr. Smarjit Jana was an epidemiologist teaching at the All India Institute. A compact, no-nonsense looking man, Jana explained that when WHO first approached him to head up the survey he was reluctant. His field of study was occupational health — planning and designing studies on occupational groups. This project was outside his field of expertise. What did occupational health have to do with the sexually transmitted diseases of sex workers? Jana had no idea where Sonagachi was, nor was he interested in HIV/AIDS. It took four weeks of steady persuasion to get him to change his mind. As he puts it, the light finally went on when he realized that sexually transmitted diseases *were* an occupational hazard for a professional group. Prostitution was, in fact, sex work. Jana came on board and the Sonagachi Project was born.

Jana explains that the first major problem was convincing sex workers to take part. It took more than three months of intensive outreach involving door-to door home visits to gain the trust and confidence his team needed to gather the necessary samples. Understanding the community's sensitivity to a survey of this sort and not wanting to repeat the blunders of the past, the project sought the advice and help of community groups like the Society for Community Development, which had previously worked with the sex workers in Sonagachi.

From the outset, the perspective that guided the project organizers was that along with surveying their subjects, it was essential to understand their lives, their issues and personal problems. As Jana put it: "The women lead a strangely confined life and lack social understanding because of an absence of social interaction. The only language they know is the language of the body, through which they interact with their male clients. This experience gives them a distinct perception of life, different from that of mainstream society. Our aim was to explore the world of their perceptions. We felt that unless we understood this, we wouldn't be able to understand them or identify the real problem."

This genuine interest in the lives of the sex workers coupled with the absence of any moral judgements was the key that opened the secret life of Sonagachi to the researchers. A random sample of 450 sex workers (around 12 percent of the community) was selected for the survey. The survey also gathered demographic data on sex workers' personal habits, customs, sexual behavior and practices, as well as their health status. The team set up a clinic in the middle of the area that offered free service for a period of three months, while the survey was being carried out. The participants were first interviewed and then motivated to visit the clinic where they were examined and tested for HIV. And although the emphasis was on sexual health, all sorts of people — not just sex workers — used the clinic to discuss general health problems as well.

According to Jana, one of the first questions that a sex worker asks at the health clinic is "Can I have a child?" This was a topmost priority, almost an obsession, with every sex worker. Their health was not so important to the women, it was their fertility they were concerned about. Jana went on to explain: "The desire to have children was a peculiar revelation. We were not able to understand their eagerness to bear children…but if the root of health care was to be addressed we realized that we first need to understand the world of the sex workers — not from our positions, but on their terms." [8]

The Sonagachi project was the only one that succeeded in completing the base-line survey. Using conventional models that involved no outreach or strategic community development methods the projects in Mumbai, New Delhi and Chennai were all abandoned after failing to collect their required number of samples.

Meanwhile, the results coming in from the Sonagachi survey were grim. They showed that of the 450 women surveyed, 45 percent used occasional contraception in some form with only 27 percent using it regularly. Only 2.7 percent were able to insist on the use of condoms. Laboratory results showed that of 360 sex workers tested, over 80 percent were found infected with one or more STDs while about 1 percent tested positive for HIV infection. Four of these had syphilis. [9] The alarmingly high incidence of STD infection led WHO and the project team to develop a longer-term project to address the need for urgent medical support and an intervention program to control the spread of HIV/AIDS. Dr. Jana and his team were once again asked to lead the project and in 1992 a six-month project called STD/HIV Intervention Program (SHIP) was started in Sonagachi. It had three components: the provision of health services; information and education on sexually transmitted diseases; and promotion of condom usage among sex workers.

In addition, the SHIP team remained clear about their approach. The team believed that sex work was a profession and had to be seen as legitimate. No attempts were made to rescue or rehabilitate sex workers, nor were moral positions taken on their work. The emphasis instead was on improving the material conditions of sex workers and the communities in which they live and work.[10] Health was central to this task. For sex workers a regular checkup is an occupational necessity as the risk of STD or HIV infection (or re-infection) is an occupational health problem that they constantly face. Isolated and easily intimidated, the women were often powerless to resist demands from men to have unprotected sex. The realization of this link between health and power was the catalyst for the birth of the Durbar Mahila Samanwaya Committee (DMSC), the instrument through which Sonagachi's sex workers began to challenge centuries-old attitudes to themselves and to their work.

The approach taken by the SHIP team in Sonagachi was unprecedented. It formed the basis for a relationship of mutual trust that built up a rapport between the project and the community. It also required the creation of a cadre of educators that could organize within, and be accepted by, the community. The project team realized that the project would be effective only if sex workers were approached directly by their peers. They needed people who were intimate with the life and culture of the community and could communicate with other sex workers at a very personal level. A group of twelve women called Peer Educators, who were either active in the sex trade or retired, were recruited from the community. This recruitment and training of sex workers to organize the work within the community was the turning point in the project. Sex workers themselves became active subjects of the work, real leaders, not simply the objects of study or treatment. It was the kernel from which a government-sponsored program was transformed into an advocacy organization organized and run by the sex workers themselves.

Peer Educators were the key that unlocked the closed world of sex work and the sex worker community. They established a new identity for sex workers and a new freedom to interact as women with value. Everything flowed from this — the creation of a community based on equality, choice and the ability to act, and react, as agents with a common purpose. This was unprecedented and news of it spread like wildfire across the city. For the first time, sex workers found, and revealed, a self-identity with which to confront the world. Sex workers began to see themselves as part of society, not just outcasts. The question of social identity and self-respect was to remain central both to the SHIP Project and to the work taken up by the DMSC later.

Peer Educators were responsible for getting sex workers to visit the clinic regularly to have their health checks done. Each of them had their own network within the community, their own contacts and outreach areas. In their new role, they made frequent visits to other sex workers in the area and established close contacts with many. But it soon became clear that this was not enough. Putul Singh, a member of the founding group put it this way: "It was not enough to inform them of the risks of unprotected sex and the threat to their lives. The sex workers had to be first made to value their own lives. If they learn to value themselves, then they will believe in the need to protect their health and their lives."

The challenge lay in the need to build a positive self-image, and for the sex workers to gain self-worth and confidence. Without this, sex workers would never develop an interest in investing in and planning for their future. HIV could not be a priority until other issues were addressed. This work in the program gave Peer Educators the space to build solidarity around a common goal and to think beyond their immediate survival. It prompted the women to reflect on the circumstances that determined their lives. Their world changed with the insight that the sex worker community was isolated, vilified and exploited not as a result of their profession, but as a consequence of unequal power relations. The social realities surrounding sex work meant that health issues were linked to the patterns of power and control that ultimately dominated the lives of these women. At long discussions among the Peer Educators and the project steering committee at the SHIP office, what emerged was not the need for behavioral change, but the need to change the power structures that surrounded sex work itself. The world of pimps and madams, police and politicians, continual violence, thugs and traffickers and loan sharks, would have to be confronted.

It was clear that all these interlocking issues could not be dealt with by the existing organizational setup. A new, permanent structure was required that would allow the community to take up these issues directly. This was the genesis of DMSC or Durbar, launched by nine SHIP members in March 1995. The word "Durbar" means "unstoppable" or "indomitable" in Bangla. DMSC's purpose was to give sex workers the power to defend their human rights, decriminalize sex work and have it recognized as a valid profession and improve the living and working conditions of sex workers and their communities. The organization was registered as a society, but from the outset its operating philosophy and structure were co-operative and democratic. These were essential elements in building the kind of mutual support and united action that were needed to give members control over their own bodies, sexuality, health and life.

At its very first meeting, the issue that took immediate priority was the indebtedness of sex workers and the discrimination they faced from the financial system. The unwillingness of banks to serve sex workers meant that they relied on moneylenders that charged from 300–1,200 percent interest for loans. It was a system of extreme exploitation which ensured that sex workers would never save money, never repay their debts, never be able to educate their children or have their daughters marry, and would always remain subject to the intimidation and violence of "collectors" and the nexus of control in which they were caught.

A number of strategies were discussed. One was to lobby the banks. This was rejected as a waste of effort. A microfinance program was debated. This too was rejected. Finally, a co-operative society was proposed. They decided that the co-op form would best guarantee direct ownership and control of the organization by the members as well as provide the flexibility to engage in other activities. What the founders eventually decided on was a multipurpose co-op that could address the manifold issues they had to deal with. What they didn't have in mind was the long, arduous struggle that ensued when they tried to have their co-op incorporated. Like so much else, West Bengal's co-op legislation was an antique remnant of the colonial period.[11] It still contained the kind of moralistic injunctions that had long since been abandoned by the British co-op legislation that had once served as a model. One of the requirements for incorporation was that members be "of good moral character." In the section of the registration form stating "occupation," the founding members had written, defiantly, "sex worker." This was a problem.

At the very best of times, the Indian bureaucrat is a species of man (always a man) requiring the most delicate handling. In a country where power and position are so heavily ritualized, and so carefully rationed, the Indian bureaucracy is the ideal habitat of the petty tyrant. It is the one place where a small man can exercise total power over someone else. The entire machinery of a vast governmental apparatus is at his disposal to help him achieve this one aim. The slightest anomaly or deviation from established form is an occasion for the exercise of this power. This clear requirement for "good moral character" was more than enough to set the stage for a bruising battle. The co-op's application for incorporation was refused. Ministry staff suggested hopefully that instead of "sex worker" the members might write "housewife" as their occupation. The irony of this was somehow lost on them.

The women refused. Aside from the deep insult, they saw recognition of their profession as a central aspect of their struggle. A huge debate ensued, in which the women argued that good moral character was a relative term. They defended their profession. Unlike others, they did not bribe people, they did not kill people, they were not corrupt — unlike more than a few government officials and their sponsors. They pointed out that they were providing a service to society. They gave pleasure. They got paid for their services as do all skilled tradespeople. What was immoral about this, they demanded. During one particularly heated exchange, when a Ministry official again proposed that they enter "housewife" on the forms, one of the exasperated women finally bellowed "Fine!" She would write "housewife." Would the official now agree to marry her? This brought the discussion to an abrupt and awkward end, with the official literally running from the room. It was soon after that Minister Saral Dev, to his credit, supported recognition of USHA and had the provision for moral character dropped from the Act.

USHA Multipurpose Co-operative was finally incorporated on June 21, 1995. It was a major victory. USHA was Asia's first co-operative formed by and for sex workers. Its 13 founding members were all Peer Educators. They had put together the seed money by pooling one day's earnings of sex work. At first, the members' aims were modest. They had no experience of bookkeeping or accounting, and had wanted only a worker's co-operative fund that they could access in times of emergency. By the time the co-op was incorporated, they had substantially expanded their vision. USHA's objectives were:

+ enable the sex workers to generate a sustainable economy
+ act as a credit co-operative and give loans to members
+ sell daily necessities at reasonable rates
+ supply condoms to various organizations who run STD/HIV intervention programmes
+ develop self-employment opportunities for sex workers
+ take up activities for the uplift of sex workers and their families

From 1995 to 1998, USHA had only 200 members. Women were fearful. The co-op's attempt to establish a credit system for sex workers was a

direct challenge to the moneylenders and their sponsors and their reaction was swift and brutal. Dr. Jana and his staff received death threats.
Bombs were used against co-op organizers and outreach workers. Sex
workers who had joined the co-op were savagely beaten up. Most vicious
of all were the "youth clubs" who were controlled by landlords and who
were in league with the loan sharks who financed their activities. These
included "community festivals," religious events and the collection of puja
(offerings) for temples and assorted Hindu deities. All these activities
were part of the trappings of local power in the district and a cover for
the more sinister role these youth played in intimidating and harassing
the women on behalf of the local bosses. It took two years of determined
struggle to dissolve the fear that sex workers had of joining the co-op.
Today, of the 16,000 sex workers that work the area, 12,800 are members
of USHA.

The work of USHA Multipurpose Co-op, in tandem with the programs developed by Durbar, has revolutionized the lives of its members.
In a pale yellow building situated at the end of a narrow lane, eight staff
run USHA's credit program out of a bustling second floor office. On the
ground floor, clustered along the benches and the stairwells in the en-
tranceway, groups of women are always present, using the USHA building as much as a social center as a place of business.

Without access to credit and the ability to save money, sex work is
akin to bonded slavery. Through their membership in USHA, sex workers have been able to save money, take out loans and even invest in businesses and property as a means of transiting from sex work, particularly
in their older years. This small measure of economic power and independence also means that a sex worker can now afford to refuse service
to a client who won't wear a condom or who is a threat to her safety.
The government, despite its original reluctance to incorporate the co-
op, quickly recognized the value of the project and became an early investor. It purchased 40,000 refundable shares, each worth 100 rupees,
to help capitalize the credit union. These were repaid with dividends in
five years. Currently, the government holds 300,000 shares and has two
non-voting representatives on USHA's twelve-member board. USHA
members hold about 1,500,000 rupees in shares.

To join USHA a member must purchase ten rupees in member
shares, plus five rupees for books and materials. They must be 18 years
of age or older. When members take out their first loan, they must also
purchase 400 rupees in investment shares. Thereafter, if members wish

to take out further loans, they must purchase an additional 500 rupees in investment shares for every 10,000 rupees they borrow. In this way the capital stock of the co-op grows as their loans increase. At the end of every year, the dividends from their investment shares are paid out to the members. No member may hold more than 40,000 shares.

In addition to its loan program, the co-op has a range of savings plans to help sex workers save:

+ a recurring deposit scheme in which members deposit multiples of 50 rupees as often as they like and can withdraw the cash whenever they wish
+ a monthly deposit scheme that allows members to deposit savings monthly and which yields nine percent interest with a five-year maturation term
+ a thrift deposit plan that again allows members to deposit multiples of 50 rupees, but limits members to loans, and yields 7 percent interest paid at year's end
+ a daily collection plan in which 38 collectors, mainly the children of members, collect savings directly from the members at the bothels and make the deposits at the USHA office

To date over a quarter of USHA members (3,228) have taken loans valued at $2.5 million. The loan recovery rate is about 95 percent. USHA charges 11 percent on loans, does not compound interest and charges interest only on the balance of the loan outstanding, not the original loan amount. How are these loans used? In order of member priority: to finance their children's education, to cover the costs of a child's marriage (usually the dowry) and to purchase or build a home.

Prompted by the success of USHA in Sonagachi, sex workers in other communities took up the fight and lobbied government to allow USHA to expand its operations into their districts. In addition to Sonagachi, USHA has now established branches in the Calcutta districts of Durgapur, Asansol, Dhulian, Konti and Siliguri. Plans are underway to expand throughout West Bengal to complement the work that Durbar is doing beyond the borders of the city.

The Stories

USHA Multipurpose Co-op is without a doubt one of Durbar's most impressive achievements. But it is only one project among many that the organization has launched in a campaign that has to fight on many fronts and at many levels. To gain some sense of the issues that Durbar and USHA have to contend with, here are three stories that touch on the realities underlying the how and why of sex work in Sonagachi.

Sonuka

Sonuka looks older than her 45 years. Small and frail, she has an aura of gentleness, of silence. Yet when she smiles her face comes to life, lit up by a flash of white teeth and the sparkle of lively brown eyes. A pair of delicate, sparrow-like feet peep out from beneath her burgundy-and-cream-colored sari. She is a figure of fragility steeled by a fierce instinct for survival. We are sitting in her room, at the back of the ground floor in one of Sonagachi's more dilapitaded brothels. I am there with Shanto, a development worker who has worked with Durbar for years and is acting as my interpreter, and three other members of the association.

Sonuka's room is perhaps nine feet by nine and painted a vivid green. The furniture consists of a platform bed that dominates the room, a glass-fronted armoire and a metal cupboard. Shelves set in the walls hold the stainless steel pots and bowls used for washing and eating, rat-proof storage containers and the brightly colored clothes, bags, and sarees that are arranged with care on the shelves and wall hooks around the room. The room is spotless. Just outside the door is a tiny anteroom where a television is playing and Durbar staff prepare chai on the kerosene burner that serves as a stove. Beyond, the dark hallway leads to an inner courtyard that rises through the heart of the building and where, in the twilight gloom, the intimate inner life of the brothel unfolds. The women, seated on the steps or leaning over the balustrade on the first floor, speak softly, passing the time by exchanging the day's gossip as they do in every village in India.

Sonuka has lived in this room for 28 years. She arrived in Sonagachi at the age of 14 when she began her life as a prostitute. Like all the young girls that arrive here, she had no idea what awaited her. Sonuka was born in the small village of Birbhum in West Bengal. At the age of 12, she was married to a man of 20. Still a child, and suffering from a variety of ailments that had gone untreated, she was unable to perform sexually for her husband who, along with her in-laws, became resentful and began to abuse her. Her first beating came because she didn't know how to properly handle the cows in her care. This was followed by endless bouts of beatings and torture and charges that she was impotent, lazy, a curse on the household. When finally her body swelled up and she became immobile on account of gout her father took her back home by force, fearing for her life.

It was during her period of convalescence that Sonuka met a young man from a neighboring village who claimed he had contacts in Calcutta. Determined not to return to her husband and in-laws, she asked her friend to look out for any work that she might do in the city. Soon, word came that he had found work for her as a housemaid and she could now escape a life of servitude and abuse. At the age of 14 Sonuka made a brave bid for her freedom — a young girl traveling far from home to an uncertain fate. When Sonuka arrived at her place of employment, she found she had been sold by her "friend" to a brothel for a price of 5,000 rupees or 50 dollars. She never saw him again. Isolated, with nowhere to go, Sonuka was trapped. It took her two years of sex work, turning six, eight, ten tricks a day and serving four or five customers a night to pay off the debt. She was lucky. The brothel owner was generous and released her once the debt was paid. By the age of 16, Sonuka was an experienced sex worker and she sought her own place, the same room she now occupies.

Today, Sonuka leases her room from the brothel owner and is an independent operator. She has three children, two daughters and a son. All of them have received an education, and her younger daughter is graduating from college. They live in Birbhum, in a house Sonuka inherited, and she divides her time between Sonagachi and the village.

Sonuka joined USHA in 2001, after she heard about the association from fellow workers. She took out a loan of 50,000 rupees in 2007 that she will pay off in 2010, and has a daily savings account. Sonuka has also taken out a second loan that she is using to pay for the marriage of her younger daughter. Her older daughter, too, had been married. But the familiar pattern of abuse at the hands of in-laws prompted Durbar and USHA to intervene on her daughter's behalf. They sent representatives to the village. They took up the case, threatened legal action against the in-laws and ultimately helped the daughter obtain a divorce. Without the organization's support this would have been unthinkable in a small village, regardless of how bad the abuse was.

When she retires, Sonuka's dream is to open a shop in the village with the help of a loan from USHA. Before departing, I ask Sonuka if there is anything in her life as a sex worker that has given her pleasure.

She breaks into a soft flow of laughter. Without a shadow of hesitation she says, "Nothing. Absolutely nothing at all."

Onima

Onima Das is an imposing woman. She sits like a monument in the center of her bed, surrounded by half a dozen men. Some of them are discussing ledgers and papers that are spread out fanwise before her. After we introduce ourselves, someone suggests that our interview take place with the men present. Some of the men seem reluctant to leave us alone. I insist that the interview take place in private and that the men leave. At a word from Onima, the men gather their papers and quietly depart.

At age 52, Onima Das has the regal bearing of a woman used to being respected and obeyed. She has a massive frame, a face that still bears the signs of the great beauty she possessed as a younger woman, and a cascade of raven-black hair that descends to her waist. Draped in a superb saree of lemon yellow and midnight blue she is the picture of prosperity and power. Hers is a true Sonagachi success story.

Onima Das was born in Calcutta. Raised in the poorer northern section of the city, she was married at a young age. Relying on her husband's meager earnings, she struggled to raise four sons. When her husband fell ill and was unable to work, Onima was forced to find employment to support her family. She found work at a tobacco packing plant. Bad as the conditions were, they were soon made worse when the men at the factory started a relentless campaign of sexual harassment, their unceasing demands for sexual favors turning her working life into a living nightmare. This went on until one day, on her commute home, an acquaintance suggested that she become a sex worker during the day and not tell her family. This way, she argued, Onima would receive some decent payment for the sexual favors she was expected to give out for free at the factory.

At the age of 37, a respectable married woman with a family, Onima arrived in Sonagachi to become a "flying sex worker" — one of the legions of women who trade sex in the day while returning home at night. Onima kept up this secret life until one day, having grown suspicious, her husband followed her to the brothel where she worked. Confronted by him, Onima defended her actions stating flatly that she had no choice, that she was constantly attacked by men at the tobacco factory, indeed anywhere she attempted to work, and that without her earnings the family would starve. Reluctantly, her husband and her family accepted her decision on the condition that she remain a day sex worker and return to her home at night. Till the day he died in 2007, the relationship between Onima and her husband remained strong, sustained by a mutual love and respect and the acceptance of a stark necessity born of desperation.

For the first three years, Onima was in great demand and she had a large roster of clients. Then she established an exclusive relationship with one man that continues to this day. Her permanent partner, known as a *babu* and a common feature in the trade, is also now a business partner and helps keep Onima's accounts. He was among the group of men we first met on arriving and he joined in our discussion near the end of the interview.

Onima has done well for herself. From her earnings and a sharp business sense she has succeeded in raising and educating her sons, she owns and operates a saree shop in Calcutta and she has been able to purchase four rooms in Sonagachi that she sublets to other sex workers. Onima has a daily savings scheme and has taken out four loans, three of which she has paid back and a fourth she is currently paying off. USHA and Durbar, she claims, are the sole reasons for her success and the reason she has been able to go into business.

Within the hierarchy of the sex trade, Onima Das is a respected madam and entrepreneur. She was also USHA's first member and a powerful advocate, recruited by Durbar staff in the course of its door-to door campaign to help lead the association's education and organizing work in the neighborhood. She has been a force to be reckoned with ever since.

Rheka

Rheka Roy was first sold to a brothel owner in Uttar Pradesh when she was eleven years old. At the time, she was working as a housemaid and living with her mother in the West Bengal village of Shamnagar where she was born, near the Bangladesh border. Like so many of the village girls she received no education, was illiterate and worked as soon as she was able to help support her family. She was spotted by a woman acting as a recruiting agent for a trafficker and was enticed to go to Uttar Pradesh with the promise of employment. Her selling price to the trafficker was 8,000 rupees, or $171.

When Rheka arrived in Uttar Pradesh, a world away from her small village, she was locked in a room with two other minors. The room had a sink and toilet; all three girls lived as prisoners and never left the room. Rheka was kept here for two years, until she began to menstruate. Then she was forced into prostitution.

Frequently, police would raid the building. They would go through the motions of searching the building for illegal activity, but Rheka and the other girls would be hidden in an underground dungeon beneath the floor, where they could hear the police tromping through the rooms just inches above their heads. All of this was a charade. The police knew about the hideaways and the traffickers were forewarned, but the raids kept up appearances and were part of an elaborate system of bribes and payoffs. It wasn't until she was 15 that Rheka was finally rescued and sent to a government hostel. She escaped, fled to Calcutta and once again ended up as a bonded sex worker in a brothel. One of her clients however, was a powerful local thug, a *goondah*, who took a liking to her. He gained her release and brought her first to Sonagachi and then back to her home village.

Back home Rheka discovered her family in a desperate economic state, just barely surviving. With that combination of cold-blooded realism and truly heroic personal sacrifice that is so often found among these women, Rheka concluded that the best option for her family was for her to return to the sex trade. She was illiterate, had no skills and her most valuable assets — a will of iron and physical beauty — would earn her far more as a sex worker than anything else she could hope for. She returned to Sonagachi.

Seventeen years later, Rheka remains close to her family. She has become a highly valued, and highly priced, sex worker. At 34, she has a voluptuous beauty and her appraising eyes glitter with bold self-assurance, defiance and the indefinable, yet unmistakable, current of sexual energy. She knows her worth. At the top of her trade, she commands as much as 1,500 rupees for a night. She has a reliable roster of 400–500 men that visit her over the course of a year and sees 4 or 5 clients a day. She keeps ten percent of her earnings for herself and her 14-year-old daughter who lives with her and sends the rest home to her mother and siblings — three sisters and one brother, all of whom are now married and depend on her. She now owns the room she has been occupying for the last 15 years. She has no *adhyas* to whom she sublets saying, "I have struggled hard all my life…I have no desire to exploit other women."

Rheka is also now a senior staff person with Durbar helping to administer the organization's many programs. She takes part in an adult education program run by Durbar for its members and for the first time in her life is receiving a formal education. She has mastered basic numeracy skills and is now literate in Bengali. It has taken her three years. These are hard-won victories, wrested from a lifetime of heartbreak and hardship. Her body still carries the marks of abuse and violence.

Like many other women I saw in Sonagachi, Rheka wears a *bindi*, the vermillion dot Hindu women wear on their forehead to show they are married. I asked Rheka, does she have any dreams for herself? Her answer contradicts her open, smiling face. "I have had so many dreams broken that there are none left for myself," she says. "My dreams live through my daughter, seeing her become independent." Will she ever settle down with one man? Still smiling, still defiant, she answers, "Love has always cheated me. I don't want to fall in love anymore. I want only to be left alone with money as my companion."

A Terrible Reflection

Braided throughout these stories, binding them together in a pattern are the three elements that underpin the sex trade in Sonagachi and most everywhere else: poverty, patriarchy and powerlessness. They are the social and economic nexus of prostitution. They combine like strands of fate to pick out who will end up in the sex trade, what their life will be and who will profit from it. Like a terrible reflection, they distill and make manifest the elemental workings of the social realities that give rise to the trade. The study of prostitution may hold more insight into the inner workings of a society than any other behavior. In Sonagachi, and throughout India, prostitution exposes a damning portrait of a society caught in the grip of gender inequity, class exploitation and caste discrimination.

All the women I spoke to, both individually and in groups, were driven to sex work by the desperation brought on by poverty. Even now in their small rooms, poverty is a constant companion. The money they earn, especially if they are new to the trade, is siphoned off to support an intricate superstructure of pimps, thugs, madams, landlords, moneylenders, police and the politicians who sit at the top of the heap. The sex economy functions like a huge pyramid where the higher echelons feed off the lower. As in all forms of organized exploitation, the weakest and most vulnerable do all the work and sustain the rest. The most powerful — the politicians and patricians at the top — simply collect the proceeds from allowing this system to continue. For them, it is essential that sex work remains an underground activity that is never legitimized. Legitimacy would mean the end of graft, the system of payoffs and bribes that feed the spectral figures that loom behind every woman working the street. This is the system that maintains the internal exploitation of the trade and the perpetual poverty at the bottom.

Outside, in the operations and relationships that still define and circumscribe the economies of the villages where most of these women come from, the pattern is the same if more difficult to discern. The women are still at the bottom, do the hardest work for the least money, have the fewest options. The subjection they endure is systemic and essential to the patriarchy that still rules India. As the stories above show, the humiliation of women through sexual harassment in the workplace is a pervasive phenomenon. Everywhere in India, women are expected to submit to the continuous sexual advances of their male co-workers. In the unskilled professions, particularly the construction industry, women workers are required to service their male counterparts if they hope to keep their jobs. It is a major factor in women's decision to take up sex work. The habitual behavior of Indian men, impelled by a mix of sexual frustration and gender entitlement, drive many women to the trade while the men themselves provide the market that sustains it. The fact that there is so little protection for women, so little recourse for complaint and restitution, is what makes this chain of economic dependence, sexual harassment, exploitation and social ostracism so profoundly unjust. As was bitterly remarked by the women of Sonagachi when they sought medical treatment, the same physicians that refused to treat them in the daytime would be their customers at night.

The ostracism and discrimination that sex workers face extends to their children. To be a known child of a sex worker means social humiliation, exclusion from schools and banishment from the innumerable social activities that make a child part of the broader community. This discrimination, coupled with the inability of sex workers to escape debt and save enough money to pay for schooling, condemns many of their children to illiteracy and a future of poverty. Beneath this—hypocrisy's most painful legacy—is the paralyzing destruction of self worth and the erasure of a social identity for child and mother alike.

Then there is the issue of human trafficking. Every day, dozens of young girls arrive in Calcutta as indentured slaves to the sex trade, many from the poor backwaters of Nepal or Bangladesh. They are part of the vast land of lost souls that populate the sex trade stretching across the face of Asia and feeding the unappeasable appetites of a market that grows daily. It too rests on the poverty, ignorance and powerlessness of the families from whence these children come.[12] Combating trafficking and the entry of minors in the sex trade has been a major priority for Durbar in Sonagachi and throughout West Bengal. Once a minor has been identified in the trade, Durbar members often intervene directly with brothel owners and pimps to encourage them to release these minors, arguing that their employment only harms the trade and provides an additional reason for police and political harassment. Durbar members also help unite minors with their families and assist them in getting into school. The association also runs its own residences, training facilities and schools that provide essential support to minors who, for one reason or another, cannot be returned to their families.

When the first base-line survey was completed by the Sonagachi Project in 1992 over a quarter of the women working in the sex trade were minors. By 2008, that figure had dropped to an astounding 0.5 percent.[13]

Through skilled and patient organizing, and a growing capacity for the creation of community through co-operation, Durbar and its constituent organizations have granted sex workers the power to defend their interests and emerge from the shadows of their trade. But more than anything, the work of Durbar illustrates that in the extreme circumstances of a marginalized and exploited community such as sex workers in India, political activism alone is insufficient. The heart of Durbar's success is its capacity to create a new community. And what made this possible was the forging of a new social identity for its members. Co-operation and the sense of mutual need were essential to this task. By working together to solve mutual problems sex workers began to identify with each other not as isolated and competing individuals but as a group with a common identity and a shared experience. Co-operation gave them a new social identity. This was, and remains, an identity they have forged for themselves. Of all the gifts that co-operation has given them, from credit and financial security to the education of their children, this sense of a new self, of a common social identity, is by far the most precious. It is the foundation and future for everything else. As every organizer knows, the first step to empowerment is the recognition of self-worth and the identification of one's interests with that of others. Political mobilization depends on this.

Since the Sonagachi Project began and sex workers started organizing, the impact on the lives of Durbar members and the broader community has been immense. The association has established 12 HIV and general health clinics that see more than 3,000 patients a month. Forty percent of these patients are male. The use of condoms among sex workers in Sonagachi has gone from 2.7 percent in 1992 to 86 percent today, the highest in India. The prevalence of HIV infection among sex workers has stabilized at around 5.2 percent. By comparison, the incidence in Mumbai and Chennai is over 20 percent. The creation of 32 literacy centers for adults and children alike has tripled the literacy rate among sex workers from 4 percent in 1992 to 12 percent in 2005. Four hundred adult sex workers and over 700 children are enrolled in these programs. Among the children enrolled at Durbar learning centers, over 77 percent have been admitted to mainstream schools, slowly reversing the institutionalized discrimination of the school system against the children of sex workers.[14] The incidence of violence and abuse against sex workers in Sonagachi has fallen dramatically. The women refuse to submit to it. The beatings and rapes that they endured at the hands of thugs and police have subsided. Perpetrators know that the impunity they enjoyed for years is over.

Despite these achievements, and despite the undisputed power of Durbar as a model for grass-roots organizing within the sex industry, the challenges faced by the sex workers of Sonagachi and elsewhere in India are still immense. A measure of visibility and grudging respect has been won within these communities. But in a patriarchy such as India's, the entrenchment of traditional attitudes is deep. These attitudes preserve the vested interests of men economically, socially and at the most intimate levels of personal identity and interpersonal power. In so many ways, the emergence of Durbar and the sex workers' movement in India has struck at the very heart of Indian patriarchy. The shock waves ripple out to trouble and make visible the dense web of social, political and economic relations that shackle the lives of sex workers specifically and Indian women generally. The buried links that condition the life of the sex worker on the one hand and the middle-class housewife on the other are the keys to the movement's long-term success. Both have a common interest in confronting the patriarchal structure and gender inequality of Indian society. For this to happen, Durbar has to broaden its political base and take up issues that extend beyond the ghetto of prostitution. Its steadfast focus on legitimizing the sex trade is necessary and understandable. But Durbar can also build bridges around the many civic and social issues that still fester in the communities of Calcutta. Insufficient health care, appalling sanitation, the absence of civic services such as garbage pickup, poor education, lack of security and police corruption — these and other issues can be taken up strategically in a bid to win allies beyond the issue of sex work.

The movement also has to contend with a host of internal contradictions. Because many madams are also members of Durbar and USHA co-op, the fight against minors entering the trade is compromised. Minors earn money for brothel owners who depend on them for a living and the line between sex worker and madam is blurred as the stories cited above illustrate. Despite Durbar's undeniable successes, there are still too many minors working the streets.

Relations between "flying" sex workers and brothel workers are tense. Women from outside the community are considered interlopers and competitors and are restricted to carefully prescribed zones in which they can work. If they step beyond these boundaries verbal battles and worse ensue. And regardless of the hard-earned solidarity that the women of Sonagachi have forged through their struggle, caste attitudes among the sex workers persist.

The legitimation of sex work, the primary political issue for the movement, is also laden with difficulty. Even among Durbar supporters this issue presents problems. Some believe that if sex work were to be decriminalized it would become an acceptable option for more women, particularly from more affluent families. Their entry into the trade could adversely affect the incomes of the mainly poor women who now work in the industry. Legitimation would also entail government regulation and oversight, something sex workers reflexively resist.

The moral questions that surround sex work are not so easily dispensed with by the claim that prostitution is a profession like any other.

It isn't. If sex work is an extension and expression of gender inequality and abuse, unless these social conditions are changed the trade itself is tainted. Legitimation without reform means normalizing the social attitudes and conditions that have driven so many of these women to the trade. This is a conundrum that has no easy solution despite what anyone, including sex workers, say.

What is clear is that the current criminalization of sex work leads neither to social change — in fact, it is essential to maintaining those very systems of abuse and exploitation — or to improving the condition of sex workers, and, least of all, to ending the practice. It is also clear that without the economic and social power that their organizations give them, sex workers will continue to labor in the shadows. Durbar is dragging these discomfiting issues into the light and, in the process, rehumanizing sex workers as women of value with a place of their own to claim in society. The co-op form, directly embodying and expressing the true voices of these women, is an absolute necessity in this struggle. The democratic and communitarian character of their co-op not only binds the women together in a shared sense of identity, it acts as the primary means for mediating their common interest with the rest of society. The co-op and the broader collective of Durbar itself provides them with a public face and a political voice.

Durbar reveals that in India what separates the sex worker from the respectable housewife is not morality but poverty, powerlessness and misogyny. It is a revelation that makes possible the reclamation of self-worth for the sex worker while damning the social conditions that make sex work a necessity.

CHAPTER 8

Fair Trade and
the Empire of Tea

The earth does not belong to human beings —
rather humans belong to the earth.

— Excerpt, UCIRI website. —

I first came to Sri Lanka 30 years ago, following the Asian backpack trail that wound through Southeast Asia from Bali through Indonesia to Malaysia, Thailand, Sri Lanka, India, Pakistan and overland through Afghanistan, Iran, Turkey and finally to Europe. It is sobering now to consider how much the world has changed. Soon after, Afghanistan was invaded by Russia, the Islamic revolution exploded in Iran and the world changed forever. Now such a trip would not be possible.

Sri Lanka seemed then like a land dwelling in a gentler light. It had a quality of otherwordly calm, a gift of natural beauty that so easily masks the violence that often flows beneath the surface. There was little sign of the tragic events that were soon to unfold, consuming the nation in a communal bloodletting that was to last 30 years until, in a final paroxysm of violence, the regime of Mahindra Rajapaksa liquidated the Tamil Tigers on the island's paradisal shores. Throughout the spring of 2009 the war played out on the television screens of the world and millions followed the extermination of the LTTE leadership and the humanitarian disaster that attended it. At the time, I was inside the country working on a project to help communities recover from the devastation left by the tsunami and watched the drama play out. I was traveling the length and breadth of the country, often only a few miles from the coastal area where the LTTE had been cornered. What was most disorienting was how little evidence there was of the war itself. Had it not been for the television and press coverage, it was quite possible to remain entirely oblivious of the carnage that was taking place. Just beyond the kill zone people carried on as if the war was a distant memory. Perhaps this was fitting, for immediately after the defeat of the LTTE, Sri Lanka sank once again into obscurity so far as the world press was concerned. But its tragedy is still unfolding.

Ethnic tensions have been a reality of Sri Lanka for centuries. The most recent violence sprang from policies leveled against the Tamil minority by the Buddhist, Sinhala-speaking majority in the years immediately following independence in 1948. At the time Ceylon, as it was then known, was under the control of the British who had deposed the last of the Sinhalese kings in 1815. Ceylon was absorbed into the colonial orbit of Great Britain after having been occupied and exploited first by the Portuguese and then by the Dutch. By 1948, the island was swept up in the great tide of colonial independence and nation building that followed the Second World War, cutting loose the colonial possessions of the European powers across the globe. In Southeast Asia, European colonial power was replaced by an uneasy blend of socialist euphoria, nationalism and a perpetual struggle between the impulse to authoritarianism on the one hand and pluralistic democracy on the other. Usually, as was the case in Sri Lanka, authoritarianism wore a populist, democratic mantle. This time-honoured tradition continues, alive and well, today. The latest government victory over the Tamil insurgency is being converted into a web of dynastic power supported by the military and the Buddhist religious orders.[1] The image of Prime Minister Rajapaksa is omnipresent. His bulbous head smiles oppressively from banners and billboards at every street corner. His voice is everywhere to be heard. Over the radio and television, his mellifluous tones are unmistakable. When speaking to his public, Rajapaksa seems like nothing so much as a lover in the very act of seduction. He sounds like Barry White in full *canto amoroso*.

Sri Lanka has always been a land occupied and fought over by migrants. The Sinhalese themselves are descendents of migrants from the Ganges valley who settled on the island around the 6th century BC. They were followed by Tamils from Southern India who crossed the 40 miles separating the island from India and settled the Jaffna peninsula at the northern tip of the island and the eastern coasts. Both these peoples displaced, and ultimately eliminated, the earlier Naga nomadic tribes that still inhabited the untracked jungles when Dutch traders first encountered them in the sixteenth century. Today the disappeared Nagas are mere specters, conjured up from artifacts and memory, ghostly presences captured in the faded photographs and dusty journals of Dutch adventurers.

As we shall see shortly, racial and religious discrimination remain unsavoury facts of life in Sri Lanka. Today many estate workers, almost entirely Tamil, continue to be denied citizenship rights and are the lowest paid workers in the country. Although the tea industry is heavily unionized, almost all the unions are controlled either by employers or the government.[2] This corruption of unionism through government control has also extended into the co-operative movement with most co-ops having been used as instruments of government policy. Sri Lanka's experiment with co-operatives as parastatal organizations is an object lesson in how not to use the co-op model as an instrument of development.

Throughout Africa and Asia, post-colonial regimes saw in co-operatives the ideal mechanism for developing national economies while advancing the precepts of socialism. In Sri Lanka, the pursuit of socialism was accompanied by the mythology of a glorious, pre-colonial past characterized by a village-based communalism that was destroyed by British colonialism and replaced by the capitalist ethic of individualism. Administrative reports of the period repeat the belief that before colonialism, rural communities were tightly knit, harmonious and grounded in the communal ownership of land. It wasn't true, but this kind of mythmaking was common during the early post-colonial period. In many Asian and African countries leaders hoped that co-operatives might heal the wounds inflicted by colonialism and restore the traditional spirit of solidarity in village life. Co-operatives were used by the state as part of an ideology of development that portrayed village people, particularly lower-caste people, as inherently different, as more *authentic*, than the English-educated elite who then ran the government. But rebuilding village society to preserve a mythically pure Sinhalese Buddhist culture was also used to legitimize elite rule — a fateful choice that contributed to the outbreak of civil war with the Tamil minority.[3] The ideology of a "pure" Buddhist Sinhala culture also required the denigration of those Sri Lankans like the Tamils and Muslims that represented other, "alien" traditions.

Sri Lanka's co-op experience after independence closely resembles the fortunes of co-op movements in other former colonies. They are tied to the rise and fall of the state's role in nation building and the displacement of government-led development by neo-liberal notions of free markets and the primacy of capital that fueled the current era of globalization that began in the late 1970s.

The British introduced co-operatives to Sri Lanka. The first co-operatives were developed around 1904 by the Ceylon Agricultural Society, a private society of English colonists who saw in the co-op model a way to promote the latest agricultural advances in local villages and to help the peasantry address the challenges of crop production, organization and distribution. In 1910, the government considered ways to introduce agricultural credit societies and in 1911 an "Ordinance to Provide for the Constitution and Control of Co-operative Societies" was passed, based on the British model. But unlike its English counterpart the Sri Lanka co-op movement did not rise up from the grassroots. It was a colonial creation, a top-down affair, but included laudable goals like the promotion of self-help among the small producers who are still the backbone of the island's agricultural economy.

In the 1930s, the British began to share power with the Sri Lankan hierarchy. The Ministry of Agriculture and Lands, which was responsible for co-ops, was handed to D.S. Senanayake, an independence leader and a founder of the Co-operative Society, who quickly expanded the co-op movement's focus to include consumer needs. When the Japanese attacked Colombo in 1942, Senanayake promoted the creation of co-operative stores which had a monopoly on the distribution of rationed war goods such as cloth, sugar and rice.[4] In the 1940s, food shortages became endemic as a result of import restrictions and the inability of local production to feed the country. Suddenly co-op membership increased to over a million and the movement acquired a national status largely as a result of these government policies promoting co-op pre-eminence in the food sector. When the British left Sri Lanka in 1948, Senanayake became the country's first prime minister.

For the next quarter century, economic policy in Sri Lanka bounced from the closed, state-controlled industrialization policies of the Sri Lanka Freedom Party (SLFP) on the left to the market-oriented industrialization of the United National Party (UNP) on the right.[5] The former took the Soviet Union and India as models for development. The latter looked to the liberal macroeconomics of the UK and the United States and adopted "green revolution" agricultural projects, less restrictive trade policies and a pro-capitalist bent that courted foreign investment. This is the trend that has taken hold in the country since a landmark election in 1977 brought the UNP to power on promises to embrace export-oriented industrialization and provide relief from the endless consumer shortages that resulted from the SLFP's ever more zealous import substitution policies.[6] This trend was in turn reinforced by the global extension of neo-liberal policies by the IMF and the World Bank, institutions to which Sri Lanka was deeply indebted. When state support to the co-operatives dwindled many co-ops failed. Of those that remained, a large number survived as dependents of state programs and extensions of state policy. However, there are some important exceptions. In the credit and microfinance sector particularly, financial co-ops play a major productive role in Sri Lanka and remain adamantly independent of government control. SANASA Development Bank pioneered microfinance in the country and its million-strong membership extends throughout the island and controls over 8,000 credit societies at the village level. As we will see in Chapter Ten, SANASA also played a major role in the recovery and reconstruction of many villages following the tsunami of 2005.

The co-optation of co-operatives by governments had disastrous results, at least for the co-operatives. It artificially increased their number and role in a misguided attempt at nation building and economic development; it destroyed their autonomy, rendering them dependent on state support; it undermined the capacity of co-op leaders and members to learn the skills essential to running co-ops as economic organizations; and it permanently disfigured the co-op idea in the mind of the populace, associating co-operatives with government control, inefficiency and corruption. Today, the most difficult task for co-op development is restoring the identity of co-operatives as autonomous economic organizations.

Co-operatives in Sri Lanka have always had a presence in the agricultural economy, but only recently have they taken on an essential role in the production and export of tea, historically the island's most important export. Previously, it was the introduction of coffee by the Dutch that drew the island into the currents of world trade. In the 17th century the Dutch dominated world trade and the traces of Dutch colonialism are still very vivid in Sri Lanka. Dutch fortifications dot the seacoasts and graceful old world lines are visible in the manors of the grand estates and the white colonial buildings that still stand in Colombo.

Dutch traders first cultivated coffee in Ceylon in 1658. In 1699 they expanded cultivation to Java, followed by Sumatra, Celebes, Timor, Bali and other islands of the Dutch East Indies. Throughout, the Dutch imposed a plantation system, brutally enslaving the populations of these countries to work the estates and recasting a small-scale subsistence agriculture into an extraction system for global trade.

When the British took control of Ceylon, they perfected and extended all the exploitative practices and brutalities of the plantation system introduced by the Dutch. On the tea estates, living conditions were unimaginably harsh. Workers lived in rows of small, stifling rooms, with each family restricted to a single room that sometimes accommodated up to 16 people. There were no windows for ventilation, only the most rudimentary access to water, and toilets were shared by dozens of families. Women and girls had no privacy from the male residents and were constantly subjected to sexual harassment and predation. Many committed suicide. Children were employed as soon as they could work and joined the rest of the workers in 16-hour days of literally backbreaking work as they stooped over the waist-high bushes, fingers flickering over the surface to pluck 15–20 kilograms of leaf a day. Workers lived on subsistence wages, sufficient only to keep them healthy enough to work and to reproduce. Women, being more deft and productive in plucking the leaf, comprised the vast majority of the workforce, working longer hours at a fraction of the wages earned by men. The entire community was isolated, having no interaction with the broader society, a rural ghetto under the despotic power of the planter. In the 19th century, the plantation economy was the perfect emblem of capitalist production, transposing exactly the power dynamics and social relations of industrial capitalism to the context of agricultural production in a colonial setting.

It was hardly surprising then, that the British had a hard time finding workers. Ceylonese farmers preferred to work their own smallholdings; only the landless and desperate worked the estates. The British were compelled to import workers from South India to work the plantations. Drawn largely from the Harijan caste of Hindu Tamils, they were bonded laborers who were transported by gangmasters under the employ of the British planters. They were boarded on boats to Northwest Ceylon and then walked 150 miles, sometimes through dense jungle, to containment camps in Matale in the central highlands of the island. From there, they were dispersed to the plantations or to the forests to clear land. Many died in the first few months of arrival. It is estimated that from 1841 to 1849 perhaps 70,000 Tamil immigrants died, or over 25 percent of the total. By 1900 there were over 300,000 Tamils in Ceylon, amounting to 7.5 percent of the population of 4 million. Today, over a million Tamils still work Sri Lanka's tea estates. Despite recent improvements, they remain the nation's lowest paid workers earning about US$3.27 a day. They also have the lowest literacy levels and the highest mortality rates in the country. Poverty among estate workers is a condition passed down through the generations.

Doubtless, the average British tea drinker of the nineteenth century had little notion of what it took to bring their favorite drink to the breakfast table. Tea was the established national drink and as much a mark of the British character as cricket and the Union Jack. It was also to become Sri Lanka's most important source of foreign exchange and a major source of revenue for the British state. Tea became the cornerstone of British Empire, founded on cheap labor, the extraction of maximum profit and the perfection of world trade as a vast instrument of exploitation. The plantation economies of coffee and tea, followed by cotton, sugar and the other global commodities were the templates on which the modern patterns of global trade were founded. And although the conditions of slave and bonded labor were widely denounced by reformers at the time it was not until the Second World War that the prevailing patterns of global trade were to be challenged. The fair trade movement arose at this time, and in precisely those areas of commodity production that are still the basis of existence for the world's most impoverished workers. Ironically, it was the Dutch who first tried to make fair trade a viable alternative to capitalist forms of production and exchange on a global level.

Fair Trade and Co-operation

Today's global trade system is based on the disconnection between poor workers and small producers in the South and wealthy consumers in the North. In a capitalist exchange system, consumers have no direct relation with producers; their relationship is mediated by the market. The market itself is controlled by an ever-decreasing number of corporations that hold monopolies in the distribution and sale of goods and almost total control in their aggregation and purchase. This is especially true in the production and sale of commodities.

Typically, a single commodity is the mainstay of a poor country's trade. For example, Zambia's trade in copper comprises about 98 percent of its total exports; Uganda's trade in coffee about 95 percent; Somalia's trade in livestock about 76 percent.[7] As a rule of thumb, a nation's economic wealth is directly proportional to its economic diversity. A study by The United Nations Conference on Trade and Development has shown that for major commodities entering world trade in 1980, the proportion of the total which was marketed by the 15 largest transnational companies (TNCs) ranged between 70 and 90 percent, and that in most cases only 3 to 6 transnational companies accounted for nearly the whole of the market.[8] These figures have only become more extreme since the wave of neo-liberal "reforms" of the 1980s tightened further the stranglehold of capital on world trade patterns. In agricultural commodities, the concentration of market power in the hands of TNCs is even more pronounced. Coffee is a prime example. The top 6 companies control 50 percent of the market. The further along the coffee chain one goes, the more concentration occurs. Just two groups (Nestlé and the tobacco giant Philip Morris) control half of the global market for roasted and instant coffees.

Capitalist modes of production based on the emergence of private property, competition, and the commodification of labor in the late 18th and early 19th centuries created the social relations and power structures that gave rise both to modern wealth and to the extraction systems that perpetuate modern poverty. The alienation between consumer and producer is at the heart of this system and this distance masks the gross inequities and social injustices inherent within it.[9] Consumers are induced, instead, to fixate on the commodity — not the process by which a product comes onto the market.

Fair trade is an international system of ethical trade that was developed to combat these inequities by establishing direct links between consumers in the North and poor producers in the South. Unlike conventional trade, fair trade is geared to draw attention to the production process, not to mask it. The system is composed of certified Southern producer organizations and Northern importers, processors and distributors. Producer co-operatives representing small farmers in poor countries are at the basis of this system.

The Fair Trade Network

The roots of the fair trade network were established in the 1940s and 1950s when NGOs in Europe and North America began selling goods produced in the South through direct purchase projects. In Europe, OXFAM was formed during the Second World War when a group of Quakers in Oxford founded a committee to raise funds for famine relief for war victims. When the war ended OXFAM turned its attention to fighting poverty. In 1950, it began selling handicrafts made by Chinese refugees and in 1965 it created the first alternative trade organization to import goods directly from producers in the South. Similar efforts were underway in Continental Europe. In 1959, a group of young Catholics in the Dutch town of Kirkrade organized Fair Trade Organisatie, which also began importing products from the South into the Netherlands. This was literally a suitcase trade. Social justice activists, usually associated with the progressive arms of Christian denominations, would bring back suitcases and trunks filled with the handicrafts of the people they worked with in the South. They then set about selling these products through their church and social networks and returned the profits to the producers through the organizations and shops they set up.

Through the efforts of OXFAM and Fair Trade Organisatie world shops sprang up throughout Europe. By the early 1990s there were over 60 fair trade importing organizations and thousands of world shops across Europe. OXFAM alone had 625 shops in the UK with a retail turnover of US$15.4 million in 1994.[10] Today, the world fair trade system is driven by a global network of alternative trade organizations, including 746 certified producer organizations in 59 developing countries, 2,700 companies licensed to use the fair trade mark and retail outlets in 60 countries. In 2008, the estimated retail value of fair trade products increased by 22 percent from the previous year to 2.9 billion euros. Over 6,000 items are now certified as fair trade products.[11] But despite this phenomenal growth in product variety, the overwhelming bulk of total fair trade retail value — over 80 percent — remains agricultural commodities. Coffee is the leading fair trade product. A close second is tea.

Tea

Few sights are as enthralling as the tea gardens of Sri Lanka. Rarely does one encounter such natural beauty so graced by the human hand. Perhaps only the glittering rice terraces of Bali and the mosaic fields of green, sienna and gold that quilt the Tuscan landscape are comparable. The tea gardens drape the land like a vast and verdant moss that flows down the valleys and up the steep slopes till it melts into the mists that shroud the higher elevations. Tall shade trees canopy the landscape and here and there the tin roofs of the estate buildings reflect the light like silver.

The tea estates of Sri Lanka are stunning but they embody a terrible reality. The cultivation of tea is a deeply tainted industry. Tea is the country's greatest source of export earnings, but the wealth pouring from one end of the production process rests on poverty at the other. For the million laborers that toil in these fields the beauty of their surroundings is no compensation for the misery they endure. The damage inflicted by the plantation system extends beyond the economic hardship of the workers. The monoculture of tea is destroying the soil. Hundreds of thousands of acres under tea cultivation in Sri Lanka are being leached of their nutrients and are sustained now by a steady saturation of chemical fertilizers and pesticides. The tea plants have become dependent on chemicals. When weaned from their chemical diet, they go through withdrawal and shrivel up while farmers using natural cultivation methods nurture them back to health with chemical-free organic compost. In conventional cultivation methods, on top of their starvation wages, estate workers work waist deep in plants covered in toxic chemicals.

In a 2003 study, the blood of workers on conventional tea estates was compared to those who practiced organic tea cultivation for the presence of perfluorated compounds (PFCs).[12] Incredibly, no study on the impact of synthetic pesticides on workers had been conducted before this time. The purpose of the study was to examine the semen quality of the two groups and its relation to PFC accumulation. Unsurprisingly, it was found that conventional estate workers had a far higher concentration of chemical agents in their blood than did workers on organic farms. The incidence of abnormalities in sperm formation was also significantly higher among workers exposed to chemicals in conventional tea estates. Another study[13] found that the presence of agrochemicals, regardless of the type, impairs the fertility of males, results in abnormal sperm, and may lead to birth deformities. Other potential health effects include liver damage, heart defects and the formation of tumors. In short, the cultivation of tea in Sri Lanka is toxic to the workers. And aside from the efforts of organic farmers, little or nothing was being done to address the use of chemical agents in the cultivation of not only tea, but in Sri Lankan agriculture in general.

The Small Organic Farmers Association

The movement for organic agriculture is relatively young in Sri Lanka. Yet it represents one instance of how co-operatives are playing a central role in reforming agriculture by blending two ideas: fair trade and organics. In the hill country surrounding Kandy, a fledgling movement arose in the early 1980s to revolutionize the cultivation of tea in the country. One of its early leaders was Sarath Ranaweena, a charismatic and passionate personality who blended entrepreneurialism, science and missionary zeal to spark the movement for organics and fair trade in Sri Lanka. Sarath is an engaging figure — tall, meticulously groomed, his handsome features alive with energy and intelligence. From his office at Biofoods, the processing and distribution company he founded, Sarath talks about the ups and downs of his journey as an organics advocate. High on a steep embankment, the Biofoods building is an attractive structure of brick and glass looking out over the tea gardens and jungle rising high around the town of Kandy. Unlike most fair trade stories, the story of the Small Organic Farmers Association (SOFA) began not with an NGO but with a private company, Sarath's own Biofoods.

Sarath's personal commitment to organics began with a brush with death from food poisoning when he consumed a contaminated bottled drink. When he recovered, he became obsessed with the issue of chemical additives to food. He devoted himself to learning about additives, their impact on health, their effect on the natural environment, their role in industrial agriculture and how to change agricultural practice in Sri Lanka. Sarath was trained as a scientist — his background was as a mathematician and statistician. But in his thirties he returned to university to earn a second PhD in food science and technology and biostatistics. He began working with small enterprises and agricultural workers. He joined the prestigious Tea Research Institute where he became one of the country's top experts on tea. There, he immersed himself in the lives of small tea farmers, especially those working in mid-altitude areas where green leaf was grown. He then decided to experiment with small-scale tea production. Sarath became convinced that three things were essential for the reform of agriculture in Sri Lanka: the adoption of organic and sustainable production practices; the survival of small farmers; and a fair price for their produce.

Sarath set up his company to purchase, process and sell organic food products from Sri Lanka to international markets. In order to do so,

Biofoods had to create a reliable supply of these products. Sarath decided to focus on tea. The SOFA project was started on abandoned land that had never been subjected to chemicals. Much of this land had been provided to small farmers by pro-socialist regimes during the heyday of land redistribution in the years following independence. These were small plots, usually under two acres and enough to subsist on, but there had been little follow-up after the redistribution. Farmers were basically left on their own with little support or training. Many of these people were new to farming. They had come from diverse backgrounds and now found themselves with a patch of jungle, no skills, little money and no social or economic infrastructure to help them. The land was left largely unworked with families subsisting on an ad hoc assortment of crops, selling any surplus in local markets when they could, and patching in work as hired laborers or sometimes running small, fragile enterprises. Turning these people into organic tea producers on their small plots would not be easy.

Sarath began an intensive educational and organizing campaign among small farmers scratching out a living in the hills surrounding the town of Nuwar Eliya, one of the most beautiful regions of the country. The hills here are carpeted in tea gardens owned by large growers. Small-scale, unorganized farmers in the area supplemented their income by selling leaf to middlemen at predatory prices. Sarath was trying to convince them that if they could provide him with organic tea, his company would guarantee them a price far higher than what they were earning by selling to these middlemen. The switch to organic cultivation would not only restore their land, it would add value to their produce. The main challenges were twofold: how to earn the farmers' trust so they would invest the time and energy required to learn and apply organic growing techniques; and how to organize the process of cultivation, collection and quality control that is essential to ensuring the volumes and product standards that a purchaser needs to run a business. Biofoods provided the farmers with the tea plants, careful instruction on organic growing techniques, inputs such as dolomite to improve soil quality, and tools. After planting, tea bushes take three years before they can be harvested. To supplement incomes while the bushes matured, Biofoods provided farmers with cows whose milk could be sold and whose dung could be used as organic compost. But Sarath was also interested in creating a structure that could become self-sustaining.

Biofoods used a co-op structure, SOFA, to organize member farmers into blocks corresponding to individual villages and then to aggregate blocks into regional societies. Over a 3-year period beginning in 1993, 30 to 60 farmers were converted to organic agriculture. Others took a wait-and-see attitude. In 1997 the participating farmers received their organic certification. Soon, there was enough organic tea being grown in the area that Biofoods could establish its Avon Lea factory for processing black tea grown exclusively on small plots. Today, SOFA has a membership of 1,682 farmers. The impact of the co-op on the lives of small farmers and the fortunes of their communities has been immense. The joining of organic cultivation with fair trade has added a deeper dimension to the fair trade system, an element that takes the fair trade concept beyond its conventional focus on producers, exchange relations and trade.

Fair Trade on the Ground

W. R. Punchibanda is a lean, leathery looking man of 64. His face is creased and crinkled and shows every one of his years. He has a thick mat of curly white hair and a scruff of silver stubble. His home rests on a lush hillside at the end of a dirt track that winds down from a dirt road. Sarath and I had driven out to his place so that I could see at first hand the work SOFA was doing and its impact on the small growers who were its members.

Punchibanda's family received this small plot of abandoned land in 1951. His father started planting in 1958 but couldn't cultivate more than half an acre. With no money to invest in plants or tools and no training, the family led a hand-to-mouth existence. The land itself was becoming degraded. Without proper care, the soil was eroding. It wasn't until 1998 when Punchibanda joined SOFA and received 30 plants from the co-op that he began to make full use of the family plot. He planted the tea bushes, received instruction on organic cultivation, was taught how to make organic fertilizer to restore the soil and was encouraged to diversify his little ecosystem by planting additional commercial crops. These included pepper, cloves, lemon grass, cinnamon, vanilla, turmeric, vetiver grass and ginger. The ginger brings in income twice a year as do the turmeric and pepper, while the vetiver is a natural insect repellent. From the 5,000 plants that now flourish on his one and a half acres, more than 1,000 came from SOFA. Walking through his little tropical homestead Punchibanda points out the plants, touching the leaves with his fingertips.

In his home, Puchibanda brings out his member's ledger. In it he records all transactions with the co-op — the number of plants under cultivation, the dates of organic inspections, volumes delivered, amounts paid, the money set aside as savings. For each kilogram of leaf tea, Puchibanda receives a fair trade premium of $1.10, which is paid directly to SOFA by Biofoods. In addition, SOFA extends to Puchibanda up to 60 percent of the estimated value of the produce he brings to the co-op. This is a crucial aspect of the fair trade system, in that it allows farmers the credit they need to tide them over until final payments are due on their crops. The fair trade premium is distributed according to the wishes of the SOFA membership at the start of the year. In the past, the premium has been used to purchase additional tea plants, planting materials and agricultural equipment and to promote community projects. These projects are a central part of SOFA's operations in the area. The co-op established a water project to supply clean drinking water to the community and built a community center which doubles as a collection and cleaning center for the tea. SOFA provided cows and goats to its members for milk and dung fertilizer and these animals are shared. It also established a loan program to help members start their own enterprises. A scholarship program for members provides all students who pass the state exams (at grades, 5, 11 and 13) with textbooks and school supplies. It is because of this program, along with the additional income earned from SOFA, that Puchibanda has been able to educate his children. They were the first in his family to go to school.

In the fair trade system, a tea farmer like Puchibanda will receive a minimum price of 23 rupees (20 cents) per kilogram. This price is established by the Fair Labeling Organization (FLO) and based on a fair market price formula for tea. However, Biofoods pays a higher price based on actual market rates. This is currently about 53 rupees per kilogram. An experienced picker can pluck one kilogram in an hour. Over an eight-hour day this means a picker will earn about four dollars. Of this, a farmer receives 20 rupees per kilogram upon delivery of his tealeaf, 23 more at the end of the month, and 10 rupees are placed in a savings program with SOFA. This is distributed to the SOFA members at the end of the year, thus ensuring that they build savings. Before SOFA, the same farmer would receive about one third of the SOFA rate for their tea.

For many of these farmers, this is the first time they have ever saved money. Puchibanda points a long brown finger to a penciled entry in his book. In 2008, he earned over 2,000 rupees in savings. In Northern terms, this may seem like a paltry amount. But this only underscores the enormous gulf that separates Northern consumers from Southern producers. For a small farmer like Puchibanda the savings represent a radical break from the past where the very idea of saving must have seemed pure fantasy.

W. R. Puchibanda is the president of his village society. He was among the 30-odd members present at a regional meeting of SOFA to discuss with Sarath an increase in the rates Biofoods pays for tea leaf. Sarath wanted to talk to members about how best to use the development fund that Biofoods has established for SOFA from a portion of the company's profits. Sarath speaks forcefully, with an air of conviction. The farmers are mostly men but there are one or two women present as well. All are sitting very straight in the moulded plastic chairs, listening very attentively. When they speak, they speak quietly. In the course of the meeting, I asked to hear from those present what membership in SOFA has meant to them personally. How did SOFA impact their lives? We went round the room. All of them wanted to tell their story, and their stories were remarkably similar.

One after another, the farmers spoke about how poor they were before joining SOFA. They talked about how neglected their land was and how depleted the soil had become. They described how local factory owners and middlemen ripped them off and how little they had to show for their labor. Then, they talked about the establishment of the co-op and the training they received, the plants and tools they could now put to use and the increase in income and living standards that came from the combination of organic agriculture and their involvement in fair trade. More than this, they stressed the benefits that SOFA brought to the community as a whole through clean water projects, the building of roads, schools and clinics, and how co-operation itself was beginning to spread through their communities. For the first time, people were seeing concretely the economic benefits of working together. As one old fellow, A. Wijethilaka, put it, "Before, my family worked alone. SOFA connected us to the outside world and taught us about the environment. In our village, we started working as a group. Only then did we realize that through team effort all of us could advance, not just a few."

SOFA's achievements are typical of how the fair trade system works through producer co-ops to benefit both members and their communities. Whether in Asia, Africa or Latin America the circuits of fair trade have had profound effects on the lives of peasant families and local communities the world over. There is no question that fair trade has brought unprecedented benefits to those communities who have been able to link themselves to the system. But the system is rapidly changing and the changes are unsettling.

The Seductions of Success

In 2000, FLO-labeled goods were worth over 220 million euros. Of this, over 55 million went directly to producers. This is about 40 percent higher than would have been the case if these products had been sold at conventional prices.[14] The direct benefits to producer families are concrete and measurable in terms of working conditions, wages, nutrition, education, health and living standards. The long-term benefits to the well-being of communities are also clear — in raising standards for health and education, in promoting economic advancement and increasing social solidarity and cohesion. These victories are not negligible, but are they enough? The question bedevils the fair trade movement. Because if the ultimate goal of fair trade is the creation of an alternative to the capitalist trade system, its capacity to make this happen is in question.

When the fair trade movement began in the 1950s and 60s there was a clear vision of building a global trade system that operated on values entirely different from those of capitalism. The drive to maximize profits and accumulate wealth by monopolizing markets and exploiting the weak was challenged by a call for a moral economy. But the vision of a moral economy has been overtaken by a strategy of collaboration with transnational corporations in order to gain access to markets. This is understandable. Unless mainstream consumers get connected to the fair trade system, fair trade will remain a marginal presence in global trade. As it is, despite the success of the labeling strategy, fair trade accounts for only 0.01 percent of international trade. Over 80 percent of this is composed of unprocessed commodities. Unless its market grows, the basic need of fair trade producers' to increase their sales cannot be met. In key sectors, fair trade channels cannot absorb producers' total output. For example, fair trade coffee producers can sell only 20 percent of their volume on fair trade markets. When producers have to turn to conventional markets to sell their goods, this poses a threat to the system. In some markets, intense competition among TNCs to lower the cost of their products has further increased the gap between conventional and fair trade product prices, making the latter less attractive to consumers.

Commodity prices are also being driven down by oversupply (as with coffee) through the entry of new players. Vietnam, for example, has emerged as a major coffee producer adding more supply to an already glutted market. The problem is made worse by the polices of the IMF and the World Bank which have encouraged Southern countries to increase exports of commodities as a means of earning foreign currency to pay off their debts to these institutions.[15] The result is a glut in these commodities that further drives down prices. This is great for large buyers and processors. It's catastrophic for small farmers. In this way, short-term gains to pay off loans undermine the very markets these farmers need to survive. The demands of capital override the interests of the people these IMF and World Bank programs were ostensibly set up to help.

The combination of these pressures has driven fair trade organizations to partner with global companies in order to reach a mass consumer market. This has resulted in a number of threats to the fair trade system. It has meant that fair trade producers and the fair trade organizations are becoming increasingly dependent on TNCs for their survival. Transnational corporations now control the largest component of fairly traded products although these products comprise only a tiny fraction of the companies' inventory. Thus, TNCs benefit disproportionately from the positive image they receive by selling fair trade products while continuing to engage in the very practices that fair trade was established to oppose in the first place. This imbalance has brought the TNCs enormous influence within the fair trade system. It is also devaluing the fair trade label.

In 2003, some supermarkets in Britain were accused of overcharging for their fair trade products and pocketing much of the premium price for themselves.[16] One of the culprits was Tesco, Britain's largest retailer and a company with a reputation for shortchanging producers and driving competitors out of town. They were reportedly marking up fair trade bananas by as much as US$1.00 per kilogram, more than twice the amount going to producers. Yet Tesco was awarded a fair trade label for a new line of flowers from Kenya by the Fairtrade Foundation in Britain.

The trend is continuing. Recently, FLO accepted the inclusion of coffee, tea and other plantations as certified fair trade organizations. It is true that these plantations must meet labor and environmental standards to become certified. This has certainly improved conditions for workers. But the principle of democratic control by producers has been compromised. It is a dangerous precedent that threatens to undermine the foundations of the fair trade system. As this is being written, TATA, a major tea producer and purveyor of their own "ethical" brand of tea, has locked out its workers in India in a bid to stall demands for improved wages and work conditions.

If the fair trade label is tarnished by the kinds of practices mentioned above, or by business-as-usual practices by the same companies in other areas, the fair trade brand is undermined. In the end, the only real distinction between "foul" and "fair" trade may be the way in which producers are involved in the trade chain and whether they control the conditions of their labor and the distribution of the profit. The more that TNCs are integrated into the fair trade system, the more crucial becomes the role of the co-op structure at the producer level. It is, in the end, the only factor that might act as a corrective to possible corruption at the higher levels of the system. And if there is anything to learn from the behavior of transnationals, it is that that they can't be trusted. They answer to a different god.

The collaboration with TNCs also threatens to hard wire the fair trade system into prevailing market structures, without developing institutional alternatives that challenge those structures. Transnational corporations would be happy if all fair trade did was supply them with products that let them pose as good corporate citizens without requiring them to alter their way of making profits for the vast majority of products they sell. In addition, fair trade labeling and the fair trade premium consign the system to the production and sale of commodities for wealthy markets in the North. This does little to develop the economies of the South by advancing them beyond commodity trade.

Like resource extraction, commodity production in the South is a long-term prescription for poverty. Global companies, despite their willingness (now) to sell (some) fair trade products, are not in the least interested in supporting the value-added processing of commodities in their place of origin. This would constitute a direct threat to their monopoly interests. But unless this happens, small producers and the entire fair trade system can become hostage to the interests of immensely powerful corporations.

This strategy of confining Southern economies to the least complex, and least profitable, aspects of the production chain is further buttressed by trade policies of rich nations that impose crippling duties on processed imports. Green coffee beans may be imported into Europe almost duty-free. Roasted beans are slapped with a 30 percent import duty. Poor countries face trade barriers for their products that are four times higher than those encountered by rich countries.[17] In fact, rich countries have cost poor countries three times more in trade restrictions than they receive in total development aid.[18] The subsidies that rich countries provide their farmers, to the detriment of Southern producers — despite the claptrap of "free trade" espoused by their leaders — drives home the point. The average European cow receives a subsidy of $2.00 a day from the EU. More than half the people in the developing world live on less than that. The total value of European, US, and Japanese subsidies to their agriculture is at least 75 percent of the total income of sub-Saharan Africa.[19] This makes it impossible for African farmers to compete on world markets.

But perhaps the most telling sign of current trends is the fact that the World Bank has begun to look at fair trade as a model for market-driven strategies that encourage companies to adopt desirable trade practices not on the basis of enforceable trade legislation but voluntarily.[20] For The World Bank, fair trade is a way to make capitalism palatable while protecting its prerogatives. But given fair trade's lack of access to mass markets, and the monopoly power of TNCs, what's the alternative?

Beyond Commodities—Going Glocal

Half a world away from Sri Lanka, the achievements of the UCIRI cooperative in the Yautepec region of Mexico resemble closely the work of SOFA. UCIRI originated at a meeting in 1981 where indigenous small coffee farmers met with Jesuit missionaries to discuss how to address the poverty in their land. At the meeting, it was acknowledged that a key source of the poverty was the low, exploitative prices paid to farmers by local middlemen known as "coyotes." The growers decided to deal directly with national and international buyers. In the first year the farmers collectively sold more than 35 tons of coffee to the state-run coffee marketing board in Veracruz. In 1983, after a prolonged struggle with local and state officials and the fierce opposition of local traders, UCIRI teamed up with farmers from other municipalities and was granted legal status and registered with the secretary of agrarian reform. The following year, UCIRI focused on the value-added processing of its products. UCIRI's members purchased a warehouse in Lachivia, a former logging compound, and installed a processing plant where coffee beans were de-pulped, sorted by quality, mechanically cleaned and bagged and prepared for export. The co-op acquired a second plant in the town of Ixtepec and became the first independent organization in the region to acquire an export license allowing it to export directly.[21]

The proceeds from these activities allowed UCIRI to launch an ambitious program to address the most urgent of the region's problems. The members organized themselves into local committees and over the next few years they built collective corn mills, dry toilets, wood stoves and, crucially, started to promote and protect the indigenous cultural values of the people. This commitment to resurrecting cultural traditions is what oriented the co-op toward organic farming methods. Organics is now at the heart of the co-operative's agricultural, political and cultural philosophy. It is rooted in the members' sense of their history and the traditions they are attempting to reclaim. It is also grounded in a deeply felt religiosity. As stated on the UCIRI website:

> With UCIRI, we want to rebuild our relationship with the environment so that it may be like that of our ancestors, and to adapt this relationship to our present circumstances so that we may live in harmony with that which gives us life.
>
> It is for this reason that we have adopted organic agriculture both as a means of labor and of education. Organic agriculture comes naturally to us, because to us, the earth is our mother who nurtures and strengthens us, and we therefore cultivate her using natural methods. By this manner, mother earth's offerings can be born and grow into fruit which gives us life and plants which give us health. We care for her, cultivate her, and defend her as an inheritance that we want to leave to our children.
>
> If the earth suffers, then so will its children, with the price being their joy and well-being. The earth does not belong to human beings, rather humans belong to the earth.

UCIRI has matured into the pre-eminent social development organization of this region, outstripping the state in the quantity and quality of

the services it provides. Its transport trucks were the first to provide public transportation over the rough unpaved roads of the area. In 1986, the
co-op founded a secondary school and training institute for the promotion of organic agriculture. Located high in the coffee-growing mountains near the town of San José el Paraíso, the Center of Rural Studies
for Organic and Sustainable Development of the Communities (CEC)
is the only secondary school outside the cities. Beyond technical training,
the school has adopted an educational philosophy that orients learning
around skills and attitudes that are needed to serve not just the individual learner but the community as a whole. All students must be children
of poor farmers between the ages of 15 and 18 years, want to work the
land and serve the community, and have completed primary school.[22]
In 1994 UCIRI established a clinic in Lachivia — a region where there is
one doctor for every 2,780 inhabitants.[23]

Although coffee was the foundation of UCIRI's development, in
1997 the co-op expanded its activities to include the processing of organic fruits and berries into marmalade as a means of diversifying and
increasing member incomes. As well as expanding and diversifying production, the co-op has played a key role in negotiating credit with state,
banking and development agencies on behalf of its members. Over time,
these institutions have come to view UCIRI as a reliable and stable organization with a commitment to the well-being of its members and their
communities. This alone is a tremendous achievement for an association
of small, peasant farmers. It has allowed them to escape the debt traps
that ensnared them when they were dependent on local moneylenders
or buyers who extracted part of their payment by forcing farmers to sell
their beans at starvation prices.

Groups like SOFA and UCIRI represent a new dynamic within the
fair trade system. Members have come to understand that their future,
and the future of their communities, lies ultimately in the maturation
and expansion of local economies. A new focus on value-added processing and the export of finished products is one aspect of this trend. The
other is the creation of trade and production alliances with other co-
ops, NGOs and business partners at a regional level. Remarkably, this
approach mirrors in many ways the development of the co-operative
production networks of northern Italy, as discussed in Chapter Three.
But whereas in Italy the manufacturing networks were a product of
the broader co-operative system already in place, in the South these

co-operative systems are being built as a defense against exploitation and as a calculated strategy to adapt the knowledge, technical expertise and industrial infrastructure of the North to the needs of the South. The incorporation of social, environmental and cultural values are central to this mission.

SOFA and UCIRI are hardly alone among producer co-ops that are looking beyond commodity production to building more complex and sustainable economies at the local level. In Costa Rica, Cooperativa Sin Fronteras (CSF), or Co-operatives Without Borders is a co-op that consolidates 21 member organizations from 11 countries that represent a total of 12,661 families. Sixteen members are co-operatives or rural farmers' associations, whose main products are coffee, cocoa, sugar, honey, fruits, nuts and guarana. Two members are non-governmental associations providing technical support, two members are business partners and one member is a co-operative financial consortium.[24] All CSF growers must be organic. And although CSF includes non-co-ops as members, producer co-operatives must always be a majority of the membership. In addition, non-co-op members such as private businesses or trade partners must be prepared "to collaborate, promote, and co-operate with projects whose main objective is the promotion of co-operative forms of enterprise,"[25] as established in the organization's objectives. CSF is linked to trade organizations in Europe and North America that provide technical, financial and trade support for the development of value-added industry at the local level while supporting the extension of the co-op model as a means of securing these goals. The entire system is set up to generate a co-operative economy locally, with global links and global skills.

These farmer associations see economic diversification as the necessary next step in overcoming the underdevelopment and dependency of small farmers in subsistence economies. For this, the co-operatives need new alliances and new sets of skills. They need trade channels not only to international markets but to local markets as well. For the creation of regional processing, marketing and distribution systems they need higher orders of business acumen, management skills, production efficiencies, and credit. Credit is the fuel that feeds the enterprises that create the wealth. And they need to be able to market their goods. This is the trade component that can ensure that wealth is created plentifully and sustainably. As pointed out by Mose Durst: "...these questions pose the challenges to producers who seek to go beyond subsistence and to enter the world of trade and prosperity."[26]

Without this qualitative shift in technical, business and networking skills Southern producers will remain at the bottom rung of the fair trade ladder. Their co-operatives are without question the best means for achieving this. In Costa Rica, Allianza Co-operative already sells 75 percent of their coffee to local markets. They have successfully opened their own café to compete with the multinational brand names, using the fair trade ethos of local ownership and the preservation of profit for local use to make their stand in the local market. For Northern fair trade partners like Equal Exchange in the US and La Siembra in Canada, the focus now is not just on equalizing trade relations but creating co-operative-based economies in the South using fair trade as a catalyst. In Europe especially, major retailing co-operatives are investing time, money and expertise to develop these regional co-op systems. The Italian consumer giant COOP is among Cooperativa Sin Fronteras' most stalwart supporters, stocking CSF products on their shelves in Italy while supporting their production in Costa Rica. In Britain, the Co-op retailing system is the chief trading partner and fair trade leader in a country where consumers are now responsible for ten percent of Europe's total fair trade sales. The UK's consumer co-ops have linked their own considerable market power on the distribution and consumption end of the chain to the production co-ops at the other end. In so doing, they have woven an alternative trade thread based on the principles of both fair trade and co-operation on a global level. It is one concrete instance of the alternative trade system that was once envisaged by the fair trade pioneers in the 50s and 60s. These filaments are being created all over the globe.

There is another reason why the expansion of co-operative systems at regional levels is central to the future of small farmers and local economies in poor countries: peak oil. The enterprises and organizations that compose the fair trade system are even more dependent on low oil prices for their survival than are transnational corporations. If the premiums paid by consumers to sustain the fair trade system are barely feasible today at current costs for transporting coffee, tea or bananas from half a world away, what will happen when the cost of oil, and thus the cost of transporting these products, skyrockets?

There is a limit to the margin that can be sustained between the higher cost of a fair trade product and its conventional competitors. The projected impacts of peak oil are threefold: higher transport and production costs, higher prices and a reduction in consumer buying power. In combination these elements, if substantial enough, can trigger a global economic crisis. The effect of oil depletion on international trade will be cataclysmic and long lasting. The small, dependent economies that rely on commodity exports to the North for survival will be the first to feel the effects. Unless co-operative fair trade systems are reoriented toward the further advancement and development of economic systems at local and regional levels, the economic and social benefits that they now deliver to members, their families and their communities, will no longer be sustainable. The role of co-operation will then become even more crucial than at present. Beyond guaranteeing small producers a fair price for their products, regional co-operation among a wide range of economic players — other co-ops, suppliers, distributors, manufacturers, credit sources — will be the only viable strategy for ensuring that small producers will find markets to sell to. Peak oil may make global trade untenable for all but the largest corporations. Moreover, apart from the survival of small producers, co-operation in this form is also a key strategy for slowing the rapid depletion of the world economy's most essential resource.

The Future of Fair Trade

In the course of securing wider markets through the labeling system what seems to have been lost to sight is the hinge on which the fair trade system turns — the co-operative structure of the producer organizations. It was the producer co-ops in Mexico that sought to penetrate the monopolies in the mainstream markets. It was only co-op control at the farmer level that could guarantee that fair trade premiums would be distributed fairly and used for the broader social benefit that was intended. This is why democratic control by producers was written into fair trade certification. The role of the co-operative model is crucial to the fair trade system. It is revealing how little known or examined this is, even though small producer co-operatives are at the foundation of the system and remain the only guarantee that fair trade will remain fair.

Given the overwhelming power of transnational corporations and the absence of state pressure to change global trade patterns, the future of fair trade as an alternative to global trade systems is seriously in doubt. Not everyone in the fair trade movement shares this vision of fair trade.

Many would argue that fair trade is about reforming how markets work. And there is no doubt that it has had this effect. Fair trade examples have been contagious. It has forced companies to reform their practices, even if for purely cosmetic purposes. Fair trade has shone a spotlight on trade exploitation and the injustices inherent in the capitalist system. It has pointed out the complicity of international organizations like the WTO and the IMF in the continuing extraction of wealth from poor to rich nations through the pursuit of policies that institutionalize exploitation. Most remarkably, the fair trade focus on exchange relations inside the marketplace has proven that, yes, consumers do have a conscience. They care about the bitter grounds that go into their morning cup of coffee. But their concern is contingent. It depends on knowing about the conditions in the South that pay for their comforts in the North and, more precisely, it depends on having some kind of relationship to producers. This is what the fair trade labeling system has brought about — a market relationship that overturns conventional notions of the self-interested consumer. Rather, it becomes a relationship based on the principle of market morality at a global level.

Fair trade is based on the premise of a moral economy that challenges the commodification of human relations. In this, it is an extension of the principles that were first embodied in the co-operative communities of the 19th century and earlier. And just as the exploitative conditions of the Industrial Revolution in Europe brought about the counter-movements of collective defence through socialism and the co-operative movement, so are these same dynamics catalyzing similar responses in the South today.

What fair trade has not done is transform the imbalance of power between consumers and producers. For this to change, fair trade needs more than a reform of exchange relations between consumers and producers. It needs to be part of a larger program of radical structural reform that moves regional economies beyond their dependence on commodities. Co-operative systems are central to this remaking of economies at the growing, picking and hauling end of the global trade system. Two things seem essential to this task. The first is leveraging the relationships and capital premiums that come from fair trade into localized expertise, resources and co-operative commercial systems. The second is devising local strategies for accessing global markets. These are essentially the two sides of a single coin.

The model that has most to show by way of example is the evolution of the co-operative producer networks in Emilia Romagna. Today, the signature food products of Italy are still produced by small farmers through their co-operatives. Small producers have concentrated on high-value-added goods intended for the most profitable tier of international food markets. They have been able to maintain both their small size and their global reach by integrating multiple sources of production across a region into a vertical system that manages processing, marketing and distribution at national and international levels. Surrounding and sustaining this model are a range of supports from specialized groups that offer credit, research, training and market intelligence. Slowly, groups like SOFA in Sri Lanka, UCIRI in Mexico, and Cooperative Sin Fronteras in Costa Rica are setting the foundations for precisely this kind of co-operative model of regional development based on one or two high priority sectors. But more importantly, the farmer co-operatives that are building these systems are in contact with their more experienced partners abroad. They are learning from the experience of those who have gone before. And if Sri Lanka and Mexico don't have the co-operative heritage of Italy or Britain to draw from, they have developed trusted allies abroad that are committed to their work. The entire fair trade system is a solidarity mission. The more sophisticated and exacting work of diversifying and maturing local economies is becoming possible because of the co-operative foundations laid down through the fair trade networks.

The global co-operative movement contains within itself the material resources to do what the fair trade movement alone cannot do. Credit is one example. The credit unions of both rich and poor nations have the capital to establish a Fair Trade and Development Bank to do what the World Bank and the IMF will never do — give direct support to farmer organizations, NGOs, business groups and local communities to build regional economies based on democratic control and ownership. An international co-operative development bank with members and progressive stakeholders from among consumers in the North and small producers in the South could provide the credit necessary to fuel the kind of value-added development that is now beginning to emerge in these areas. Among its top priorities would be to build up local credit unions that can play a regional role in this development process. This has already begun. The World Council of Credit Unions (WCCU) and the national co-operative federations of many countries have been working to build the development infrastructure of Southern regions for many years. But, as usual, the problem is one of scale and coordination. Each country's development efforts are separate from those of other countries. Their expertise and resources aren't pooled and coordinated. In the area of credit, research, marketing and the establishment of trade links, pooling and co-operative coordination at a global level are fundamental.

At the international level, established co-operatives can expand their solidarity work with Southern groups by promoting their products. This is already happening in some areas, as indicated above. But not everywhere. In Canada, for example, while consumer co-operatives in the Atlantic region have started to promote fair trade products, the consumer co-ops in central and western Canada have not. In the US and Europe too, the retail co-ops have yet to establish a coherent and aggressive policy with respect to fair trade. Their relationship with the fair trade system remains ad hoc and fragmented. There is a difference in the history, outlook and culture of these two movements that accounts for some of the absence of co-operation. But the continuing avoidance of more formal links harms the long-term prospects of both movements.

Politics

Finally, there is the issue of how the fair trade system is going to address the absence of government action with respect to trade regulations. Regardless of how successful the efforts in building local co-operative economies are, the larger issues of trade inequity have to be addressed at a political level. This means state action and intervention. International fair trade organizations and local co-operatives have to join forces with the global justice movement to increase pressure on national governments. In this, the established co-operative movements have a key role to play, a role they have so far shied away from.

Closely linked to the question of political action at the state level is the radical reform of those international organizations that operate outside political accountability. The IMF and the WTO, to take two obvious examples, effectively control the rules of the global trade game and they do so at the behest of powerful corporate interests led by the United States. Like private corporations, they are controlled by whoever has invested the most capital in them. The IMF is controlled by the US because American capital comprises its largest capital pool. The WTO discriminates against poor countries by imposing on them membership barriers that aren't required of existing members. These organizations are profoundly autocratic and unfair to the interests of the vast majority of the world's nations. But they can continue to operate in this way because there is no recognition that trade policies should embody the actual interests of participants. Such a principle is possible only if it is embedded in the power relations of regulating organizations.

As Joseph Stiglitz has pointed out, bad governance is at the heart of the trade inequities in globalization. Governance structures in global trade organizations are biased and lopsided and designed to produce precisely the types of unfair deals that benefit the already wealthy at the expense of the poor and the weak. If the IMF and the WTO were reorganized to fairly represent the interests of poor countries, they would have to adopt a democratic structure with each country having a greater share of control. Something like a co-operative model for the regulation of global trade is absolutely central to any real hope that globalization will ultimately benefit the poor as it now enriches the wealthy. For at the bottom of unfair trade is an imbalance of power between rich nations and poor ones. This, in turn, is based on an imbalance of power between the rich and the rest *inside* individual countries. Globalization as a *process* is a mechanism that is geared to perpetuate both. Unless these imbalances are addressed at the political and regulatory level, the patterns of global trade that determine who benefits and who loses will continue and the ongoing transformation of markets into permanent systems of exploitation will only accelerate.

The abandonment of state intervention in the reform of global trade is a grave mistake. The reform of global trade institutions requires at minimum the formal involvement of national governments to push for these reforms. Just as citizens, producers and consumers alike, have to reclaim economics and markets for social purposes, so do governments. As always, it is citizens who will take the lead. If corporations can't be trusted, neither can governments. From the complicit governments in the North to the corrupted governments in the South, unless there is a political movement to democratize economics and economic policy, the narrow interests that now write the rules of the game will continue to do so. Fair trade is a bridgehead in this battle. It crystallizes the underlying community of interests between consumers and buyers in a moral marketplace. It is one crucial aspect of the remaking of markets along moral lines. But the broader struggle lies beyond fair trade in the demand that trade and economics embody fundamental principles of morality and social justice in the models and mechanisms that govern their operation.

Meanwhile, the work of building up the co-operative systems that embody these purposes continues, both in the South and in the North. This work will go on, regardless of what governments do. The movement to humanize trade is growing and setting down roots in the consciousness of millions of consumers in the North. The benefits of co-operation and empowerment are becoming obvious to the least sophisticated of small farmers from Sri Lanka to Costa Rica. And regardless of what happens in the corridors of the IMF and the infamous Green Room of WTO negotiations, the slow, painstaking work of building alternative trade systems will continue. Fair trade and the co-operative systems it rests on are opening up spaces within the global marketplace for these alternatives, and these spaces will grow regardless of what corporations do or what governments refuse to do. Consumers are waking up to the uncomfortable human and environmental costs that underwrite their consumer comforts. They want other choices and small producers are learning how to provide them.

For W.R. Puchibanda and his small band of farmers in the green hills of Sri Lanka, there is no turning back because there is no longer any real alternative. Despite the worrying trends and the dispiriting spectacle of greed and destruction, of outright nihilism, that fuels and follows the course of corporate capital in its search for profit, there has never been a more opportune time for change. The models for viable alternatives are all around us in embryo. The disgrace and discredit of the status quo has never been more obvious. It is now a question — a most difficult one to be sure — of linking the ideas, practices and models of fair trade to the political work that will force governments to act. On their own, they will not. They require the moral force of an awakened citizenry to compel them.

CHAPTER 9

Argentina:
Occupy, Resist, Produce

*Life and physical integrity
have no supremacy over economic interests.*
— BRUKMAN FACTORY EVICTION ORDER. —

Two days before Christmas 2001, Argentine President Adolfo Rodrí-
guez Saá, announced to the world that Argentina was bankrupt. The
country couldn't meet the payments on its national debt, totaling US$132
billion. It was the most spectacular default of a sovereign nation in history. Mr. Rodriguez Saá made the statement to a packed Congress after
having just been sworn in as the country's third president in four days.
The previous president, Fernando de la Rua, had been forced from office
following weeks of rioting in the streets. Unlike the policies of De la Rua,
the new president declared, the people would take priority over crippling
debt payments. De la Rua's policies had punished ordinary Argentines,
he said. "They gave priority to the payment of the foreign debt over the
payment of the debt to its own people," cried the President, to shouts of
"Argentina! Argentina!" roaring up from the assembly.[1] One week later,
President Raá had also resigned. The government was in chaos. Argentina was a country set adrift.

The Argentine crisis of 2001–2002 has been exhaustively recorded
and reflected upon. It is one of the seminal events of the new century.
As political economist Dani Rodrik put it, "…fingers have been pointed
at enough culprits to explain the Argentine crash many times over."[2]
This is true, and who the culprits are usually depends on one's political

viewpoint. Yet, the key factors that pulled down the economy are not in question. While the particulars of the crisis are complex, the overall picture has at its center the question of foreign debt and the country's inability to pay it. Everything leads up to this cliff edge.

A number of streams combined to produce the torrent that eventually overtook the country. The first was the accumulated debt of decades — foreign borrowing that was used to shore up a weak and uncompetitive agricultural economy that relied on beef and grain sales to European markets. According to Esteban Magnani, a journalist and author of *Silent Change*, the roots of the debt go back to the days of the dictatorship, from 1976 to 1983, when the junta used debt to finance corporate theft.[3] The second cause was hyperinflation and the desperate attempts of the government, prodded by the IMF, to combat it by propping up the value of the currency. This was done by tying the value of the peso to the American dollar. The third cause was the skyrocketing interest rates that followed an increase in the value of the dollar. The cost of servicing Argentina's debt ballooned. The global recession of 2001–2002 made matters even worse. Finally, after having saddled the country with unprecedented, and unsustainable, levels of debt, the IMF pulled the plug.

The Argentine Crisis has been described as a case of catastrophic mismanagement of the affairs of a country by the IMF. But this is misleading. Mismanagement implies unwitting mistakes, the absence of knowledge concerning the consequences of one's actions. This wasn't the case in Argentina. The Argentina debacle was a repeat of the very mistakes made by the IMF in the Asian Crisis just a few years before. The actions of the IMF at that time had transformed a regional currency crisis into a global financial meltdown. It seemed the IMF had learned nothing. Or worse, it knew the consequences of its policies but deliberately ignored the lessons. The IMF had been forewarned, in gloomy detail, that an economic catastrophe was about to engulf the nation.[4] Argentina's crisis was the culmination of a long, traumatic collapse of its political and economic foundations, the final act in a slow-motion unraveling that had begun decades earlier. But the unfolding tragedy was made infinitely worse by the policies of the IMF which, under the cover of fiscal prudence, put the interests of international finance ahead of the country it was supposed to help. Its fixation on reducing inflation made the lives of Argentina's most vulnerable far worse. Unemployment rocketed to over 20 percent. But since inflation reduces the value of the capital that the IMF and the banks are owed, reducing it at any cost is the first priority. Creditors hate inflation. The second priority was ideological as well as practical—to reduce the role of government.

By forcing massive cuts in public spending and the privatization of national assets—including water, electricity and Argentina's social security system[5]—the IMF contributed to the contraction of the Argentine economy, which plunged Argentina into a recession. This was one example of the "structural adjustment" policies that the IMF liked to impose on sovereign governments.[6] The IMF also insisted that Argentina's banks be sold to foreign capital. And so just when local investment to stimulate growth was most needed, the foreign-owned banks refused to supply it. Indeed the opposite happened. There was a massive hemorrhaging of capital, made easier by the government's removal of capital controls, another IMF prescription. The wealthiest depositors and the country's ruling elite were allowed to ship their cash out of the country literally in the dead of night. According to accounts at the time,[7] an estimated $26 billion was bundled onto trucks and transported to Ezeiza airport in Buenos Aires where it was then flown out of the country before the government panicked and froze bank accounts on December 3, 2001.[8] The IMF's response to possible illegal activity on the part of banks like Citibank and the Bank of Boston in looting the capital was to demand that Argentina's subversion law be repealed so that banks couldn't be charged. As a report at the time made clear: "The IMF, whose most important member is the US, was emphatic that the economic subversion law must be repealed, leading to the heated debate in the Argentine legislature and the huge public protests across the country. The change in law is likely to bail out businesses and banks accused of playing a role in the veritable stampede of financial capital from the country at the end of last year."[9]

Capital flight was the final touch that pushed Argentina over the edge. The government's capitulation to IMF demands, and the collusion of its political class in what could only be described as a treasonous sellout of the country's sovereignty were essential ingredients in this very sordid story. The cuts to public spending and the freezing of people's deposits triggered an outpouring of rage onto the streets of Buenos Aires. The sellout and humiliation of Argentina by its politicians and ruling classes was scalded into the conscience of the population.

On December 19, 2001, people took to the streets of the major cities. In Buenos Aires, from middle-class suburbs to the squatter districts of the city, thousands joined in a massive and spontaneous occupation of the Plaza de Mayo, banging pots and pans and smashing the ATMs and windows of banks along the way. There was looting. A state of siege was declared. The following day the protests grew, reaching out to the surrounding cities and provinces, the metallic rhythms of the *cacerolazos* sounding a frightening symphony of the streets. Behind the barricades, the arias of protest swelled, letting loose the accumulated grief and rage at a system and a political class that had sold out the country, squandered its wealth and left its population to suffer the consequences. On the night of December 20, President De La Rua fled. With the sound of street fights and the sting of tear gas wafting up from below, an Air Force helicopter lifted away from the presidential palace bearing the president to the safety of his residence in Olivos. By the end of the day 26 people lay dead, 5 on the pavements of Buenos Aires.

New World, Old Habits

By the time the crisis came, Buenos Aires had acquired the worn appearance of a city whose former grandeur only emphasized its current decline. The broad boulevards and crumbling Belle Epoque facades of the city's grand buildings seemed to have materialized from another reality. And they had. The Paris- and Barcelona-inspired sensibility that adorned the city reflected the peculiar cast of mind of colonial rulers who, at the start of the 20th century, composed in their mind's eye a city that would be like no other in Latin America. They would replicate the glories of European civilization on this pliant and barbarous land at the end of the world. Buenos Aires would serve as the necessary backdrop, like some colossal operatic stage set, to vainglory and a mythology of conquest that rationalized domination while erasing the vanquished. The Spanish conquests that commenced in the 15th century conceded nothing to the land or its native people. They have become a synonym for colonial savagery. Like holy fire, spurred on by missionary zeal, the New World conquests consumed everything before them.

From the start, as V.S. Naipaul paints it, Argentina was a land of blood and plunder. It is a heritage that defined the country and established the traits that were to become inseparable from the collapse in 2001. Argentina was always the land of the strongman — machismo on the street and the military man in the palace. Underneath, there remained a narrow ruling class that displayed all the decadence of a Spanish court and whose profligacy and indolence siphoned off and wasted the wealth of the country. Unlike the small homesteaders of North America who were at that time populating the western prairies, the landlords of the vast *estancias* did no work. Indian slaves came with the land grants they received. Later, it was European immigrants who came to work the land. In the 1860s and 1870s, the landowners regarded rural life and the actual practice of agriculture with contempt.[10] Instead, they sent their sons to Eton to acquire the habits proper to those who were born to rule. The "lords of the pampas" crop up in contemporary accounts as a familiar type, strutting the salons of Paris and Berlin. But unlike the Americans, this was a landowning class that never possessed that capitalist spirit of entrepreneurialism, the willingness to invest and to risk (as well as exploit) that drove the emergence of the mass industrial forms of North America. The aristocracy merely used its wealth to purchase luxuries or buy more land.

It took the rise of a populist dictator, himself a product of the military class, to force Argentina into the modern industrial age. As a member of the military coup of 1943, Colonel Juan Domingo Perón became the transmitter and standard-bearer for a newly empowered political force, the mass of workers and stifled middle class that for the first time emerged from under the shadow of the aristocracy and the political parties it had controlled.

Organized labor was a primary source of untapped social and political power. Perón built up the labor unions to the point that they became semi-government organizations. From a membership of some 260,000 embracing mainly skilled workers, they swelled under his patronage to encompass practically the whole wage-earning force. But it wasn't only the trade unions that grew under his tutelage. The co-operative movement too, came under his influence. State sponsored co-ops were introduced into agriculture to boost production and rationalize a fragmented and inefficient sector. Credit unions, perceived as a national alternative to foreign capital, were supported in their role as lenders to small businesses and farmers. When the military clique grew panicky at the empire Perón was carving out and tried to depose him in 1945, it was already too late: the *descamisados*[11] flexed their proletarian muscles and triumphantly restored Perón to power.[12] The whole of civil society seemed to have been swallowed up in the fervent populism of the time. And if Juan Perón emerged as populism's king, Eva Perón was its patron saint. Together, they parented a political movement that has persisted to this day.

In its ideology and practice, Peronism was mystical, authoritarian, yet deeply enmeshed in the aspirations of working people. It was also all consuming; it ultimately undermined any autonomy reform movements might have had from the power of the state. All the progressive currents of the country's civil society were absorbed into Peronism. At one point, Peronists took over a general meeting of the Federation of Argentina Consumer Societies, expelled its president and installed their own officers. Large sections of both the labor movement and the co-operative movement became extensions of the Peronist party machinery and working-class culture in Argentina today remains steeped in Peronism. The divide within labor and co-operativism is still alive today, with both movements split between groups that retain their clientist affiliations with the Peronist party and those who maintain their independence. The corrupting force of this apparatus has leached deep into society and exerts its power wherever people attempt to organize as independent actors. It has played a role throughout the recovered factory movement that arose as factory after factory closed their doors in the wake of the 2001 crisis.

Occupy, Resist, Produce

Of all the stories of resistance and resilience that emerged from this traumatic period, few have captured and crystallized the spirit of the time like the movement of recovered factories. Today, 10 years later, there are still some 300 factories that have been taken over by their workers and turned into co-operatives. During the crisis, when their world seemed to be pulling apart, this act of workers seemed a gesture at once concrete and supremely symbolic, a powerful fusion of defiance and hope. At the time, the takeovers were not motivated by politics. Mostly, they were simple acts of desperation. At the height of the crisis, in Buenos Aires alone 3,900 factories were declared bankrupt and abandoned by their owners.[13] Workers who had been left with nothing, without work and without the wages they were owed, had simply nothing left to lose. They needed to feed their families. But they had also passed a threshold. The familiar subservience to power and authority had fallen away. The atmosphere of the time had corroded the old class mystique inside the workplace and beyond. Perhaps bosses weren't so indispensable after all. And although it wasn't entirely clear at the time, what was being recovered in the factory takeovers was far more than work and the "means of production." People were also recovering something essential about themselves and about their society.

Two names in particular have come to symbolize the struggles at this time — Zanon and Brukman. These two factories, whose histories and characters could not be more dissimilar, were caught up in a current of change that exposed not only the underlying rot and corruption of a society, but also the redemptive powers of transformation that lay in the simple acts of solidarity and co-operation.

Zanon

Luigi Zanon was the son of an Italian immigrant, one of the multitudes of southern Europeans who came to Argentina to seek their fortunes at the end of World War II. In 1981, in the western province of Neuquén, Zanon built a ceramics factory. He built it on public land, using public funds and subsidies from the provincial and national governments, which were never repaid. Throughout the nineties, Zanon's factory became a state-of-the-art facility, the largest ceramics factory in Argentina, growing steadily through a regular infusion of government loans. Luigi Zanon was a close friend of former president Carlos Menem, the golden boy of Argentina during the country's infatuation with neo-liberalism in the 1990s. Menem was the IMF's man in Argentina. It was Menem who enacted the IMF's demands that labor standards be made more "flexible" and friendly to "investment." Zanon, like so many others, was quick to take advantage of the new flexibility. He colluded with corrupt union leaders and ratcheted down wages and work conditions for the rank and file while rewarding the leadership. This included paying an extra salary to union bureaucrats and making cash donations to their union to buy its compliance. Throughout the 90s the factory was making money. Zanon was averaging $45–50 million a year and in 1996 the company turned a profit of $67 million. Yet wages and work conditions continued to decline. Intimidation of workers became routine. According to Reinaldo Giménez, one of the young workers at the time:

> They began cutting materials and supplies, they took away half of the
> work, all with the union's complicity. Zanon was very false, he would

come in a couple of times a year, tour the factory, pat someone on the back. To this guy they say: we have ways to identify those who don't like you. A typical tactic: If they wanted to lay off five guys, they'd announce 20 layoffs. Then the union would intervene, fight, negotiate, and would end up saying, OK, we managed to have 15 brought back. And so they'd get rid of the five that management wanted to fire.[14]

Workers decided to take back their union. With the help of Lista Marrón, a branch of the Internal Union Commission, workers started organizing to replace their union leadership. Tensions with Zanon and the company management intensified. Conditions got worse. Layoffs increased and union activists were targeted for reprisals. It was an atmosphere that made organizing inside the factory impossible. So, like a scene from a Hollywood film, the workers hit on the idea of organizing a soccer league outside the factory. With a footprint of almost 96,000 square yards, the plant covered 22 acres and was organized into 14 sections. The workers organized a team for each, and each section elected a delegate to attend league meetings. Here workers communicated clandestinely, organized, accumulated data and did the math. It soon became apparent that the crisis that the management was complaining about was a fabrication. As one worker put it: "What crisis, if 20 trucks are going out every day, they have 25 percent of the domestic market and export to I don't know how many countries? What crisis, if they get tax incentives in the province and loans and every kind of advantage imaginable because Zanon, in addition to everything else, was Sobisch's shadow?" Jorge Omar Sobisch, a right-wing politician with political ties to the Peronist president, Carlos Menem, was the governor of Neuquén.

By 2000, the company was withholding payments to its employees despite the fact it had been receiving government loans to pay back wages. It simply pocketed the loans.[15] The boiling point came in June of that year when 22-year-old Daniel Ferrás died of cardiorespiratory arrest inside the factory because the oxygen in the first aid supply was empty. There was no ambulance and no doctor either. Enraged, the workers stopped production for eight days, demanding and finally receiving an ambulance and nurse. In December 2000, the workers ousted the union local's leadership and Luigi Zanon responded with mass layoffs. From a workforce of 330, his proposal was to downsize to just 60 employees, which the workers understood as a means of "cleaning out" the union.

The workers struck. They rejected the layoffs, burning the termination slips in bonfires outside the presidential palace in Buenos Aires. They erected a tent in front of the company gates for five months, launched an education campaign and turned to the community for support. Mr. Zanon had already abandoned the factory.

By this time the country was spinning out of control, both politically and economically. Across Argentina, neighborhood assemblies were becoming a widespread phenomenon, especially in Buenos Aires. The masses of unemployed workers, the *piqueteros*, had begun organizing roadblocks and demanding reform. They had also teamed up with neighborhood organizations to stage protests, organize self-help programs and debate the accelerating national crisis in impromptu, open-air symposia. These neighborhood assemblies became the political firewall of the recovered factory movement, lending critical popular protection and moral support to the striking workers and their eventual decision to take back the factories against much larger forces. Chilavert Artes Gráficas, a print shop in Buenos Aires, was supported by the assembly of Pompeya; E. I. Aquarite by the Assembly of Carapachey; and Nueva Esperanza (formerly Grisginopoli), the Bauen Hotel, and others by several assemblies at once.[16]

In March 2002, 220 of Zanon's 330 workers decided to occupy the factory and resume production under worker control. Through an assembly they agreed to receive the same salary and formed commissions on sales, administration, security, expenditures, production, planning, safety and hygiene and public relations. The indigenous Mapuches, who, up to then had been exploited by the ceramics company, gave the workers access to their clay quarries. On April 5, 2002, the first production of 20,000 square meters of tiles left the factory. Three months later they produced 120,000 square meters, half of what the company had produced under the previous owner.[17] With help from the Universities of Comahue (Neuquén) and Buenos Aires, they modernized the production process and within two years invested $300,000 in improvements to the machinery. From the 300 accidents per year that occurred under the previous ownership, the rate was brought down to 33. There was not a single death, while previously an average of one worker died every month.[18] In a final, flamboyant gesture the workers changed the factory's name to FaSinPat (Fábrica Sin Patron, or Factory Without Bosses) and formally incorporated as a co-operative. The name carried a certain proletarian panache.

Co-op and Community

Had it not been for the solidarity that was forged between the Zanon workers and the surrounding community it would have been impossible for the recovery of the factory to be sustained. From the outset, the workers were confronted with a determined campaign to keep the factory shuttered and to allow the owner to strip and sell off its remaining assets. They fought off wave after wave of police assaults. What saved them was the willingness of community members to turn out en masse whenever the police descended on the site. Lookouts were posted and word of an imminent police action spread through the district. Thousands turned out, planted themselves in front of the police lines and held vigils in support of the workers. The more militant among them joined the workers at the factory windows and rooftops and fired back at the tear gas and rubber bullets with slingshots and marbles.

On April 8, 2003, when police attempted to evict the workers, thousands surrounded the factory to stop them. Thwarted, the police dispersed and 9,000 people gathered inside the factory for a rock concert to celebrate the fragile victory and their solidarity with the workers. It was a nerve-snapping game of cat and mouse that lasted on and off for nine years, broken occasionally by a temporary reprieve won by court order or political pressure while the unending, demoralizing work of winning legal recognition of the co-op's right to produce was pursued through a corrupt and arbitrary judicial and political system. Meanwhile, the factory continued to turn out the tiles. Despite lack of government support and capital investment, it hired more workers and inside of 4 years increased production from 15,000 to 400,000 square metres a month.

The co-op became integrated into the life of the community. Once the workers took control of the designs, they started making changes. Instead of the old-world designs of medieval Italy, the tiles began to carry Mapuche forms, created with the help of Mapuche communities themselves, with the objective of restoring the marginalized culture of the people who in the co-op's hour of need had offered the ceramists their reserves of clay. The co-op started making countless donations to the surrounding neighborhoods. It donated materials, money and labor to hospitals, schools, nursing homes and soup kitchens. It helped indigenous groups and groups with disabilities, supported firefighters and the Red Cross of Neuquén. The most important, and most symbolic, donation was the construction of a medical center for the impoverished community of Nueva Espana. In 2005, under the guidance of 400 families who had been running a first-aid center for 40 years, the FaSinPat members donated the materials and constructed the clinic in 3 months. The community had been waiting for a clinic from the provincial government for two decades.[19] Subsequent research into the degree of aid that recovered factories received during the darkest days of the struggle revealed a direct correlation between their commitment to the local community and the political aid they received. In other words, they earned this solidarity. Those recovered factories that formed bonds with the community in their hour of weakness also felt obliged to reciprocate when they were strong.[20] This was most certainly true with FaSinPat.

It took a crisis for workers and community members to see that workplaces are never the atomized and isolated entities that conventional notions of capitalism like to portray. Workplaces are social organisms. They are sustained as much by the social investments of schools, roads, legislation, and very often capital, as they are by the investments of their owners and shareholders. Takeover of these factories by their workers and the widespread support they received from the communities in which they were located aimed an arrow at the heart of the notion of the pre-eminence of private property. The recovered factory movement became at bottom a moral claim of labor and the public interest.

Inside FaSinPat, work life was transformed. It was humanized. As one former employee put it: "We were not allowed to leave or go to the bathroom. The pathways were marked out with different colors. Red indicated places where there were automatic machines and you had to move with caution, and blue was for places you could go. Back then, the kiln operators had to wear red clothes, electricians green, and so forth. That way, they could tell if someone from another sector was somewhere they weren't supposed to be. It was like a jail."[21]

As in a prison, the company managers and the union bosses were located on the upper floor with offices looking down into the interior of the factory so they could survey the workers. The union stewards shadowed the workers on the floor. This went on 24 hours a day, 7 days a week. When the workers took over, they ended this tyrannical and demeaning system. Instead, each production section was organized into a workers' assembly and each assembly selected a co-ordinator to take charge of the production process and dialogue with co-ordinators from the other assemblies. There are 36 sectors and the co-ordinators of each assembly rotate every few months so that every member takes a turn in this position. During his tenure the co-ordinator has more responsibility, but the salary remains the same as the other members.

According to one employee, "Each Monday there is a co-ordinating meeting and there they decide what each shift needs; problems of individual sectors are resolved and if they cannot be resolved, they are brought before an assembly of all the shifts. But the final product that goes to market is the responsibility of everyone, not just the person who makes it, because we all work on the same level, in conjunction with each other from the raw clay until the final ceramic piece is finished and put up for sale."[22]

Once a month there is a general workers assembly in which each member participates. This is the co-op's governing council and its sessions cover every aspect of the factory's work, from production targets to community donations, to the type of footgear needed for each section. It is intense, demanding and idealistic. And it works. The factory's operations and finances are totally transparent, while the workers' personal investment in the creation of a culture of reciprocity inside the workplace is now a cornerstone of the co-op's success. Throughout this evolution, the bonds that have been forged with the surrounding community have grown. The changes inside the factory are an extension of a wider transformation, an awareness that the life of a factory and the life of a community are connected and that the fortunes of one are bound up in the fortunes of the other. The allegiances and the alignments of power have opened up, become reciprocal and breached the walls that formerly isolated workers within the hierarchical bonds of capital.

Brukman

The Brukman garment factory was the first to be taken over by its workers. By December of 2001, when the economic crisis was reaching a head inside the country, the 12-year-old Buenos Aires plant was in deep trouble. The Brukman family had been whittling down wages to the non-unionized work force. Over a period of 5 months, wages had been slashed from 100 pesos a week (the equivalent of 100 dollars) to 2. This was not enough to pay the bus fare to get to work. The workers had shouldered the cutbacks with sullen tolerance. At the time, unemployment in Argentina was running at 22 percent. To be left without a job was to sink into destitution. It meant scavenging and begging for food.

Already, with the government buckling to IMF demands to cut back social services, 58 percent of the population had slipped below the poverty
line. This was an anxious and compliant workforce. But the cut in wages
to less than bus fare pushed the workers, mostly middle aged women,
over the line. They had not been paid in three weeks. On the 18th of December, one day before the mass of citizenry hit the streets, the workers
shut down their machines and refused to leave until they received the
money they were owed. The owners told them to wait until they came
back with the money. They never returned. Instead, Jacobo Brukman offered them two suits apiece in lieu of pay. They refused.

As veteran seamstress Mathilde Adorno recalled, "If we hadn't taken
the factory then, the bosses would have closed it. We held meetings all
morning; we were all very nervous. When the bosses didn't turn up, we
decided to wait. That evening we held our first assembly and 23 people
stayed locked in all night. When I got here the next morning the others
had put up protest banners all over the factory. We'd taken a decision
without knowing what we were up against."[23]

The following evening was the first of the workers' official occupation.

"We were all inside, laid down on the floor out of fear. We'd put card-
board over the windows so nobody could see us and switched off the
lights. Then we felt a noise swelling up from outside. We thought it was
the police. It was coming from all sides. We didn't know where to run to.
Then someone opened a window and saw what it was — a *cacerolazo*!"[24]

Outside, the clatter of spoons banging against saucepans accompanied the mass rallies that soon put the administration of Eduardo de la
Rua to flight. Inside the factory walls, the atmosphere remained tense.
Workers did not yet dare to produce without a boss. "We thought the
equipment was sacred," remarked Adorno. It took another month before workers abandoned their fears. At some moment, imperceptible in
its gathering, the old, familiar fear dropped away, like the popular turning of a tide against a tyrant. People started to work. The tailors started
chalking cloth, the women took their seats at the sewing machines
and volunteers set off in search of sales. All that was missing were the
bosses.

Like at Zanon thousands of miles to the west, the police launched
an attack. In March, 100 police officers dressed in riot gear stormed the
factory at dawn looking for "activists and criminals." They found three

workers and a baby. While they ransacked the factory, the neighbors surrounded the building. The police left, but not for long. They returned again, evicting the workers in the middle of the night and turning the factory into an armed camp, surrounded by machine guns and dogs. Again the community turned out by the thousands. It's a scene that is vividly captured in Avi Lewis and Naomi Klein's film, *The Take*.

> Unable to get into the factory and complete an outstanding order for 3,000 pairs of dress trousers, the workers gathered a huge crowd of supporters and announced it was time to go back to work. At 5 PM, 50 middle-aged seamstresses in no-nonsense haircuts, sensible shoes and blue work smocks walked up to the black police fence. Someone pushed, the fence fell and the Brukman women, unarmed and arm in arm, slowly walked through.
>
> They had only taken a few steps when the police began shooting: tear gas, water cannons, rubber bullets, then lead. The police even charged the Mothers of the Plaza de Mayo, in their white headscarves embroidered with the names of their "disappeared" children. Dozens of demonstrators were injured and police fired tear gas into a hospital where some had taken refuge.[25]

No one who had the least notion of the history of police repression in Argentina could have been surprised at the outcome. Klein's reference to the attack on the Mothers of the Plaza de Mayo is particularly revealing because it highlights the persistence of the repressive reflex inside the police establishment. These are the same forces that, during the "dirty war" immediately following the military coup in 1976, were responsible for the abduction, torture and "disappearance" of 30,000 people deemed to be enemies of the state. This included the usual roster of labor organizers, academics, journalists and human rights activists that would figure prominently on the hit list of any self-respecting despotic regime. They were plucked off the streets in broad daylight, thrown into the back of a Ford Falcon — the car of choice for this operation — and reappeared some time later floating in the River Playa or dumped onto the streets. But the depravity and paranoia extended even further, approaching the realms of science fiction. Many of the disappeared were the hapless children of these "enemies of the state." Once their parents were imprisoned or murdered, they were simply handed over to more upright families who might instill in them values more in tune with the corrective moral codes of the military men who ruled the country.

Surprisingly, the police actions against the factories, although unrelenting, have not been decisive. They haven't succeeded in turning back the tide. The recovered factories have held on. The broad public support they enjoyed bolstered their moral case and the political impact of their appeals for state support and legitimation. Those few that have gone under have done so not from police intimidation or violence, but as a consequence of the near-impossible constraints they operate under as they try to run a successful business. The most damaging effects flow from the absence of investment capital which, in turn, is one consequence of the disputes over factory ownership. When they saw that these factories had begun to be profitable under worker control, many of the very owners that had driven them into the ground and then abandoned them demanded them back. This was the case with FaSinPat.

There is a remarkable scene in *The Take* in which Luigi Zanon is making his claims on the factory. When he is confronted with the litany of grievances against his past actions, both by his former employees and by the community at large, he remains sanguine, utterly untouched by any notion of injustice associated with his behavior. Smiling indulgently in his ornately carved armchair, speaking as if dealing with a child, he is certain he will have his factory back. "Who will give it to you?" asks the interviewer. "The government will give it to me," says Mr. Zanon, with an air of such complacence and entitlement that in that one moment he has embodied in his person the entire tragic logic of his country.

An Awakening

Both inside and outside Argentina, the success of FaSinPat — like that of the other recovered factories — has come as something of a revelation. From the start, the notion that workers could take on and manage these factories, and succeed where the previous owners had failed, was met with ridicule from the former owners, from "experts" and from the governing class in general. With little experienced management (in most cases the management left along with the owners), and with little prospect of capital investment it was expected that the factories would fail. Everything was done to help them fail. If the owners who had abandoned the factories couldn't have them, no one should. Above all, the sacred notion of the inviolable rights of property should not be questioned.

No matter that many of these factories had been floating for years on public funds and subsidized through tax exemptions, gifts of public property and the elimination of workers' rights to fair pay and decent working conditions. The rights of labor, unlike the rights of capital, were dispensable. But it was curious indeed how the same doubts concerning the innate ability of workers to manage these firms somehow were never leveled against the owners and the policy experts who bankrupted the businesses to begin with.

Throughout the nineties, under the terms of the IMF's "strategic adjustment policies," the administration of Carlos Menem agreed to make labor conditions inside Argentina more "flexible" using the rationale that this would increase foreign investment and tamp down unemployment. Every visit by Michel Camdessus, the managing director of the IMF, and the "technical missions" dispatched monthly to Buenos Aires drove the country further in this direction.[26] The results were catastrophic. Not only did unemployment triple, but the conditions of workers plummeted. Collective agreements were torn up. Social security and health benefits were scrapped. The working day was lengthened and overtime pay was ended, not only in the private sector but in schools and hospitals as well.[27] Millions of jobs were made temporary and labor was casualized. The cumulative effects of these legislative measures were evident in the Survey of Labor Indicators published by the Ministry of Labor in March 1997. Eighty percent of jobs created in 1996 were either fixed-term or probationary. Between January 1996 and the same month of 1997 "the number of wage workers on permanent contracts fell by 5.9 percent, while the number of those of a casual or probationary nature increased 3.2 times." The impact in the countryside of the rise of unregistered workers was beyond belief. According to ministry figures, there were one million people employed in agriculture in 1996. Of these, a total of 11 workers received any pension rights.[28] There arose an army of dependent, insecure, unprotected workers who could now be rehired by employers at a fraction of the cost with "rigid" labor conditions in force. The other result was that the destabilization of work spread from the traditional working-class jobs up into the white-collar jobs of the middle class. Employer abuses of these types of labor contracts became pandemic.

All of this amounted to a legislated subsidization of capital, an enormous transfer of wealth and resources from labor and society-at-large into the hands of the country's ruling elites. Even worse, the Bankruptcy Act of 1995 rendered collective agreements unenforceable in bankruptcy proceedings. This made it nearly impossible for workers to collect money owed to them. Employers took advantage of this act to concoct bankruptcies, fire workers, strip and sell the assets of the company and sail off with the proceeds.[29] Fraudulent bankruptcies were made legal and became a major contributing factor in the destruction and abandonment of these factories. As noted by Magnani, this went far beyond the limits of industrial failure.[30] The policies enacted by the Menem government at this time were a model for de-industrializing a country. The IMF and the Argentine ruling class, with the enthusiastic collusion of the government, were engaged in a systemic looting and wrecking of the country's manufacturing foundations. Even today, the IMF continues to oppose attempts to hold factory owners accountable for their actions.

From the perspective of the workers and the communities that relied on these factories for jobs, there was a harsh awakening. After years of subservience and acceptance, they saw that these supposed rights of property were based on a mixture of myth and manipulation. While the rights of capital were protected, the rights of labor and the public — of society at large — were being trampled. Public investments in these factories were essential to their success, both in terms of capital and in the legal concessions that favored factory owners and private capital in general. The Zanon factory had been built with 90 million pesos of public money. Now that these investments had been squandered and never repaid, people demanded that the public interest in these enterprises be recognized and legitimized. If the debts owed to capital must be paid, why not the debts to labor and the public?[31]

Across Argentina, at the point where the national economy was sliding over the edge, an unprecedented conviction arose among both the middle and the working classes that the entire political class had betrayed the country. It was no longer a question of this administration or that policy being questioned — it was a wholesale rejection of the political system and the parastatal institutions that had for so long been a part of this apparatus. The vacuum of legitimacy left by the collapse of the previous systems also provoked a break with the hierarchical structures that had become deeply ingrained, socially, politically and psychologically, since Peronist times. Horizontal power relationships became much more possible. A new type of organizational logic began to take hold, a form radically opposed to the authoritarian moulds imposed in Argentina since the days of Perón and before, through the dictatorship of the '70s, and up to the individualist neo-liberalism of the '90s. All of these structures conspired against the very idea of civil and industrial co-operation.

The recovery of some 200 enterprises became the most tangible embodiment of a new sentiment, incorporating as it did an affinity between factory worker and community member, blue-collar seamstress and middle-class housewife, and most profoundly, a recognition and reclamation of social rights over and against the rights of private property. Beyond this, there was the extraordinary revelation that alternative forms of organization that embodied these values could work. Not only in factories, but in hotels, hospitals, schools, childcare centers, printing houses and public services, worker co-operatives were not only saving jobs but remaking the nature of work itself, humanizing labor through the application of democracy and reciprocity in the workplace. In the words of one Zanon worker: "What we've learned is that in a business participatory democracy is more efficient. Because if you vote often, you get used to winning...but you also get used to losing, you learn to accept the decision of the majority."[32]

But contrary to the rosy-hued reports of some commentators, the process was difficult and remains difficult still. For if the spirit of defiance and the rejection of conventional authority was an essential factor in the rise of this movement, it has also worked against it. So too, has the suddenness of its emergence and the continuing influence of attitudes that have been internalized over generations. Old habits die hard. In some factories, the initial impulse toward egalitarianism and solidarity became stalled. The familiar individualism and deference to authority reappeared once the conditions of crisis began to abate. New cliques began to emerge and sometimes they were aligned with the old trade unions, which had begun to make deals with the previous owners to wrest back control of the factories.

The trade unions had a vested interest in the status quo — that's where their power came from. They had offered little help in the first days when the occupations began. Not only was their power vested in the old structures of collusion with owners on the one hand and government on the other, but they were genuinely perplexed by a movement of people who had been so passive for so long. The Bonacrendi Federation of Graphics Workers during the occupation of the Chilavert printing plant, The Textile Workers Union at the Brukman factory, and the Union of Food Industry Workers in Grissinopoli all abandoned their members to their fate and pulled their lawyers out when the workers decided to occupy their factories.[33] There were many cases of this. Workers were promised help, but none came. When help did arrive it came in the form of food boxes or advice to negotiate for fewer layoffs, or for a better severance, or a reduction in the debt they were owed.[34] Certainly, the mainstream unions had little notion, and less interest, in how to set up an entirely new form of industrial enterprise, one that explicitly rejected the top-down power patterns that were the ruling logic of these union organizations.

The co-op movement presented its own set of problems. Historically, the Argentine co-op movement traces its roots back to the early 1900s when many of the Italian immigrants that first arrived in the country brought with them the co-operative and socialist ideas they were familiar with from their home country. Other immigrant groups, including Jews, also brought their own co-op traditions. And as in so many other places, the movement put down its earliest roots in the agricultural economy of the country.

Today, over 600 co-ops are active in marketing and processing and handle 45 percent of Argentina's tea production, and 35 percent of the domestic grain market, dairy processing and cotton production. Co-ops produce 30 percent of the rice and 20 percent of the wine in the country. Other key sectors include savings and credit, telecommunications (where 350 co-operatives collectively serve about 8 percent of the country's population), and health, education, housing and tourism. In total, Argentina's 12,670 co-operatives have over 9.3 million members and provide direct employment to over 87,400 individuals. Their membership represents approximately 23.5 percent of the population. The movement has an established and rich tradition.

But some of the leaders within the traditional movement were suspicious of the recovered factory phenomenon. They had no prior relationship with these worker co-operatives that had sprung up almost overnight. They had seen how fragile the co-op idea, much less the co-op organization, was within these plants. For most factories, the adoption of the co-op form was at first a matter of convenience. They needed a legal framework that would enable factories to operate under worker control; the co-op structure provided such a framework. But few had any real notion of what a co-op really entailed. They had no connection to the culture, history or attitudes that underpin the decision to join or form a co-operative in a normal sense. And so workers that had just occupied their factories weren't motivated by the co-op idea per se; it had simply risen in their midst like a genie as a consequence of their predicament. To be sure, in the first wave of occupations there were those who understood that the co-op form was an obvious choice not only for the question of industrial organization under worker control, but also as an idea that embodied the values that a newly radicalized populace was struggling to make real. From the perspective of the traditional co-op movement however, there was real ambivalence. How "real" were these co-ops? Who was truly in control? Did the workers really call the shots? Had any of them ever run a co-op? Who the hell were these people?

These were all very good questions. But in asking them, and then waiting for the answers, the mainstream co-op movement ended up following, not leading the new wave. Some few individual co-operatives had provided modest assistance and recognized the significance of what was taking place. They provided legal advice, organizational help and moral support. But the co-op movement as a whole took a hands-off attitude.

Other factors also weighed against the movement taking a leadership role. The truth was that large sections of the co-op movement were politically compromised. Like the trade unions, a portion of the Argentine co-op movement was still connected to the Peronist power structure. Many of them were co-ops in name only. I remember vividly an occasion when I saw this with depressing clarity. During the winter of 2005, I was in Buenos Aires to witness the recovered factories at first hand.

A rally had been called to demonstrate co-op support for Nestor Kirchner, the Peronist governor of Patagonia who had recently been elected President. In the course of his campaign against former president Carlos Menem he had pledged support for the recovered factories. This particular event was designed to capture some much needed media exposure. The venue was situated in one of those barren non-locations one finds in the industrial suburbs of any large city. Featureless blocks of utilitarian buildings squatted along the near-empty roads in neat rows, extending endlessly in every direction. Lines of buses had drawn up outside a stadium and people were piling out. Hundreds upon hundreds were filing into the stadium, filling it up, and still more buses kept coming. Inside, the space was cavernous, like a hangar. Up among the steel girders at one end stretched a long banner depicting Kirchner in profile alongside Castro, Che and President Lula of Brazil. At the other end billowed a ten-foot portrait of Evita. Elsewhere, there were signs proclaimed Kirchner as the saviour of the co-operatives.

People continued to pour in. These were mostly poor, rural folks who had been bussed in from across the province and beyond. They now filled every possible space inside the stadium and were roaring in anticipation of Kirchner. Roving bands of drummers started pounding out ear-splitting rhythms, lending the scene an unsettling aura of delirium. Countless handheld signs of the assembled co-ops were pumping up and down in tempo. Outside, Kirchner's helicopter landed. The temperature mounted, the noise reached a deafening crescendo, and Kirchner mounted the stage with his retinue. The cameras whirred away.

I was accompanied by colleagues from a small co-op that did work in adult education. What we were seeing, they explained, was the unsavoury side of the co-op movement in Argentina. Their co-op, and others like theirs, had nothing to do with this aspect of the movement. Those co-op "members" who had been screaming their enthusiasm for Kirchner had been paid to be there. The price was a sandwich lunch, a bottle of Coke and the good graces of the Peronist organizer that had recruited them. The same technique was used to corral their votes at election time. Whether any of them knew the first thing about co-ops was anyone's guess.

The complicity of sections of the co-op movement in this kind of politics was one cause for unease. But far worse was the tenor of the gathering. For what was on display here was the unmistakable air of the mob. It was that crude and unthinking populism, the hero worship that was perfected by Peron and then revived through the years by the political machinery that he and his wife had erected. In its spirit and its practice, this frightful demagoguery was the opposite of everything the co-op movement should have stood for. But it would have been impossible to convince very many at this rally. The trappings and the mannerisms may have been bought and paid for, they may have derived from another time, but these were the attitudes and the psychology that still held sway under the surface for a large number of ordinary Argentines. And if the economic disaster had for the moment united the poor and the prosperous in the same sinking boat, would the spirit of solidarity and reform that characterized the first wave of popular defiance outlast the immediate crisis? Was there the staying power that was needed to remake Argentina's economic and social institutions? Would the new-found spirit of co-operation and mobilization prevail?

In part as a reaction to the type of unthinking authoritarianism that was on show at the rally, a fierce spirit of independence and resistance to centralized control of any kind arose inside the recovered factories. But resistance to authority also gave rise to unthinking independence. For the recovered factory movement to exert an influence beyond its immediate material concerns, it needed a high degree of co-ordination and organization. Because of their inherent vulnerability the factories needed the solidarity and support of other factories. To a very great extent, it was fear that bound them together. But beyond this, the factory co-ops needed to share information, tactics, experiences and lessons learned with one another and with the more established co-ops. They needed to develop organizational expertise, master the complexities of democratic governance, acquire training and the myriad other things that can be transferred and shared when there is some form of centralized organization. Politically, the coordination of information and strategy and the mobilization of people is crippled without such a structure and its absence remains a grave weakness of the movement.[35] After decades — generations — of domination, many newly empowered workers see centralizing authority as a source of corruption, with good reason. There is a pride in the worker autonomy and freedom that prevails among the factories. But it is a limiting freedom, born of the mistrust that followed in the wake of countless betrayals. It is not yet the freedom born of trust.

What this has meant is that while idealism remains at a high pitch, the practical skills required to run complex enterprises are in short supply. Much energy and time are wasted precisely because the systems have yet to be built to enable a common stock of skills, concepts and resources to be shared. Basic procedures like bookkeeping, accounting, inventory control and marketing have to be learned co-op by co-op. Most pressing of all is the absence of managerial expertise. For enterprises that are fragile to begin with, these are things that can spell disaster.

If the political legacy of authoritarianism at the societal level was the corruption and co-optation of the organizations of civil society — the trade unions, co-ops and cultural organizations — inside the factories the psychology of control became a primary impediment to establishing just that understanding of reciprocity that places in balance the interests of the individual with the collective interest of the worker community. The ingrained habits of egoism remained. The tendency to defer to leaders had to be unlearned. Personal responsibility and mutual accountability in the context of a workplace without bosses had to be learned anew. In short, the absence of a boss meant that the entire pattern of work had to change. Workers could no longer wait for orders and rest assured that a paycheck awaited them at the end of the month. Everything was now up to them. The transition from dependence and obedience to democratic ownership and control was a transition that affected not only how work was organized but what it meant.[36] Workers had to create new modes of working and relating and in so doing they were forced to develop dimensions of their personalities they had never used. They were forced to become different people. Work took on a deeply social meaning. The simple act of creating and operating a co-operative in the circumstances of Argentina in these days was transformative and no one was untouched by it. This profoundly personal impact is attested to continuously.[37] It constitutes perhaps the most revolutionary and far-reaching effect of the recovered factory movement. It is captured in the words of a worker from Forja San Martin, an auto parts factory profiled in *The Take*: "This is what we are doing here today, this co-operativism is our way of making a new world — to sweep away the old one."

The Road Ahead

From 2004 to 2008, Argentina was on the rebound. Having hit rock bottom in 2001, the national economy began to recover only after the government defaulted on its debt. The administration of Nestor Kirchner began to focus on building up the national economy without recourse to the crippling policies of the IMF and the encumbrances of international debt. Soon, the economy was growing again at a rate of nine to ten percent annually. This continued until the American bank crisis of 2008 cast a pall over the global economy. But Argentina weathered the crisis better than most countries. This was because the economy was no longer entangled in the international financial structures that had ensnared most national economies. It was a touch of unexpected luck from the 2001 default, which was still technically in force. In addition, the present administration of Cristina Fernández de Kirchner, the former president's wife, has resisted determined efforts to re-engage Argentina with the IMF. Saying no to the IMF is a popular policy. It appears that the IMF's contribution to the 2001 collapse will not soon be forgotten — or forgiven. It's a lesson that has still to be learned by other governments in other countries. Argentina's story, if nothing else, has everything to teach dependent economies about their relations to Northern banks and their instrument, the IMF.

Naturally, the crushing debt burden of the world's poorest economies has long occupied a central place in deliberations of how to address third world poverty. But there is as yet little solidarity *among* debtor nations on how to cut this Gordian knot of dependence. It is only in the extreme case of an economic catastrophe, as happened in Argentina, that debt default is ever considered an option. But poor countries do not yet perceive default as a deliberate *strategy* to pull themselves out of perpetual poverty. In the accepted wisdom, such an action would bear consequences too horrible to contemplate. But what could be worse than the present purgatory, where debt, historically incurred by tyrannies with little accountability to their people, consigns entire populations to penury? Would the strike of international capital be worse than the current situation where the primary consequence of foreign debt is not only poverty for the vast majority and the loss of a country's patrimony, but the perpetuation of parasitic ruling elites that make the prospect of true reform even more remote?

In the end, there are only two options to address this question: debt forgiveness, essentially a form of charity from the North, or debt default — either as a result of economic collapse, or as a strategy for recovery taken by poor nations themselves. Consider how interesting it would be if the poorest countries of the world co-operated on just this one issue and issued an ultimatum to their creditors that unless a debt forgiveness plan was enacted, they would take the initiative in their own hands, stop asking for favors and default as a moral duty to their people.

Inside Argentina today, the recovered factory movement retains a strength and resilience undreamed of in the crisis days of 2001–2002. Despite the obstacles, there are now well over 300 factories that have been turned into co-operatives by their workers. They employ some 15,000 people. In the last 6 months of 2008, 33 factories that had been declared bankrupt were taken over by their employees. Most remarkable of all, the co-ops continue to produce and retain their workers despite the current economic downturn. Workers weren't fired, unlike at other factories during this same period. Wages may be temporarily scaled back, or hours shortened, but the hardship is shared. This has had an enormous effect in minimizing the damage of the economic downturn on workers, their families and their communities. Moreover, the movement has catalyzed similar actions in other countries. In Uruguay, Nicaragua and Bolivia, factory takeovers in the wake of bankruptcies are becoming more common. In Bolivia, the mining sector has witnessed a massive takeover by the largely Indian workers who for decades had labored as literal serfs in the mines of the country. Bolivian mining co-ops now employ some 60,000 people.

There are almost no failures among the recovered factories. Of the original 200 that were occupied in the first wave of takeovers, only 2 have shut down.[38] The grim predictions of failure intoned by the former owners, the politicians and the endless parade of "experts" have been proven false. That these factories continue to produce, to survive while others fail and go bankrupt, continues to astound even the workers themselves. As a model of industrial organization, and as a prescription for a broader economic policy, the factory co-ops are providing daily evidence of an alternative that has the power not only to weather the storm in economic bad times, but a means of rebuilding the manufacturing base of a national economy on a far more sustainable and equitable basis.

Attitudinal change within the factories however, continues to be hard and comes slowly. Not only the control psychology of an authoritarian culture must be overcome, but also the traditional mentality of the industrial worker in a capitalist system. The two share the common logic of control and command. The inability, or unwillingness, of many to make the transition from industrial worker to co-owner of an enterprise is a major impediment. Most workers have not yet learned to think like co-operative entrepreneurs. As shown by the experience of successful industrial co-operative systems like those in Emilia Romagna, this takes years of work and the intentional recasting of perceptions — from submissive individualism to responsible communitarianism, and from the salvaging of one's own factory to the building of a co-operative culture. Many workers are still content to survive on a day-to-day basis. They resist the management imperative to plan long-term. This thinking is further reinforced by the uncertainty concerning the eventual fate of their factories. The spectre of eviction still haunts them.

But there is reason for hope. Of the original recovered factories, over 50 percent have been granted legal expropriation. This usually entails a settlement with the previous owners, with the state being responsible for paying it and recovering the cost over time from the co-ops. Within the movement for reform generally there is now an acceptance, and a familiarity, with the experience of the recovered factories. Their survival is exerting a progressive influence throughout society, including the judicial and political systems. Judges have gained confidence in the ability of workers to manage these factories through their co-operatives. Lawyers have developed expertise on how to handle occupations and expropriations within a legal framework. Politicians are more prepared to support the drafting of effective legislation, including rewriting the regressive legislation covering co-operatives generally, which was gutted during the junta years. Most importantly, worker takeover, expropriation and the creation of a co-operative have now become part of the mental vocabulary of workers and surrounding communities. When factories now go bankrupt, the possibility of worker ownership is a natural part of the equation. Almost everyone now knows someone who has participated in, or is employed by, a recovered factory. The positive effects of the movement are real and undeniable.

More broadly however, the reform impetus of 2001–2002 has lost its momentum. The Peronist party is back in power and it has been masterful in absorbing the political currents of the grass-roots movements and channeling them into conventional neo-Keynesian nostrums for economic and social policy. However, faced with a resurgent right wing and the loss of congressional elections, the government has been forced to radicalize. It appears Kirchner understands that unless the government moves to the left it has little chance of winning the elections in 2011.[39] Argentina's political institutions remain fundamentally unchanged. The ideas that first accompanied the radicalism of the reform movement are still in play, but they have yet to find expression in the broader social and political structures of the country. And this is perhaps the signal lesson of the Argentine economic crisis of 2001, and a regular lesson of history. The threat to material economic security may be sufficient to spark revolt and unite formerly disparate interests, but to sustain the social impulse for reform beyond crisis, social relations and the institutions of an economy must themselves be changed through the materialization of transformative ideas.

On August 14, 2009, the provincial legislature of Neuquén voted to expropriate Zanon and grant legal control to the co-operative by a count of 26 for and 9 against. The state also agreed to pay the principal creditors 22 million pesos (roughly US$7 million). Chief among these is the World Bank from whom Luigi Zanon took a substantial loan to start the company. The co-operative is resisting these moves, claiming that these creditors participated in a fraudulent bankruptcy and that Zanon himself should be liable for these debts since the money enriched him personally and not the plant. The struggle continues...

CHAPTER 10

The Crisis of Community

There is no society,
only individuals and families.

— MARGARET THATCHER —

With the sound of helicopter rotors thumping in the background, the video image showed three black figures on a rooftop. One held a long pole with a bright red towel attached, waving the banner in a slow arc over his head. Off to the side two women held up a handwritten sign that read simply, "HELP US." Around them, the rising floodwater lapped at the roofline. New Orleans was underwater.

On the satellite images, the approaching storm had appeared as a jerky, red and yellow vortex spiraling slowly like a nebula just off the south coast of Florida. For days, meteorologists had been warning that the approaching hurricane was unlike anything seen in the last 30 years. By the time it made landfall on August 29, 2005, the storm had been jacked up to a category 5, gathering lethal force as it sliced across the Florida panhandle and slammed into the Gulf States of Louisiana and Mississippi. When its fury was spent, Hurricane Katrina had become the worst natural disaster in the history of the United States. Its material toll was estimated at $100 billion. Five hundred thousand homes were destroyed.

But New Orleans was lucky...the storm only grazed the city. What destroyed New Orleans was entirely a man-made disaster—the failure of the city's levee system due to shoddy design and engineering. The political fallout that followed marked a watershed in public perceptions not only of the Bush administration but of government itself. At a deeper level, Katrina emerged as a freeze frame of the shocking dysfunction

219

beneath the surface of contemporary American society. Images of those desperate, isolated figures on the rooftops were added to the iconography of the collective American consciousness.

What happened to New Orleans in the aftermath of Katrina was a horrifying portrait of a society falling to pieces in the face of crisis. Wynton Marsalis, a New Orleans native and one of the city's proudest proponents, put it this way, "I feel that in this moment we see a lot in what's wrong with us, it's a signature moment…this is like you stood in front of the mirror and you couldn't turn away from it. You stayed in that pose, and everything in that pose shows us what's wrong with us."[1]

What was it that Americans saw in that shattering reflection? It was social breakdown — a primal descent into a struggle of all against all, the abandonment of a people by their government, despair and desperation, a turn to savage individualism. As soon as the storm had subsided, a tide of crime and violence swept through the city. With many of the city's police officers preoccupied with their own families' misfortunes, there was an immediate breakdown in law enforcement. City residents, black and white alike, turned to looting. It wasn't just food. Pharmacies were picked clean by armed gangs seeking drugs. Gun stores were emptied out. One could see people leaving stores with armloads of expensive sneakers or television sets. There was no one to stop them. Often, the few available police were dispatched to protect the properties of the well off. Many stranded and storm-battered survivors had to defend their lives and property unaided. There were reports of police officers abandoning their posts and joining in the looting. In the stadium where some 25,000 people were stranded without food, water or communication with the outside world, rumors of rape and murder spread panic through the exhausted, anxious crowds. Most appalling of all, there were confirmed reports of snipers firing on doctors, nurses and rescue workers struggling to evacuate critically ill patients from the Tulane University Hospital and the nearby "Charity Hospital."[2]

The social fabric of the city was coming apart as an astounded nation witnessed not only the collapse of an entire community, but also the total inability of government to provide help. Americans were finding it hard to believe they weren't witnessing some distant disaster in a third world country. But they were. They were watching the tragic truth of third world America right at home. Deeply shaken, they were coming face to face with the kind of society they were now living in.

And despite the fact that the media focused almost entirely on these appalling images and events, ignoring or overlooking instances of mutual aid, the record remains depressingly clear — Katrina provoked a social breakdown.

Even before Katrina, New Orleans was not one city but two — cleft along the fault lines of class and race. There is a small, affluent city of great beauty and charm, centered on the French Quarter, and almost entirely white. But New Orleans is two-thirds black. If one took a map of the city's black population and laid it over a map of the poorest districts, the two would correspond almost perfectly. These are also the lowest-lying neighborhoods — the ones most likely to flood. The city's black sections comprise an unlovely sprawl of boarded buildings, broken sidewalks, low-slung strip malls, and deadly violence. New Orleans was the murder capital of the country, with an average of 200 murders per year. The annual arrest rate was 100,000 for a population of 485,000.[3] The city ranks as the sixth-poorest big city in the US. In the Lower Ninth Ward, an almost all-black neighborhood that was swept away by the flooding, only six percent of residents had a college degree. The national average is 22 percent.[4] Average household income in this neighborhood was $27,499 a year, compared to the national average of $44,000. Over a quarter of the Lower Ninth's households survived on less than $10,000 a year.

It would be easy to dismiss the lawlessness that followed Katrina as a symptom of endemic poverty, or rage at the injustice of a system that had turned its back on so many, both before and after the catastrophe. But poverty and anger do not explain the apparent failure of empathy for one's neighbors, the collapse of moral obligation to the plight of others that was perhaps the most disturbing aspect of this tragic spectacle. For what seems to have been laid bare by Katrina was the underlying condition of American society. It is always in crisis that the truest character of a society comes to light. At a socio-psychological level, Katrina's legacy was even deeper and more painful than the terrible toll the storm took on the lives of the thousands of unfortunates that lay in its path.

But did it need to be so? There is no avoiding the material destruction and the immense personal suffering that such an event must entail. But the collapse of a community itself is something else altogether. To highlight this point, all we need do is compare the aftermath of Katrina to the events following the devastation of the tsunami in Sri Lanka in December of 2004. The differences are revealing.

Despite decades of ethnic conflict and a war in progress, the small island nation was able to rally a truly remarkable restorative effort that quickly repaired much of the damage left in the wake of the largest natural disaster in modern history. Over 250,000 people were killed throughout South and East Asia. Sri Lanka was the most heavily affected in relative terms. Within a few hours on December 26, 2004, without prior warning (unlike Katrina), 35,000 Sri Lankans were killed. Unfamiliar with the deadly warning signs of such an event, curious Sri Lankans wandered onto the exposed seabed as the ocean gathered itself back in the eerie calm preceding its catastrophic return. Some were running happily about, gathering up the stranded fish. When the tidal waves came, everything within half a mile of the affected coasts was obliterated. So powerful was its force that the main train running along the southern coastline, The Queen of the Sea, was picked up and scattered like a child's toy. Fifteen hundred people were killed, making it the worst train disaster in history. At the small coastal town of Peraliya, some of the torn and twisted rail cars can still be seen as a grim reminder of that day.

For a small developing country of 20 million with a per capita annual income of US$1,000, the destruction was a terrible blow. In the immediate aftermath of the tidal wave, the government was overwhelmed. There were worried predictions of civil breakdown and the spread of epidemics among the homeless. But a different story emerged. Communities across the entire affected region banded together. Within hours of the tsunami, local groups had established shelters in neighborhood homes, schools and temples. Among the very first groups to start organizing relief efforts was SANASA, the close-knit credit union system that mobilized its members throughout the affected areas.[5] Private relief supplies also began to pour in from across the nation. Food, water and shelter were provided to survivors, while bands of volunteers combed the affected areas to remove thousands of decomposing bodies before they became a health hazard. (By contrast, bodies were still being found in boarded-up homes in New Orleans seven months after the storm.) Most tellingly, incidents of lawlessness — looting, violence and predatory behavior — were minimal. Just ten days after the tsunami hit, a broad range of civil society organizations were meeting to co-ordinate efforts and ensure maximum deployment of available resources. A comprehensive action plan for recovery and renewal was drafted and delivered to government on behalf of civil society and a full report was sent to the Second UN Conference of Disasters held only a few weeks later in January 2005. By February 20, over 100 miles of track that had been torn away by the tidal wave had been repaired and re-opened through the combined efforts of 1,000 railway employees, troops and countless village volunteers. It was the largest development of the railway in a century and it had been completed in just 57 days.

If anything, the immediate social impact of the tsunami in Sri Lanka was to strengthen the social bonds that existed before its onset. Even the ethnic fighting between the Tamil Tigers and the Sri Lanka army was put on pause as Tamils, Muslims and Buddhists joined their rescue efforts in the weeks immediately following the disaster. What accounts for this profound difference in the social effects of Katrina and the tsunami? The answer to this question, and its relation to the creation and social role of co-operative institutions, is the central focus of this chapter. It requires us to take a look not just at the external signs of social dysfunction, but also at the profound changes being wrought on the interior life of the individual at this advanced stage of consumer culture. For this we need to take a brief excursion into social and psychological theory.

The Decline of Social Capital

At the start of the twenty-first century, ordinary Americans share a profound sense of civic malaise. The rampant lawlessness that followed in the wake of Katrina was an unsettling spectacle that both crystallized and amplified this sense. But the feeling had been growing for years. In his book *Bowling Alone*, a study of the decline of community in America, Robert Putnam provides compelling evidence of the growing isolation and disengagement of Americans from their communities and the profound social and personal costs of this withdrawal. Signs of this decline have been accumulating for decades. On every measure of civic engagement, from voter participation to involvement in religious organizations, from membership in social clubs to giving dinner parties and visiting friends, America has experienced a catastrophic decline in the willingness of individuals to become active members of their communities.[6]

Political involvement is a case in point. Voter participation in the US has declined by 25 percent over the last 30 years, from 62.8 percent in the Kennedy-Nixon election of 1960, to 48.9 percent in the Clinton-Dole election of 1992. What Putnam documents in his study is the progressive "hollowing out" of civic life commencing in 1960 down to the present day.

The high-water mark of civic engagement, it turns out, was in the period between 1945 and 1960, when the generation born just after 1910, who grew up during the Great Depression and fought in the Second World War, dominated the American demographic. It was with the succeeding generation of baby boomers and Generation Xers, born between 1965 and 1980, that the decline of community life became epidemic in the US. The one thing that distinguishes these generations from the preceding one is precisely their rejection and distrust of mainstream politics and institutions. As Putnam notes, they are defined more by "what they don't like and don't do, than what they like and do."[7]

Boomers became "free agents" — disengaged, atomistic, less deferential to authority and uncommitted beyond a relatively narrow circle of friends and family. They volunteered less and contributed less to charity than their parents or grandparents. They became more materialistic. The trend was further amplified among Generation Xers. When asked by Roper pollsters in 1975 to identify the elements of "the good life," 38 percent of all adults chose "a lot of money" and an additional 38 percent mentioned "a job that contributes to the welfare of society." By 1996, those who aspired to serve society had slipped to 32 percent while those who aspired to "a lot of money" had grown to 63 percent.[8] In addition, Xers have adopted an extremely personal and individualistic view of politics. They emphasize the private and the personal over the public and the collective. They share no collective sense of a higher purpose in political or civic involvement. Their political engagements are narrow and specific and relate to one-off issues that affect them personally.

How have these dramatic changes affected the American social fabric? To begin with, American society has become more atomized. The fraying of civil institutions such as social clubs and religious organizations has also meant that the civic structures that brought disparate people in relationship with one another are no longer playing this role. One consequence has been a general decline in trust.[9] This, in turn, has increased social isolation among individuals. At a personal level this is one of the most disturbing effects of the generalized decline of community in the US.

Since 1940, the onset of depression has struck earlier and more pervasively in each successive generation, culminating in today's alarming levels among youth. The rate of depression over the last two generations has increased tenfold.[10] Between 1950 and 1995 the suicide rate of teenagers between 15 and 19 more than quadrupled. In that portion of the population born just after 1910 and that also felt a stronger connection and had a deeper involvement with their community, the trend was exactly the opposite. What is more, this rising suicide rate among Generation Xers is apparent not only in the US and Canada where rates are almost identical (11.1 per 100,000 versus 11.4) but throughout the West. Inconveniently, suicide rates overall are even higher in Norway, Sweden and Denmark — those countries that have attained what many would imagine a kind of contemporary welfare state utopia — where suicide rates per 100,000 number 11.7, 13.6, and 13.7 respectively.[11]

The crisis in community life that has arisen in the last few decades seems to correlate with the rise of personal anxiety, insecurity, isolation and personal unhappiness. But how has this come to pass? What are the reasons for this disastrous decline? Putnam identifies two main culprits: the advent of isolating technology, television in particular, and the rise of a disengaged, disenchanted generation that took the place of what he termed the "long civic generation" of the first half of the twentieth century, a generation that is now fading away. The result has been the loss of social capital, the norms of reciprocity and trust that make civic life and healthy communities possible. In its shocking clarity, New Orleans displayed the end results of such decay. But the decline is not confined to that city alone. It is pervasive and apparently a by-product of the socio-economic system that now defines American culture specifically, Western culture generally, and global culture increasingly. But the question remains: what is the cause of this generational disaffection and discontent? Not only in America but also around the world? Putnam doesn't provide an answer.

The question draws us back to the central theme of this book — the widening rupture between the economic imperatives of capitalism, especially since the Second World War, and the requirements of an authentic form of human living, a form of life in which economics is an extension of humane societies. How might co-operative economic and social relationships help heal the wounds of our present economic system? We will turn to this question in the closing section of this chapter.

In his description of the generations that succeeded the "long civic generation" and that now dominate American life, Putnam identifies two cardinal characteristics: the intensified sense of individualism and the devotion to materialism. This is not a novel perception. Possessive, or perhaps better to say, *acquisitive* individualism, has been the defining feature of this curious creature that, for a long line of thinkers, typifies the postmodern personality. In their book *The New Individualism: The Emotional Costs of Globalization*, sociologists Anthony Elliott and Charles Lemert attempt to correlate the effects of globalization with the remaking of personal identity. They too focus on acquisitive individualism as the psychological substratum that conditions the life choices of the consumer personality. And like many others, they trace the rise of this hyper-individualizing condition to the influence of a global economic order. They describe its effects in stark terms: "Individualism today is intrinsically connected with the growth of *privatized worlds* (emphasis added). Under the impact of privatism, the self is denied any wider relational connection at a deeply unconscious level, and on the level of day-to-day behavior such 'new individualisms' set the stage for a unique culture of anguish, anxiety, fear, disappointment, and dread."[12]

According to Elliott and Lemert, this does not mean that collective ideals have come to an end or that the public sphere has died. Rather, it means that social matters are increasingly understood and responded to in individualist ways. This new reality signals a fundamental breakdown in the historical connection between the individual and society. As C. Wright Mills pointed out in the 1950s, social problems cannot have personal solutions. But this is precisely the delusion under which much of Western society has been laboring over the last 30 years, the years during which the current crop of "lost generations" has grown up. This is the period when market forces were deified by the state itself, a golden age of privatization ushered in first by Thatcher and then by Reagan. The decline of "the public" as a meaningful concept has cost us dearly, and not merely in political terms. More profoundly, it has unmoored any sense that the individual is an organic part of the society she lives in. In turn, both society and the individual must pay a price. On the one hand, the erosion of a common sense of connection to broader society beyond strictly selfish or instrumental interests, renders society less capable of providing its citizens those social goods like security and safety that are of such fundamental value. On the other hand, the individual feels more and more stranded, more vulnerable to the twists of fate, more isolated in the fear and anxiety that must surely follow.

But there is far more at work here than the failure of government to uphold the idea of the public as a social and political value. The decline of everything social is commensurate with the rise of the individual as the key to the attainment of the good life. As outlined at the very start of this book, this is a concept as old as liberalism itself. The "new individualism" that Elliott and Lemert talk about is merely the radical extension of an evolution in human psychology that commenced in the 15th century. But something has altered over the last 50 years. Somewhere around the midpoint of the 20th century the postmodern personality took on a decisive form, and this was the point at which purely commercial forces became the determining influences over human behavior. Zygmunt Bauman, one of the world's pre-eminent sociologists, locates this transition at the point where humans changed from being producers to becoming consumers.[13] It is possible that this transition marks a point of mutation in the evolution of capitalist society itself. For the primary illusion of capitalism — the founding myth of the autonomous individual — now becomes an object of mass manipulation and an instrument for the unlimited expansion of impersonal corporate power. In a supreme paradox, the ideal of the autonomous individual has become the primary means for ensuring the final entrenchment of market values over all else, including that of the individual itself.

We opened this chapter with a rather dismal portrait of a society in deep trouble, exemplified by the trauma of New Orleans in the wake of Katrina. But there are other, subtler and equally disturbing aspects of the destruction of community. A personal anecdote helps illustrate this point.

The End of Authenticity

In northern Arizona the small town of Sedona is surrounded by pillars of red rock that rise up from the floor of the Sonoran desert. It is one of the most spellbinding landscapes in all America. A land of spaces and sagebrush and silence. Countless westerns have been filmed here. Think John Ford and Jimmy Stewart. Zane Gray and John Wayne. Thelma and Louise fleeing across the desert in a cloud of red dust. This is the quintessential backdrop of the American frontier.[14]

The town of Sedona has flourished here, profiting immensely from the beauty of its locale. Tourism is its lifeblood. It has become a kind of Mecca for New Age (if not daffy) spiritualism, a crossroads of spiritual and "healing" paths that originate from sources as diverse as Shamanistic and Yogic spirituality and as improvised as the latest self-help therapies with offerings like the "Sedona Method" (Your Key to Lasting Happiness, Success, Peace, & Emotional Well-being!) and guided tours to something called "The Sedona Vortexes" — spiritually powerful spaces that emanate from the landscape itself. All this is augmented by the more hedonistic pursuits of spa vacations, golf courses, art galleries and upscale shopping.

For the unwary visitor like myself, this fabled beauty should give little reason for second thoughts. But trouble starts from the very moment of arrival, at the airport car rental. My wife Catherine and I had booked a mid-sized vehicle, quite sufficient for two people to scout the area. But the rental clerk at the desk started talking about the attractions of a larger vehicle, the increased comfort, for only a marginal increase in cost. We said no thanks, the mid-sized was fine. He went on, pointing out other features, the better sound system, the bigger engine. We dug in. No thanks. To our astonishment the guy pressed on, his voice climbing now to a panic pitch, almost pleading with us that the terrain out there was treacherous, that we were in a desert after all, that it would be folly to travel without a larger, more powerful car. This was a matter of our personal safety. We were stunned, somewhat disoriented by this manic persistence, but we declined. With complete reluctance and something like bitterness after having put up a fight that lasted some 20 minutes, he gave us our vehicle.

This strange episode stayed with us. We mulled it over and talked about it. It was very nearly incomprehensible. But it was also clear that this guy was on a mission, that he had failed, and it would cost him.

Once in Sedona itself, it's hard to imagine a more captivating place. Everything from the color palette of the buildings to the food and the clothing seemed to be an extension and a complement to the natural environment. All the locals seemed prosperous and in beaming health. We came upon an attractive collection of tasteful buildings in a park-like setting, with cafés and boutiques sprinkled throughout. A young woman near the entrance path invited us to look around, enjoy the setting, no obligation. Encouraged by her upbeat charm we wandered in and soon discovered that we couldn't leave without first being subjected to a hard pitch to buy property.

Back on the streets we took in the scene, somewhat more discerning now. At some point, we found ourselves in conversation with a well-dressed, middle-aged man who had very casually engaged us in discussion as we sat in a café. It wasn't long before it dawned on us that he too, was intent on selling us something. And so it went. In our entire stay in Sedona, we did not experience a single encounter with residents that was not motivated by a desire on their part to sell us something. It could be claimed that this should be expected in a tourist town, or that we stood out as particularly inviting rubes. But what was so unnerving was that these encounters seemed to take place everywhere. Not just in obvious places like stores, but on the streets. And they were disguised, covert. Where in another place the expectation of a commercial encounter is clearly defined by the nature of the space and the context one finds oneself in—a market stall, a shop—here the very notion of a social encounter in a purely social setting had been overturned. *Any* chance encounter in *any* place could be a mere ruse for someone to profit off you. We had stumbled upon the full-blown realization of a Thatcherite world. Sedona was the end point of this imagined capitalist utopia—a parallel universe in which every encounter came with a price. No encounter could be trusted on its face. The collapse of fundamental trust that this entails, whether between friends or strangers, must in turn spell the death of any meaningful notion of community.

I do not mean to imply that *every* relation between individuals in such a place is purely commercial. If that were so, Sedona could not subsist as a social community at all. What I am saying is that the market ethic, the use of objects (and people) as instruments for personal gain, has invaded every sphere and become the pre-eminent norm of human interaction, not only disfiguring, but *displacing* traditional modes of human relating in what one would normally assume to be social environments. American culture has produced a mindset that no longer distinguishes between the social and the commercial. It may appear that this is old news. After all, the shopping mall is one expression of this fact and malls have been with us for decades. So has the privatization of formerly social goods. But shopping malls are recognizably commercial spaces *within* a social setting that borrow the *forms* of community—walkways, gardens, streetlights, etc.—in an attempt to socialize shopping. The Sedona experience is something else—the appropriation of the social, and one might add the *natural*, as mere instruments for the pursuit of profit. Nothing holds any value in itself. Everything is instrumentalized, fitted to the measure of gain and loss. The contamination and counterfeiting of social and public space by market logic, however, has profound personal consequences. It eventually entails the colonization and remaking of personal perceptions, interpersonal relations and ideas about who and what we are as individuals. In the end, personal identity and interpersonal relations also become means to some other end.

Much has been written about this recasting of individual identity in our postmodern era. The subject has acquired an almost obsessive power in contemporary thought and cultural studies generally. One need only visit a contemporary art show to see the extent to which art, and artists, are transfixed by this question of personal identity. Indeed, a huge amount of contemporary art is focused on the identity of the artists themselves, as the artists' subject — a narcissistic self-absorption that mirrors perfectly the reality of the society beyond their studios. This inward turning and self-fascination is the hallmark of our age. It is intimately bound up with the influence of powerful market forces that have come to mould our lives and motivate our choices. For now, at the onset of the millennium, we find ourselves wandering in the untracked regions of hyper-individualism, looking for ever-new ways of recreating ourselves, in search of that elusive ideal of success or personal happiness or "self-actualization" that, like a mirage, draws us further into our own private desert. And here too, Sedona is an emblem of the age. The New Age spirituality that has found such a welcome home in this desert idyll is just the flip side of the cult of self that is at the heart of consumer culture.

The transition from a production society to a consumer society has recast the means by which capitalism regenerates itself. It is not possible here to provide a complete account of this process; that would carry us beyond the scope of this chapter. But I want to address one key aspect of the change that is underway and its effect on ourselves as individuals and on the societies in which we live. This is the manipulation of personal identity as a principle means of controlling consumer behavior. It is perhaps the defining characteristic of a capitalist culture that has crossed the threshold from a scarcity to a post-scarcity, indeed post-industrial economy. For the first time in human history, individuals are free to choose who they will be. They are not locked into the class or caste identity they were born into, as in previous scarcity economies. With the removal of survival as a problem the challenge in post-scarcity societies becomes the feasibility of constructing mobile identities as the mechanism for constructing meaning. By mobile identities I am referring to the malleability of identity as a strategy for personal gratification.[15] Success in controlling this process is now the holy grail of advertising.

Corporate advertising has always been in a state of evolution, perfecting over the years the art of commercial seduction. But in the postwar era, and especially during the sixties and the decades following, a radical change took place. Advertising shifted from selling *products* to selling *lifestyles*. In this, the central instrument of advertising — the ultimate vehicle for transmitting the underlying meaning of the commercial message — was not the product but the projected persona of the consumer *buying* the product. This is very different from earlier days of advertising when the qualities of the product itself were the selling point, whether it was the dependability of a car or the cleansing power of a detergent. To illustrate from a hugely successful campaign currently running on television: cool guys buy Macs — they are slim and wear jeans and casual Gap-style sweaters; well-intentioned but clueless guys buy PCs — they are puffy and dorky and wear bad suits and glasses. This campaign says nearly nothing about either Macs or PCs. It says everything about who buys them. The same strategy can be applied to jeans, or cars or holiday vacations.

Branding, therefore, is a central element in this process. Unless you brand a product, you cannot brand the consumer that buys that product. So the branding process — the means by which a product acquires a set of pre-determined attributes — is intimately linked to the creation and manipulation of commercial identities that actually *sell* that product to you, the consumer. The trick is always to focus on the identity of the buyer that selects this or that brand. Identity creation and manipulation is now the chief preoccupation of advanced capitalism. For such a strategy to succeed, and for a consumer society to continue to drive the wheels of capitalism as we now know it, the notion of identity must remain malleable, ever evolving, never satisfied, always hungry for the next acquisition. The most sophisticated technique in commercial advertising today is how to instil in people the desire to recreate in their own lives the personae they find attractive in ads. Once this happens, all that remains is to manipulate the commercial stand-ins that, through a process of refraction conveyed through mass media, influence the behavior of individuals in the real world. This, in summary, is the contemporary theory and practice of brand marketing. It's an Avatar reality in reverse, perhaps the true meaning of the digital age. Except that the brand really being marketed is an ever-shifting version of the human personality.

The cynical glorification of fake individualism may be necessary for purposes of consumer manipulation, but it also undermines people's inclination to relate to each other, and to their communities, in authentic ways. That is to say, in ways that understand and value the intrinsic worth of people and social relations as ends in themselves, not as instruments to serve other, usually selfish, ends. Capitalism is hollowing out the intrinsic value of experiences precisely because it sets a market price on them. Once something has a market value, that value can fall to zero. That is one reason why the term "human capital" has such a chilling quality about it. It is also the reason why people travel to the ends of the earth in search of "authentic experiences" uncontaminated by commercialism. But they are getting harder to find, in part because the "authentic" has itself been absorbed as an object of commercial value. Authenticity itself is now a prime selling feature that is attached to countless products, from cuisine to culture.

A great deal of debate is now focused on what this process means for the interior lives of people, and for how they understand and interact with the world around them. Pessimists and conspiracy theorists have a field day with this theme, pointing out the ease with which these techniques are capable of manipulating the perceptions and choices of millions of consumers. And it is easy to credit their alarm. For it is precisely the perfected techniques of mass commercial advertising that are also driving the mechanisms of politics, from the selection and marketing of politicians to the framing of political messages to the manipulation of news and mass media. On the other hand, it is just as easy to point to "branding backlash" and the many ways in which growing numbers of people have become hypersensitive to commercial coercion and remarkably fluent in decoding the hidden mechanisms of control that these techniques embody.

Both these realities are true but at very different scales. Millions are aware of the image game and resolutely resist its impact on their lives. This is a minority, but it is a growing minority (at least in the West). But the effectiveness of identity manipulation as a commercial technique is undeniable. The contemporary cult of celebrity and the inexhaustible conduits of magazines, tabloids, television shows and films that carry its influence magnify its effects immeasurably. Most people not only fall under its spell, they are also unaware of the extent to which their behavior is a mimicry of commercial prototypes. In the information age, the building blocks of identity are the images cast by media, primarily television. Individuals are more and more interacting not with the real, but with a controlled *image* of the real. Their lives, to the extent they are conditioned by commercial messaging, have taken on a counterfeit quality, a borrowed reality. And how could it be otherwise? Since the triumph of the television age we have been immersed in this world of illusion almost since birth.

Shadowland

Plato once used the allegory of a cave to illustrate the deceptions that men live by. In his story, humans are like shackled cave dwellers who see shadows on a wall and take them for reality. The real forms — what he called the ideal forms — were behind them, beyond their line of sight, passing between them and an enormous fire at the cave mouth. It is their motions that cast the shadows on the walls. Modern consumers are in a similar plight. Except that we have become the shadows on the cave walls and the ideal forms are now the fabricated identities that provide the values, lifestyles and attitudes by which we model our lives. In the process, we have become strangers to ourselves and to each other. In short we are living in delusion, which our economic system depends on perpetuating. The moment we waken from this shadow play, capitalism is in trouble.

I don't want to imply here that only capitalism engages in this kind of identity manipulation. All ideologies have recourse to it, and essentially for the same purpose — to exert control over mass behavior. But the question of personal identity has a different resonance for different worldviews. The fascist *weltanschauung* of National Socialism was essentially a race logic that absorbed personal identity within race identity. The focus was not the individual but the mythologized tribe, the *volk*, of blood and soil. State communism did the same, substituting class for race. In both, the essential social consequence was the practical erasure of the individual both as an ideal and as a value. To glimpse the soul-destroying effects of this process on the individual and on social relations, one need only read the writings of the Czech novelist, Milan Kundera. In capitalism, the techniques of identity manipulation have been perfected through the dark arts of advertising but in service of wholly different ends — the inflation of the individual as the prime mechanism for driving consumption.

The one thing that is almost universally recognized (by pessimists and optimists alike) is that one result of this process has been a near pathological preoccupation with the self. Whether it is the acquisition of this or that product as an accessory to one's ever-changing self-image, or the attainment of the perfect body or the pursuit of self-fulfillment through yoga, postmodern man is compulsively focused on himself. The constant arousal of new needs and desires in an endless stream of stimulation is the fuel that feeds this perpetual remaking of our selves. But the interior logic of such desire is that it can never be sated. Consumption is addiction. To use an apt Buddhist term, we have become "hungry ghosts."[16] Moreover, self-deception is the only strategy available for creating an identity that is linked to consumption. The consumption of goods to create identity is necessarily the consumption of mass goods; this in itself is antithetical to the formation of any sense of identity that could be called authentic. What does happen however is the crystallization of false difference among individuals. In a consumer culture, identity formation is competitive. The futility of consumption per se as a source of meaning translates into a form of identity that derives satisfaction from the denigration of others — I have meaning and a valued identity and you don't. This is one result of being unable to invest our lives with a meaning that extends beyond ourselves.

There is a deeper, even more debilitating aspect of this remaking of human values and perspectives. We have arrived at a point where people are less able than ever before to perceive, and therefore act upon, the source of their sorrow and frustration. With the displacement of all other competing worldviews and value systems, with perhaps the single exception of religion, individuals have no other value references to gauge the true worth of their life choices.[17] They have lost the means to imagine alternatives. It's at this level that the most important dimension of transformative social change must take effect.

In view of the above, is it really such a mystery why the generations that grew up in the hothouse decades of unbridled consumerism should be so inward-looking, so little engaged with their communities, so unhappy? And is it any wonder that despite the unprecedented wealth of choice and material comfort that surrounds them, these people are apparently the least satisfied with their lives?

Happiness, the sense of well-being, is inextricably linked to relationship with others. It has little to do with income level or material possessions,[18] a very ancient truth that is now being carefully studied and documented by economists in a most welcome new field of study, the economics of happiness. One of the most far-reaching, and heartening, conclusions reached by this research is that the presence of social capital and the widespread practice of reciprocity, are fundamental not only to individual well-being, but to broader social and economic well-being as well. Why is this heartening? Because there are actions we can take to make things better.

Reciprocity and Restoration

Social capital is at the heart of healthy, vibrant communities and this is highlighted by a community's response to crisis. To return to our earlier discussion, how a society restores itself in the wake of a catastrophe like Katrina is largely a function of social capital. This is not the only factor, of course. The role of government is also essential. But how effective government is in responding to the diverse demands of the public interest is closely related to the strength of social capital within a society. This point is powerfully documented in Robert Putnam's fascinating study of the performance of governments in the regions of Italy. The direct correlation between social capital and a strong civil society on the one hand and honest and effective government on the other is the most revealing finding of this groundbreaking study. Another key finding is a similar correlation between social capital and economic performance. Those regions that had the most abundant expressions of social capital (as shown in measures like voter participation, number of social clubs, levels of union membership, number of co-operatives, etc.) also registered the best economic performance.[19]

The restorative power of social capital has also become a central theme in disaster studies. There is now empirical evidence that it is not the material condition of communities, their relative prosperity, that determines their resilience in the face of disaster. Rather, it is the presence of dense social networks based on relations of mutual trust that turns the tide. The work of SANASA and civil society in general, in the hours, weeks and months following the tsunami is a prime example of this. However, the presence of civic organizations, whether formal or informal, is a primary indicator not only of a community's capacity to recover from crisis but also of its quality of life generally, both before and after crisis. Beyond this, social capital, which is one product of such organizations, is also linked to the quality of life at a personal level — individual happiness.

The key to addressing the current crisis in community is rebuilding the stock of social capital in society. And the key to this is building up the kinds of organizations and institutions that develop social capital and the relationships of reciprocity and generalized trust upon which community rests. Co-operatives are a central part of such a strategy. This is not to say that other forms of organization that operate on the principle of reciprocity are not also important (charitable organizations, volunteer organizations, social clubs, etc.). But co-operatives, as illustrated throughout this book, have a unique capacity not only to build a sense of community but also to challenge and reform the economic structures that are so often the cause of social breakdown. Because quite apart from the truly diabolical efforts of corporate powers to deliberately manipulate human feelings and thought processes for commercial advantage — the essence, after all, of modern advertising — the very nature of a capitalist enterprise is to consume social capital without replacing it.

Capitalist enterprises, like all businesses, need trust to function. So do the institutions that sustain them, like banks and stock markets. Once trust is lost, business becomes impossible, stock markets crash. If contracts can't be relied on, business comes to a standstill. You need only witness the sorry state of trade and economic development in societies where corruption is rife to see the economic effects of mistrust.[20] But the direction of contemporary capitalism is driven by an ideology of predatory competition and profit maximization at any cost, whether material or psychological. Unchecked, the logic of this system will sooner or later deplete a society's stock of social capital, just as if it were water, wood or oil. Capitalism and the consumer culture it generates are not only environmentally unsustainable, they are socially and psychologically unsustainable as well. Social poverty and personal unhappiness are the hidden costs of consumerism.

Conversely, co-operatives generate social capital even as they draw on it for their sustenance. Their use of reciprocity means that trust is regenerated and repaid both to their constituent members and to the surrounding society. The more that trust is used as the basis of social exchange, the stronger it becomes.[21] Co-operatives and other social economy organizations are like batteries that recharge a society's capacity to link people together, establish networks of mutual trust and undertake collective action around shared goals. In short, to behave like healthy societies ought to behave.[22]

Co-operatives replenish social capital in other ways as well. Members of co-operatives (like members of other social groups) are more likely to volunteer with other organizations. When they do, they bring the skills they acquired in their co-ops. Often, co-op staff and volunteers first learned their civic skills in the course of setting up and running their own co-ops. They learned how to clarify goals, how to identify and recruit supporters, how to assemble needed skills and resources. They had to learn how to plan and run meetings and how to raise money. How to set up and run the kinds of complex organizational structures that mobilize people around common goals, sort out conflicts and allow for the democratic give and take that is at the foundation of successful co-operative organizations. The relational imperative that these organizations run on teaches individuals not only how to work with others, but at a more intimate level, how to identify their own interests and well-being with that of others. Co-operatives socialize individuals without extinguishing their individualism. If any social form were the ideal template for remaking society in the midst of rampant individualism, it is the co-operative.

The Meaning of Work

We saw in the story of Argentina's recovered factories how seminal was the change that workers experienced when they had to learn for the first time to become co-operators. Their experience of creating a co-operative enterprise recast their understanding of themselves and their relations with others in two fundamental ways. First, it revealed their connections to others through the bond of mutual interest; second, it enlarged their sense of personal power and personal worth. They saw that they were capable of controlling their own fates, not being mere instruments in the hands of others. What made all this possible was the simple calculus of collective power through co-operation. The same was true of the sex workers in Sonagachi and the small farmers of Sri Lanka. Participating in these co-operative organizations provided ordinary people with the social mechanism they needed not only to reclaim and revolutionize their own lives, but to carry this transformative power out into the society around them. Their organizations gave them the means to do it.

The restorative power of co-operation in the world of work goes beyond a worker's connection to others, powerful as this is. It can also provide an individual with a coherent sense of what work means beyond a paycheck or as a steppingstone to some other end. Everyone knows how insecure work has become in modern societies. Part of the language of self-construction is the ability to remain flexible, to continuously "upgrade" our skills, to remain marketable — like commodities — on the ever-sinking sands of the labor market. At any moment, even the most skilled jobs can be shipped overseas to where labor is cheaper. This is one of the most pernicious effects of globalization and a primary source of anxiety for people everywhere, from the industrial towns of the American rust belt to the free trade camps of the Mexican *maquiladoras*.[23] This is possible because our places of employment are not our own. So long as the workplace remains a mere mechanism for the generation of wealth, so long as labor is an instrument of capital, this will not change. It can only get worse as capital extends its dominion over more and more dimensions of the economy.

The privatization of the public sector and the casualization of work in Argentina are object studies of a process that is undercutting the sense of permanence in work everywhere. But the episodic and transitory quality that now characterizes the working life of millions is also making it impossible for people to construct a coherent story line of what work signifies to them, or to integrate the work experience as a meaningful dimension of their self-image. How meaningful can work be if it is likely to change every few years? How does one commit oneself to a job if that job is constantly under threat of export? The old Marxist notion of the alienation of work has extended farther and deeper than even Marx may have imagined.

Worker co-operatives provide a way of making work meaningful by sustaining employment in situations where those jobs would be sacrificed — not because they were untenable but because the business didn't generate the insane levels of return demanded by shareholders.[24] Second, co-operatives invite worker-members to invest their identities in their work, to see their work as extensions of themselves through the mechanisms of shared ownership and personal control. Any workplace can undergo a profound change in meaning if it shifts from being primarily a mechanism for the generation of profit over which one has no control, to being a community of relationships with an inherent worth of its own. This is perhaps the quintessential difference between the co-operative and the capitalist firm. In one, the enterprise is a means to the human fulfillment of all through the creation of community. In the other, the enterprise is a means for the fulfillment of some through the subordination of others. It is strange how such a simple and self-evident truth seems so foreign in our culture.

At some basic level co-operation is hard wired into human behavior — otherwise there could be no possibility of human society — but the instinct is unrefined and atrophied in a society in which the norm of social relations is competition, dependence or subservience to authority. Further, in a society like Argentina's where the procurement of needed goods and services is so often a favor bestowed on those below by those above — the hallmark of a clientelist power structure — lateral co-operation among equals is difficult and actively undermined by those in power. This is why in such societies co-operation of any sort is the object of attack and ridicule. Its very existence is a threat to hierarchies. In the regimes of the former Soviet bloc all forms of civil co-operation were deliberately destroyed by the state through sheer brute force. Such crude measures are unnecessary in the sophisticated economic structures of contemporary capitalism. The frontlines here have moved onto the far more slippery terrain of psychological attitudes that no longer recognize there is a problem.

We need to be thinking about the organic structures of society that play formative roles in moulding personal identity and interpersonal relations. As thinkers from Aristotle to Tocqueville have pointed out, one of the chief virtues of democratic civic life is that it teaches people how to be citizens. This is the political dimension of an open and inclusive society. At a personal level, the nature of the organizations that mediate the interests of people have a defining influence on how these individuals see themselves and their connection to others. Institutions that promote selfishness, individualism, competition and dependence on authority have the predictable result of simultaneously isolating and disempowering people. On a mass scale the effects are clearly visible in the societies we have created. On the other hand, social institutions that identify and reinforce the mutual interests of people, that invite them to seek common solutions to common problems and that link individual fulfillment to the support and co-operation of others, create those habits of mind that are the building blocks of healthy societies.

This is probably the only route, a most challenging and difficult route to be sure, for reweaving the social fabric that has grown threadbare around us. What makes it especially difficult is that precisely at those times when co-operation is most needed it is in least supply. We are in this predicament *because* the instinct to co-operate, to relate to others, is so weakened. The hardening of peoples' sense of self-interest works against the attitude that sees others not as competitors in some race to realize our personalized utopias — an autistic dream — but as fellow travelers on a common road to building a better society for all. But as will be discussed in the final chapter, work at this level is only part of the task at hand. For as Putnam himself has pointed out, building social capital and replenishing the civic organizations that help to sustain it cannot be a substitute for effective public policy, but is rather a prerequisite for it and, in part, a consequence of it. Effective political action is therefore part of the puzzle that must be pieced together.

CHAPTER 11

Humanizing the Economy:
Co-operatives in the Age of Capital

Good ideas are contagious.
— STEFANO ZAMAGNI —

When, on January 20, 2009, US President Barack Obama took the oath of office it seemed for one glittering moment as if America had restored itself to its own highest ideals. The terrible waste and wantonness, the utter folly of the Bush era seemed at last to have been purged. It was like wakening from a very long and very dark dream.

Eighteen months later, the American people continue to come to terms with the enormity of the challenge that political action faces in the attempt to reform, let alone revolutionize, the economic template of our times. On every front, from regulating the worst excesses of Wall Street, to squeezing the feeblest of reforms from a corrupt health system, corporate power in the US has remained as intransigent and immovable a force as ever. The disrepute and crisis of trust that the capitalist system endured during the financial meltdown of the summer and fall of 2008 continues to cast a lengthening shadow despite the optimistic reports of "recovery" that still find their way into the news.[1] The massive bailouts of the financial sector seem to have broken the free fall that everyone feared. But they have left a crushing legacy of debt that will cripple the American economy for decades to come.

It is only in the face of the most extreme resistance by the banking industry, and the protracted obstructionism of its proxies in the Republican Party, that Congress finally passed legislation to reign in the practices of a system that consigned the economic fate of the country, and much of the world, to the gambles of financial speculators. But it fell far short of what was needed. Using portions of the bail out cash they received from Washington to bribe politicians with campaign money, the banks succeeded in blocking the kinds of protections that would have prevented a repeat of the crisis. The credit-default swaps that were at the bottom of the collapse may still be traded, and there is no firewall preventing banks from speculating with depositor's money.

Nothing at all has changed in the culture either of the financial institutions that brought the US and other economies to the brink, or within the wider culture of corporate America. The unconscionable bonuses, incentives and wage packages that became so repellent in the heat of the crisis are still being doled out, with the excuse that things are now turning around, banks are making money again, talented people need to be fairly rewarded. On the ground, things feel very different. The federal bailout money has failed to reach those that most need it. In countless communities, neighborhoods are being gutted as the wave of foreclosures continues at a rate of one every 13 seconds.[2] (On the bright side, hopeful house buyers can take a ForeclosuresToursRUs bus tour in places like Cape Coral in Florida and survey the wreckage with an eye to picking up a bargain.[3])

It took the prospect of a catastrophic collapse not only of the US economy but the global economy with it, that prompted the change so urgently called for. Yet these changes, essential as they are, are a form of legislative triage. They target the emergency symptoms of a system fatally infected with an incurable malady — the market's separation from its social moorings. For this to be addressed, more than legislation is required. What is now needed is a recasting of the economic paradigm. And so the question must be asked: Was the enormous hope for change that was placed on the outcome of the 2009 election — was that, too, a massive act of self-deception? This is not a rhetorical question. It points to the essential contradiction of our time. For despite the hard-won battles in the US Congress, we are still speaking of a corporate system, centered in the United States, but spreading, that is beyond control. Yet there remains a fervent desire, a spirit of hope for something better that is deeply moving, powerful and undeniable. America seems to be at the tipping point of something momentous, of hope affirmed and further propulsion toward reform, or hope denied and a turn to bitterness and disillusion — a most precarious moment.

If the hopes placed in the Obama victory turn out to be hollow, if the reforms achieved don't start to repair this fundamental schism between economics on the one hand and social values on the other, something terrible will befall America. For failure may well break the back of a fragile reform movement, one that is already growing doubtful of itself, uncertain of its capacity to prevail inside the bounds of America's deeply compromised political institutions. Having flared up so suddenly after three decades of reaction, the aspiration — or, more accurately, the *belief* — in change, may just as quickly be snuffed out. Nothing would reinforce the status quo more than this and the opponents of change know it fully. The most promising recent opportunity for saving the US, and much of the world, from plunging further into a very dark age will have been lost. A charismatic and intelligent leader with a wave of popular support firmly at his back will have lost the one best chance for recasting the American story.

I am not using the phrase "dark age" lightly. I am speaking of an age in which the values that are essential to the prosperity and well-being of a society are eclipsed. One might debate what such values consist of. What I mean by them includes at minimum intellectual and political freedom, the value of both the individual and of community (not the exaltation of one at the expense of the other), equity *and* economic opportunity and the notion of citizenship in an open and democratic society. But more than this, I am speaking of social and economic institutions that embody and advance these values.

We have been speaking in this book of how fundamental the organization of economic life is, not only for the character of our societies, but also for the make-up of our personalities and the conduct of our relations with others. Should we lose sight of those elements that define a fully human life and truly humane societies, no amount of material prosperity could ever substitute for their loss. As discussed in the last chapter, our sense of alienation and discontent will grow in proportion to the displacement of our social values by material ones. Not only are the Western democracies set firmly on this path, but even more troubling, the contaminating influence of consumption ideology has drawn in resolutely anti-democratic states such as China, where prospects for the democratization of economic life are even more remote than they are in the West. Any time or place in which a single worldview comes to dominate the hearts and minds of men is almost by definition a dark age. Ideologies of this type diminish people and society to the small and stifling measures that always serve narrow and self-perpetuating elites. Ideology always serves power. It was so in Communist Russia, it is true in the fundamentalist theocracies of Islam, and it is true for the corporate capitalism that has crystallized throughout the West and is being spread now like a contagion through the forces of globalization.

As most readers know, there was a long time in the West when the spirit of free intellectual and spiritual development that flared in the brief light of the Classical Age grew dim. It was eclipsed by a Christian religious dogma that over time became totalitarian, sustained by absolutist religious institutions that were utterly intolerant of dissent. Europe entered a long sleep of forgetfulness. There were periods of awakening, of relative openness and discovery, but they were rare and insufficiently strong to alter the overall stagnation of the era. Not until the rediscovery of classical knowledge in the 14th century, especially the works of Aristotle, did Europe as a whole recover from its stupor. It was thanks to the preservation and study of classical works in Islamic centers of learning in Spain, Morocco, Alexandria and Baghdad that the ideas of a lost age eventually returned, along with the philosophical and scientific works of Islamic thinkers like Avicenna and Averroes who had been influenced by them. In the monasteries of Europe as well, those works that had survived were carefully preserved and diligently copied out by monks for a time when they might again reveal their worth. When they did, these works not only opened out the horizons of cultural and scientific achievement, they enriched and deepened the understanding and practice of Christianity itself, leading to the revolution in theology prompted by the marriage of classical philosophy with Catholicism by thinkers like Abélard, John Duns Scotus, William of Ockham and Thomas Aquinas.

There is a parallel to be drawn between the omnipotence of the church in the age of religion and the analogous influence of the corporation in our own age. In each, the requirements of an imperial ideology spawned the social, cultural and psychological forms that were necessary to its preservation, not only in public life but, even more importantly, in the interior life of the individual. The external and internal aspects of each of these systems were, and are, mutually reinforcing. But there is a profound difference between these parallel worlds. It concerns the radically different conception of humankind that each personifies. They are like the inverse of each other. In Christianity, the religious attributes of faith and obedience predominate, fixing individuals inside the immutable structures of class while uniting them in the spiritual body of the holy church. As an ideal this is a universe that is both social and spiritual, drawing forth and embodying the human attributes of service, sacrifice and, ultimately, the redemptive power of faith. It is also profoundly conservative, anti-democratic and authoritarian. In capitalism, materialism and the satisfaction of personal desire predominate. In the ideology of consumerism avarice, not faith, is the propelling force. In turn, the idealized human personality is individualistic, self-serving, competitive and implicitly anti-social. The ideal of our capitalist age is a privatized paradise, one that is realized by the satisfaction of our bodily desires here on earth, not in some hoped-for afterlife. The liberal notion of personal freedom as the pursuit of selfish ends is intimately bound up with this strange vision of the good life. On its surface it appears as a system of perpetual change, as a constant process of destruction and reinvention, but at bottom it too ends up serving authoritarian ends.

It is easy to see that in both systems these idealizations are simplistic and one-sided. But that's what makes them idealizations — they are not meant to be descriptive, but rather prescriptive. They are symbolic representations that embody our ideals and guide us toward their realization. Given this fact, how can we say with any confidence that the human ideal of the modern age is superior to the one it displaced? From the standpoints of economic achievement and personal and political freedom, it most assuredly is. But the individuation and secularization of the human personality has also cut us off from our social and spiritual foundations.[4] The challenge of our time is to reclaim them without sacrificing the enormous achievements in material prosperity and human freedom that have come with modernity. We have to humanize our economies. This is the essential role of co-operation in the age of capital.

In his book *Greed, Inc.*, Wade Rowland likens the modern corporation to an alien life form that has taken over the planet.[5] It's a good analogy, for two reasons. First, it captures the anti-human and sociopathic attributes of the most powerful institution of our time. Second, it highlights the essential abnormality of the modern corporation as a social institution. Wade traces the intellectual antecedents that gave rise to the corporation, linking them to the kinds of utilitarian ideas we examined earlier, and to the philosophy of Rationalism pioneered by thinkers like Thomas Hobbes and René Descartes who viewed society as a construct mirroring the impersonal, mechanical laws of nature. The practice of economics was a perfect reflection of this worldview, systematically eliminating from its theories any consideration of moral or ethical principles in the workings either of the market or the behavior of people as economic agents. The corporation arose as the instrument that came to personify and perpetuate these ideas, just as the church embodied the religious values of an earlier age.

Rowland's analogy of the corporation as an alien life form is more than a useful metaphor. The very real concept of corporate personhood has breathed life into a legal fiction that was originally intended to facilitate the contractual and commercial requirements of socially chartered entities. Today, with its assumption of human qualities and due protections, corporate personhood is the final consummation of the power of capital at the cost of human powers and freedoms. Ever since 1886 when the US Supreme Court abused the 14th amendment — originally intended to protect the rights of freed slaves — by applying the idea of personhood to corporate entities, business interests have used the concept to extend the power of corporations by assuming every right and protection normally afforded to human beings.[6] The most recent case was the Supreme Court decision on January 21, 2010, to strike down government limits on political spending by corporations on the pretense that such limits were an infringement of the constitutional right to free speech. In one stroke, overturning every precedent, the hold of capital over the political process was not only legitimized, it was extended and perpetuated. Thus, in a perverse twist of fate, the very rights and freedoms to human liberty and democracy that were won at such cost by opposing the divine rights of kings and property have in our age been eclipsed by the extension of those same human rights to property in the guise of the corporation.

The rise of the corporation, and of consumer society in general, was in no way a natural process in the sense of being an inevitable product of human nature or a kind of culmination of social, much less natural, laws. Our consumer society is an artifact born of sustained and laborious effort in the service of a privileged minority. The countless billions spent on advertising alone testify to the abnormality of such a system. It requires a colossal effort, a specialized industry in itself, to sell people the concept that they should devote their time and money and sacrifice the best years of their lives to the proposition that the consumption and accumulation of unneeded things will make them happy. Perpetuating such a delusion is necessarily very costly.

In the West, and particularly in the United States, the rise of material prosperity was accompanied in the last half of the twentieth century by a commensurate decline in social capital — social connectedness. The result has been material wealth shadowed by social poverty. But it needn't have been so. Economic prosperity need not entail the exclusion of moral or social goods. Following in the trail of Polanyi and others, I have been arguing that the divorce of social from economic ends has been catastrophic for society. It has proceeded from a disastrous misreading of human nature *and* human society, and has culminated not only in the creation of institutions that make it ever more difficult to correct the original delusion but, more profoundly, in distorted perceptions of ourselves and of our societies that mask our ability to even recognize the problem. We are left with a lingering sense of unhappiness and frustrated desire at a personal level and growing inequality at a societal level, both of which are the inevitable consequences of an inhumane system. Moreover, even as the social and personal costs of this system are mounting to the point where they can no longer be ignored, globalization is extending and replicating its worst excesses.

The Future of an Idea

The neglect, and decline, of reciprocity as a value has its roots in classical economic theory.[7] But through their accumulated weight and momentum, the social, political and economic institutions that have accompanied the rise of neo-liberal ideology have acquired a life of their own. Like biological organisms, institutions, once established, develop a paramount instinct for self-preservation independently of their actual utility, worth or effects on society. In our age, critiques of the damage done by institutions like the WTO or the Wall Street banks are plentiful, and almost beside the point. Such institutions, like the giant corporations they serve, will adapt to the demands and pressures around them; but they will not change their reason for being and they most assuredly will not self-destruct. A central condition of their survival instinct is to undermine any viewpoint or practice that presents a challenge to their power. The most effective strategy is to ridicule or demonize alternative worldviews not from the standpoint of verifiable evidence in the real world, but at the level of ideology. Chief among the endlessly deployed fallacies is the inevitability of capitalism as the culmination of human progress. The supposed superiority of the capitalist form of enterprise over all other alternatives is just another facet of this fallacy.

One very influential example of this defense of capitalism is the supposed necessity of a trade-off between social goods and economic efficiency. This has been a staple of liberal economic theory for nearly two centuries. But it is a fallacy. Social goods need not be traded off for the sake of economic efficiency. Nor, at the other end of the political spectrum, is it true that personal freedom must be traded off for the sake of equity — the fallacy that lies at the bottom of communist ideology. Social and personal worth can both be embodied in an economic paradigm that is based on the social-personal dynamics of reciprocity. The co-operative enterprise is one way of combining these elements. But the co-operative does something more. It democratizes the operations of the marketplace and provides a means for the democratization of economic institutions, beginning with the form and function of the workplace. Co-operatives expand democratic space. And, to return to the central thesis of this book, just as the replacement of despotic regimes by democratic systems was the key to humanizing politics, so is the supercession of democratic values over authoritarianism in economics the key to humanizing economies.

But to be absolutely clear on this point, I am not advocating the transformation of all economic institutions into co-ops or the imposition of the co-op form on individual enterprises. Such a policy would be folly. It would immediately negate the democratizing and humanizing value of co-operatives and make the model an instrument of yet another controlling ideology, this time one that would turn co-operation into an authoritarian dogma, a contradiction in terms. Rather, I am proposing that the idea of co-operatives and co-operative economic systems, based on the principle of reciprocity, be promoted, extended, studied, taught and reinvented, not only as a matter of public policy, but as a far higher political priority within the co-operative movement itself. For if the co-op model is not promoted far more vigorously by the co-op movement, its role as an alternative to contemporary capitalism will remain as tenuous and marginal in the future as it is today.

What then, is the future of the co-operative in the age of capital?

Let us begin by acknowledging that if they are to progress, all social orders must incorporate a number of economic principles, each of which responds to a different aspect of a fully functioning society. They include *efficiency*, which minimizes waste of resources; *equity*, which is the basis of economic and social justice; and *reciprocity*, which is the basis of human solidarity. In turn, each of these principles has found its most developed expression in very different economic forms. The principle of economic efficiency is most embodied in the conventional capitalist enterprise; equity is embodied in the policies and institutions of government; and reciprocity has found its most developed expression in co-operatives and other social economy organizations. But there is nothing that dictates that one or another must dominate over the rest, or that the market should become the exclusive domain of any one form. It is this compulsion to achieve supremacy for one or another paradigm that has been the source of so much pointless waste and suffering. And what this really boils down to is the belief, distilled and frozen in ideology, that the human values that are idealized in any one of these structures (equity in one case, efficiency in another) are inherently superior to the others. In fact, all societies are composites of all these values and the forced dominion of one set over the others results not only in dysfunction but despotism, because their very imposition is a violation of natural human qualities.

I do not imply that all human attributes, as they are embodied in particular economic systems, are equally beneficent to the workings of a humane society or the realization of a fully human life. Both the glorification of personal greed, which has become the basis of capitalism, and the exaltation of conformism at the expense of individual freedom, which characterized communism, distort and pervert the human personality and by extension, human societies. But each, held in check by other values, opens a particular space for the economic expression of the human personality. Not everyone is inclined to co-operation. The natural entrepreneur's risk-taking individualism is absolutely crucial to the ingenuity and wealth creation that comes from the capitalist form which gives freedom to this impulse. Who can deny the benefits that flow from this recognition and promotion of individual initiative? But we have noted its dark side when left unchecked. On the other hand, contrary to the simplifications of economic theory, everyone is not motivated solely by individualistic goals. Many find fulfillment in service, in helping others or in the profound joy of collective effort. Where is the space for these individuals to express this fundamental aspect of the human personality?

Most societies in the West have been organized around economic paradigms in which either efficiency or equity have been paramount. The principle of reciprocity, however, has never yet been the basis for an economic system in the modern era.[8] The closest contemporary analogy is the co-operative economy of Emilia Romagna in northern Italy, but even there the co-operative system is but one dimension, influential as it is, of a vibrant mixed economy. What is needed today is a paradigm that achieves a balance between all three principles, an economic model in which all three may find a home and are not excluded. The development and realization of a reciprocity paradigm is essential to this.

Co-operatives are vital because they help to institutionalize reciprocity. They make reciprocity in society intrinsically possible and replicable, independent of public policy or the actual conduct of governments or corporations. They are the materialization and economic expression of the very specific human instinct for social bonding. What is more, the reciprocity generated by co-operation is essential if the human race is to respond effectively to the truly unprecedented challenges it faces in this millennial age. But such statements mean little if the conditions that make their actualization possible are not present. What are the realistic prospects of co-operatives acting as a means of humanizing economies?

As Stefano Zamagni has argued, there are three obvious possibilities. The first is that the co-operative model will continue as it is today — an alternative form of enterprise, but one that operates in restricted sectors or pockets of the market, resembling an archipelago of co-operative islands set in a sea of capitalism, sometimes expanding and sometimes receding as the fate and fortunes of capitalism rise and fall with the times. The second is that co-operatives will in time become extinct. In this view the inherent inefficiencies and anomalies of the co-op form will drive it further to the periphery of economic life until it is eventually overtaken altogether by the capitalist system, spelling the end of the co-op movement as a viable alternative to capitalism. The third, and most controversial possibility, is that the co-operative model will eventually increase its power and influence and will in time come to displace the capitalist enterprise as the primary engine of economic activity. The co-op archipelago will come to resemble a connected landmass, and the capitalist sea a series of ponds, lakes and rivers surrounded by a now dominant co-operative economic system.

What evidence could possibly sustain such an optimistic view? Zamagni lays out a number of arguments. It helps that Zamagni, one of the world's leading theoreticians on co-operative economics, is an unapologetic optimist with a cheerful faith in our human capacity to change, to respond to crisis and to remake ourselves and our institutions in service both to our own happiness and to more humane ideals. But this optimism is neither sentimental nor idealistic. It rests on a very careful reading of economic history and of prevailing trends in capitalist society. Zamagni is not the only optimist. Elinor Ostrom, the Nobel winner for economics in 2009, takes a different tack, focusing instead on the absolute imperative of reframing our approach to managing the resource commons of our global ecosystem. Combining her studies, and the stark prospect of impending environmental collapse, I conclude that reframing the prevailing economic order along co-operative lines is now an issue not only of social values and human decency, but also of human survival.

Happiness Matters

The case for the gradual ascendance of the co-operative model rests on at least three factors. The first is the changing nature of advanced capitalist societies and the transition from scarcity to post-scarcity economies. The second is the accelerating crisis of environmental degradation and resource depletion. The third is the growing movement for global justice and the search for economic models that institutionalize fairness.

The transition from scarcity to post-scarcity societies in the latter half of the twentieth century represents a watershed in human development. By "post-scarcity" I do not mean the elimination of poverty. As illustrated in the last chapter, poverty remains a problem in advanced capitalist societies, as does the growing disparity in wealth. In scarcity societies, poverty is very much a function of whether economic systems can generate the wealth necessary to meet the basic survival needs of the population as a whole. Even in these societies, as we know, a minority will always accumulate the resources they need to meet, or surpass, their basic needs. In post-scarcity societies, poverty is not primarily a consequence of the productive capacity of the economic system. Rather, poverty is a consequence of the unequal distribution of wealth which, in turn, comes from the inequality embedded both in the economic paradigm and the political system that sustains it. Moreover, even the poor in post-scarcity socieities are living at a level that is far above basic survival.

The solution of basic survival needs on a mass level in much of Western society has given rise to an entirely new kind of civilization. For the first time in human history, societies can be organized around the pursuit of non-survival ends, not only for a privileged minority as in the past, but for everyone. As noted in the previous chapter, this has had a revolutionary effect on concepts of personal identity, on the prospect of personal freedom and on the pursuit of meaningful life goals. Post-scarcity has made the pursuit of happiness a viable goal for societies as a whole, not just privileged individuals.[9]

But the enormous liberation of human energy and capacity that the resolution of scarcity made possible is now being consumed in the pursuit of ends that are not only contrary to the realization of happiness at a personal level, but lead to the erosion of the social basis of happiness as a sociocultural possibility. Post-scarcity society is for the first time capable of realizing happiness as a broad social project while simultaneously undermining the basis for its realization. For this paradox to be resolved, the restoration of social capital through institutions that incorporate and generate reciprocity is essential. The social poverty trap that Western capitalism has set for itself is being recognized at different levels — academically, politically, culturally, socially — and the decline of social bonds along with the growing alienation of individuals in society is being noted with alarm. At a personal level there is a growing thirst for something other than material consumption, and co-operatives are being viewed as a means of delivering the kinds of social and relational goods that commercial culture depletes. Throughout Europe and North America, co-ops that provide personalized services are the fastest growing sector for new co-op development, representing a new wave within the movement. Co-operatives increase the availability of relational goods, which are central to the production of happiness. Whether in elder care, services for the disabled or health services, co-ops are responding to a growing public concern over the depletion of social goods. But there is a deeper, far more intimate dimension to this new, post-scarcity reality.

If it is true that personal identity has become the locus of consumer culture in post-scarcity economies, then the co-operative assumes a central role in providing individuals a means of realizing a sense of personal identity that is both meaningful and attuned to the need for profound change at the level of economic practice. Because co-operatives recognize and reinforce the social dimensions of identity, they offer a means of realizing meaningful objectives that supersede instrumentality or consumption.

In a post-scarcity identity economy, the central issue becomes, "How do I create an identity that can deliver a high level of life satisfaction?" Past a $30,000–$40,000 survival threshold, this question is not related to income.[10] And if consumer culture and the economic forms that embody it are incapable of delivering life satisfaction and well-being at this basic emotional level the human need for social connection as a vital dimension of personal happiness will drive people to the kinds of institutions that can provide it. Co-operatives are chief among these. They build in people the capacity, and the satisfaction, of creating complex social relationships that are part of a truly meaningful personal identity. Religious organizations provide another way of meeting this need. But unless co-operatives and other organizations within civil society clearly recognize the urgency of social connection, as well as their role in responding to it, the danger is that other, less positive, forms of belonging will inevitably arise to fill the void. The tribalism inherent in fascistic or nationalistic movements, for example, feeds on this. The power of a perfected art of identity manipulation, combined with broad social disaffection and insecurity at this most elemental level of human psychology is a truly frightening prospect, and the signs of its emergence in contemporary political and religious propaganda gives little room for complacence. The extremist populism that is now disfiguring the political culture of the USA is one example. There is much at stake and the role of social institutions that can help to repair the dysfunction caused by our consumption-obsessed culture cannot be overstated.

Post-scarcity economies also mean that individuals can make the kinds of economic choices which express values that go beyond the satisfaction of basic needs. As we saw in the chapter on fair trade, there is a growing movement among consumers to align their economic choices with their personal values. This is the positive aspect of identity formation as an extension of consumption. But ethical choices about consumption are redeemed by their social dimension. They are directed to outcomes that reflect a social connection to others who, in turn, are affected by that choice. Co-operatives allow consumers, as well as producers, to humanize markets by incorporating values which increase in relevance as societies solve basic issues of survival. From this stand-point, the nature of co-operatives as socially directed enterprises makes them uniquely suited to the ethical standards that will be increasingly expected of enterprises in the future. The degree to which this is the case may already be judged by the behavior of capitalist firms today. The entire movement toward corporate social responsibility is a strategic response to the growing importance of market ethics in the mind of the consumer. Co-operatives have had a profound influence on corporations in this regard. Their conduct in the marketplace as socially conscious en-terprises has become contagious. When corporations like Microsoft en-courage their employees to do community work and pay them to do so, or oil companies like BP rebrand themselves as environmental organiza-tions, something has shifted. Corporations are attempting to human-ize their image and, sometimes, their behavior. But in the era of ethical consumption co-ops have a natural advantage, and the more important that ethics and social responsibility become for selling a dysfunctional economic model, or the survival of the planet, the more corporations will be compelled to adopt the appearance, if not the substance, of the co-operative model.

This introduces at least some notion of social accountability into corporate behavior. But it is not enough. Sooner or later the gap be-tween appearance and reality that is inherent in the structure of corpo-rations becomes manifest. Rarely has this been more starkly presented than in the case of the rebranded BP. As this is being written, the largest environmental disaster in US history is unfolding in the Gulf of Mex-ico. For over two months, upwards of 50,000 barrels of crude oil have been gushing into the Gulf every day, fouling the shorelines of Louisi-ana, Alabama, Mississippi and Florida and imperiling not only the Gulf fishery but an entire way of life. By the end of June 2010, the cleanup cost had surpassed $2 billion. This was a predictable catastrophe that mirrors at an environmental level the systemic and ideological failures that led inevitably to the 2008 financial collapse on Wall Street. Behind the sunny, leafy, environmentally-friendly new logo of BP, the company's true character now stands naked. It turns out that the oil giant, despite rebranding iself as an environmentally conscious company, had devoted a mere 0.03 perecnt of its profits to ensuring the safety of its operations. No amount of spin or marketing manipulation will ever address the utter disconnect between social values and social controls over corporate behavior on the one hand and the immoral thirst for profits at any cost on the other. For this to happen, the business model personified by BP has to be reconstructed along democratic principles if it is ever to be truly accountable to anyone beyond its shareholders. Sooner or later, the appearance of corporate social responsibility has to give way to substance.

Commons Sense

In 1968, ecologist Garret Hardin published an influential paper that has become a classic formulation of the dilemma between self-interest and the common good. It was titled "The Tragedy of the Commons"[11] and in it Hardin constructed the following scenario: Consider a commons in which individual herders are free to graze their cattle without restriction. All the herders depend on the common pastures for their survival. But given their nature, each herder will behave like a "rational" user, and will therefore utilize the resource to their own maximum benefit, regardless of the effect on other herders. The "rational" user of a commons, Hardin argues, will make demands on the resource until the expected benefits outweigh the personal costs. What inevitably follows is the tragedy of overgrazing until the resource collapses to the detriment of all. What Hardin proposed as a solution was either imposition of external control by the state,[12] or privatization of the resource.

Since then, the phrase "the tragedy of the commons" has entered the common lexicon and is trotted out every time someone proposes a co-operative approach to the management of common goods. The inevitable, and unmanageable, selfishness of people is simply taken for granted. But it is astonishing how little evidence has been supplied to support this view. Few have bothered to test the underlying assumptions on which the argument rested. Instead, the metaphor simply recast and reinforced the view of human nature that has underpinned classical economics since the 18th century. Hardin doesn't *prove* that the users of a common resource will always act in a way that destroys it; he *assumes* that the rational economic choice is to behave selfishly and then uses a circular argument to show the tragic results.[13] Hardin's gloomy view of human nature has since been used by policy makers and scholars to rationalize centralized government control over common resources or, more recently, to argue that the privatization of common goods is essential to their protection. This stark, pessimistic, disabling portrayal of the human condition in which users are condemned to fail in a situation they cannot control has been the basis for the imposition of external solutions to the management of local resources. The underlying premise is that any organizational activity involving several people has to be closely supervised to prevent it from dissolving into chaos and anarchy. Once again, the ghost of Hobbes sets the terms of the debate. But is this view warranted? Few bothered to check.

But Elinor Ostrom did. Ostrom was the recipient of the Nobel Prize for Economics in 2009. She developed an interest in the *actual* behavior of people with respect to the commons and decided to test Hardin's assumptions with empirical research. What she discovered, which may come as no surprise to readers who have made it this far in this book, is that Hardin was wrong. Ostrom found that in cultures all over the world many groups found ways to overcome the obstacles that he described — by creating contracts, agreements, incentives, constitutions, signals and media to enable co-operation for mutual benefit. From the management of water by farmers in California, to the grazing of herds in Mongolia, to the sharing of irrigation systems in Nepal, Ostrom showed how people have organized themselves to manage common resources and to devise long-term, sustainable institutions for governing them effectively. Ostrom's research also revealed a set of conditions that underlay the development and use of co-operation as a means of regulating common goods.[14]

By comparing communities, she found that groups that organize and govern their behavior successfully also share some basic design principles: users have a say in how the resource is managed; monitoring of the resource is done by those who use it; sanctions are applied against miscreants; group boundaries are clearly defined; and community members have access to low-cost mechanisms to resolve conflicts. In addition, for resources that are part of a larger system, the governance and monitoring activities are organized in multiple layers of nested enterprises. In short, Ostrom's research showed something that should have been obvious to anyone that cared to look — people have been managing common resources co-operatively for centuries. Far from being trapped in a set of conditions over which they have no control, they can change the rules of the game. They can agree to co-operate and to create the social mechanisms that normalize co-operative behavior.

Two contemporary examples serve to illustrate the point.

Japan's Fishing Co-operatives

Hime-Shima (Hime Island) is a tiny island of abut two and a half square miles located in the western part of the Seto Inland Sea in the southwestern part of Japan. It sits about three miles off the northeast coast of Kyushu Island, the most southern of Japan's major islands. The island has a population of 3,200 inhabitants that live together around a small village. Since time out of memory fishing has been the sustenance of this community. There are today about 300 fishermen and they are all members of the Hime-Shima Fisheries Co-operative. The small fishing vessels rising and falling in the harbor, all under six tons, characterize the village as a typical small-scale fishing community in Japan. The fishing gear is all traditional, including various types of angling/lining, bottom longlines and gillnets, boat seines, pots and traps, and compose a typical multi-gear fishery in the region. No mechanized trawl fishing is allowed in the waters around the island. The number of fishing vessels is also strictly controlled by common consent.

Japan is one of the world's pre-eminent fishing nations. On a per capita basis, the Japanese are by far the world's greatest consumers of fish and their fishing industry is among the world's largest. What is less well-known is that Japan's fishery is organized entirely on a co-operative basis, with over 2,500 fishing co-ops just like the one on Hime-Shima managing the fishing industry up and down the Japanese coast. By law fishing co-ops in Japan are granted exclusive rights to fish in local waters that are carefully defined and linked to specific villages. Co-op membership is restricted to fishermen who live in the village and their fishing rights are not transferable. They may be inherited. The co-operative management of fishing has been a traditional feature of Japanese village society since pre-feudal times when Emperors granted exclusive fishing rights to communities located in areas where rivers flowed in or out of lakes. Later, this territorially based co-operation was expanded to take in the whole of fishing in Japan's coastal waters.

Today, Japan's fishing co-ops are the backbone of the industry. They are responsible for the management of all aspects of fishing including the provision of banking and credit, the supply and sale of gear, fuel, ice, food and other daily necessities, mutual insurance and welfare, transportation, wholesale operations and the processing, storage and sale of catches and fish products. One of their most important functions, however, is to monitor and implement regulatory practices related to managing fish stocks. Four basic principles have been established for this regulation. They include the conservation of resources, the harmonious carrying out of all fishing operations, a guarantee to ensure the highest economic return within the framework of the management limits and equity among the entire community of fishermen in terms of profits.

This locally-controlled system, based on the twin principles of equity and collective responsibility, has been the world's prime example of how to co-operatively manage a fishing commons. Throughout the time when many of the world's fisheries were being depleted through overfishing, Japan's fisheries remained stable and sustainable. Mechanized fishing trawlers were prohibited. Fishing practices were calibrated to preserve stocks by diversifying the species that were fished. Local fishers, tasked with managing the resource through their co-ops, were vigilant in policing illegal activities and worked closely with government authorities in fashioning fishing policy and practices. The success of this complex, self-managed co-operative system continues to astonish observers whose expectations have been moulded by the tragedy of the commons scenario painted by Hardin. Meanwhile, a growing number of studies recommend the adoption of similar locally-based co-operative practices for the sustainable management of fisheries in other countries.[15]

Ozone

In the seventies and eighties, the depletion of the ozone layer was the climate change issue of the day. Following the demonstration of the depletion of the ozone layer in the early 1970s, two international treaties for the protection of the ozone layer were negotiated under the aegis of the United Nations Environment Programme (UNEP). They were the Vienna Convention and the Montreal Protocol and they were signed in 1985 and in 1987 respectively. In particular, the Montreal Protocol aimed at protecting the ozone layer from damage caused by the use of industrial chemicals known as ozone-depleting substances (ODS). The Montreal Protocol was among the first multilateral agreements to achieve universal consensus on how to address global environmental issues. Between 1986 and 2004 the Protocol, in concert with the Vienna Convention, has succeeded in reducing the production and consumption of ozone-harming substances by more than 90 percent. In addition, the Protocol established a fund to help developing countries phase out their use of ozone-depleting substances by the deadlines set in the agreement.

Between 1991 and April, 2006, the Ozone Fund provided us$2 billion to finance 5,250 projects in 139 developing countries.

Since it was signed, the terms of the Montreal Protocol have been implemented successfully with most major industrial and commercial concerns in industrialized countries having found alternatives to the substances banned by the treaty. The result has been a stabilization, or even decrease, in the concentrations of harmful substances in the atmosphere. The hole in the ozone layer that appeared over the Antarctic seems to have stopped growing. As a result of these actions the ozone layer is expected to return to normal levels from 2050 onwards.

The Montreal Protocol is almost universally regarded as a real success story of international co-operation, a signal achievement that secured the collaboration of governments, academia, industry, NGOs and the broader public in the pursuit of global aims. Its success in co-ordinating a global response to the common issue of atmospheric pollution is now serving as a model for tackling climate change. On September 16, 2009, the Democratic Republic of East Timor became the 196th nation to ratify the Montreal Protocol.

Globalizing Localism

One way of looking at the long arc of civilization since the emergence of agriculture 8,000 years ago is as the gradual evolution of co-operation as a means of managing resources — the growing capacity of societies to turn zero-sum games of winners and losers into games of mutual gain by creating institutions that facilitate collective action. In the past, these strategies have often been limited to small, tightly-knit communities where face-to-face relationships facilitated reciprocity through the trust one could place in a person's reputation. But the question that emerges now is: Can such co-operation be effective in the context of resource depletion and environmental degradation on a global level? Can we really apply the lessons of irrigation management in Nepal or Bali to the truly daunting task of managing the world's oceans or cleaning up the world's air? The examples cited above show we can. Another way to answer such a question is with a further question. Is there any other alternative?

Of all the reasons why the co-op model is fated to play a major role in the age ahead, the most compelling is the threat to our common survival posed by the damage humans are inflicting on the natural environment. In a very real sense, a truly global instance of the tragedy of the commons is playing out, with potentially apocalyptic consequences. The irreparable effects of overfishing, rainforest depletion or greenhouse gas emissions are beyond question. On local levels, such uncooperative behavior is tragic, but limited. Globalization changes everything. When corporate institutions amplify the effects of selfishness, the extension of harmful impacts through their global reach makes the results catastrophic. Greenhouse gases generated in one locale produce global warming everywhere. It's not just multinational corporations that inflict damage. Global circuits of exchange also magnify the consequences of incompetence or weakness at governmental levels. Avian flu that originates in lax standards or the failure of state oversight for poultry production in China ends up infecting people across the globe. Unchecked consumption on the part of individuals will, finally, make life on this planet untenable.

But just as countries have become more globally integrated, they have also become more interdependent. Solutions to global warming require the consent and collaboration of everyone. When the Wall Street banks started to collapse, the ensuing global economic crisis required a global response. But collaboration at these levels is often sporadic and reactive, not normative, especially in those areas where the regulation of economic behavior is concerned—international trade, the monitoring and regulation of capital flows, the management of international debt, tax policy—in short, any constraint on capital. This is because not only have globalized systems of economic power outpaced the capacity of our political institutions to regulate them, our political institutions have come under the control of these very corporate systems. When it comes to the management of global public goods, like breathable air and healthy oceans, there is a structural conflict between the prerogatives and interests of corporate power and the adoption of co-operative solutions for the sustainable management of resources whether at local or global levels.

One can argue that the sustainable management of resources is also in the interests of corporations, and that if the world's oil or forests are depleted the companies that rely on these resources will go out of business. They have a long-term interest in their protection. But what drives corporate behavior are short-term interests, market competition and the imperatives of stock values from one quarter to the next. There is a total disjunction between imminent profits and end results. If ever there was a compelling real world analogy to Hardin's tragedy of the commons, it is the behavior of corporations with respect to natural resources. But given their structural imperatives, how can corporations be expected to do otherwise?

Any change to this scenario must include a political solution. That is to say, the use of political power to identify, articulate and advance social interests — in this case the survival of the human species — over narrow economic interests. In this sense, the dynamics that resulted from the separation of economic and social reality at the dawn of the Industrial Revolution have remained the same, except that they have now been transposed to a global level. The squalor and suffering of the Victorian-era factory worker in Manchester is now replicated in the industrial slums of Mexico and the Philippines. Just as new political institutions were needed to contain the destructive forces of unrestrained capitalism in the 18th century, so too the international community must develop similar constraints to corporate capital in the 21st. As democracy in the West led directly to a rise in equality and economic well-being in those nations where it found a home, so its absence in the global arena has led to the rise of inequality and economic insecurity for billions.

In his book *Making Globalization Work*, former World Bank chief economist (and Nobel laureate) Joseph Stiglitz diagnoses the manifold problems of globalization as it is unfolding today. This work is a follow-up to his widely read *Globalization and its Discontents*, which disclosed the many sins of contemporary economic practice as they have been applied by global economic institutions, in particular the IMF. Stiglitz dissects the inner workings of these organizations from the perspective of one who knows them intimately from his experience as a one-time insider. Stiglitz pinpoints their key failures as failures of governance.[16] These organizations are controlled by technocrats from the financial and treasury departments of the countries that have controlling interests, primarily the United States. In turn, these governmental departments are beholden to multinational corporations. As a remedy, Stiglitz proposes reforming institutions like the IMF, the WTO and the World Bank to better reflect the interests of poorer nations by addressing what he calls their "democratic deficit."

Of course, Stiglitz is correct. Unless the democratic deficit in these institutions is fixed, there is little hope that they will address effectively the broader questions of poverty and exploitation in developing nations.

But beyond this, unless these institutions are democratized, there is little hope that the enormous environmental challenges facing the human community at a global level will be addressed either. Both crises flow from the same source — the absence of democracy in the structures that drive economies. This is why any strategy that focuses solely on political reform to solve economic dysfunction is likely to fail. The political structures of these institutions merely reflect the despotic nature of the corporate powers that control them. It is also why talk of "sustainability" that ignores the lack of accountability inside corporate structures also misses the point. This is one reason why Stiglitz's proposals for reforming globalization tell only half the story. For so long as corporations remain the dominant form of economic power, the conflict between social good on the one hand and the profit motive on the other, will remain. Moreover, it is simply not credible that undemocratic institutions will serve democratic ends. The economic domain must itself be humanized through the democratization of its institutions.

Among other things, the power and size of corporations must be curtailed just as the absolutist power of the church and monarchs was curtailed in an earlier age, and for the same reasons — the happiness and privileges of a few should never be sustained at the cost and misery of the many. The remedy for this was, and remains, the protection of social values through the democratic distribution of power. At the same time, alternative forms of economic life that embody and advance more humane social values must be sought out and encouraged. This also is a function of politics and public policy.

I am under no illusions about the difficulty of such a prescription. If nothing else, I am reminded of the cardinal law of politics: once gained, power is never given away — it is only taken away. Institutionalized power at the level we have been discussing is on an unprecedented scale of concentration, extension and sophistication. But then again, the threats to human happiness and welfare are also unprecedented. Not the least of them is the disfiguring of the human desire for happiness that is now embedded in the culture of consumption. There is a flip side, however. The knowledge and tools that are at the disposal of those who wish to make a better world are also unmatched. This too, is a product of our global age.

We now know what democracy looks like. The democratic impulse is no longer a novelty to be ridiculed or ignored, as it was a mere two hundred years ago. Even the most despotic regimes feel compelled to legitimize their power by appealing to democratic principles. There is shame in power for power's sake. Today, though, everyone knows the difference between sham and reality. No one is fooled. The social technology of democracy has become diffused throughout the global human community. Like those instances where learned behaviors among animals in one part of the world are replicated among the same species in another part, democracy has now become a kind of social instinct. This in itself is a precondition for progress unknown in previous ages. And while corporate capitalism still relies on replicating the exploitative conditions of the early industrial age in the poorest of the world's nations, people in these countries need not start at the beginning for the creation of democratic institutions as the Chartists and trade unionists and co-operators did in 19th century England. It is easy to forget that visionaries like Owen and Engels relied largely on the power of ideas; their dreams had yet to materialize. Today, the ideas, institutions and practices of democracy are fully understood, if not yet realized in every country. What is more, the models for democratizing economies exist almost everywhere. Trade unions and co-operatives already have a long history in most countries, surviving repression and outlasting even the most reactionary regimes.

The challenge in our global era is threefold: to mobilize existing knowledge, organizational capacity and resources at those levels where the globalization process is managed; to extend the principles and forms of reciprocity and co-operation at both local and global levels; and to link the co-operative movement's ideas, experience and resources to the political reform work that needs to be done. This means a much more explicitly political vision for the movement, and a linking of the movement to those social and political currents that are at the forefront of the struggle for global justice. Clearly, the democratization of global economic institutions requires political change in those countries that control these institutions. Here again, though the environment for pressing such change has rarely been better, it remains to be seen whether the moment will last long enough to realize the kinds of reforms that begin to rein in corporate power. But regardless of this, the effort to democratize economies directly through the creation of co-operative economic forms will continue. The environment for this too, is positive. The capitalist paradigm is in trouble and will remain so because the crisis of legitimacy that it is living through is not resolvable by economic recovery alone. The crisis is ontological — the social and personal requirements of modern capitalism are a violation of human nature. And unless the social and economic aspects of human culture are reconciled in a new paradigm for a global age, the crisis will deepen and the damage will soon become irreversible.

Another lens through which to view the rise of civilization is the degree to which societies have been able to realize and advance the essential interconnectedness of humankind. The progression of political institutions from the tribal level to the city-state, and from thence to nation states and to multi-state federations reflects this process. The creation of the United Nations and the European Union were in themselves possible, despite their flaws, because of the growing capacity of human beings to organize around common interests at higher and higher orders of inclusion. Most of the dysfunction present in these institutions is precisely the incongruity between the common good for which they were intended and the disparate particular interests that still hamper their operation as co-operative entities. Restructuring them in ways that allow them to fully embody their purposes means incorporating principles that have always defined reciprocity-driven organizations. The management of common interests demands recognition of all those affected. Gradually, this is happening. The economic crisis of 2008 required an overhaul of the G7 to include, at minimum, emerging economic powers like India. It is now the G20. Sooner or later, this too will expand to include other countries. Likewise, global economic institutions like the IMF will function effectively only if they incorporate the interests of all their stakeholders, not just their largest bankrollers.

It is possible to re-imagine the World Bank, the WTO and the IMF being restructured along co-operative principles, in which each member state has an equal vote. Countries making up these bodies could include representatives not only of governments, but of civil society as well. Such a reworking would ensure that the global community would at last have governance structures that, in principle at least, incorporate social and political interests in the management of global economic systems. At worst, they would do less harm than the incompetence, mismanagement and degradation of weak nations for the benefit of the strong that these institutions display today. This is one area of political action that links the global with the local in ways that could crystallize alliances across a broad spectrum of reform efforts from every corner of the globe. And to those who are tempted to roll their eyes at such a dreamy proposal, I would point out that unless something like this happens, and soon, these institutions will become irrelevant from an utter lack of credibility. If they wish to survive, the democratization of their governance structures is ultimately in their interest. For those millions who have to suffer the economic and social consequences of the status quo, democratization is not only a critical necessity in a system that impacts daily on their material welfare. It is increasingly being viewed as a political right. The ongoing story of Argentina and the IMF should serve as a warning. And just as political pressure at local and national levels is driving governments to grapple collectively with environmental problems like global warming, so too can similar pressure be brought to bear within individual countries to radically reform the governance structures of the global economy.

Humane economies are a lot like healthy ecosystems. They depend on the creation and recreation of a diversity of economic forms that respond to the different dimensions of human societies and provide scope and freedom to the broad range of human needs and talents that compose them. Just as the domination of any one species to the exclusion of others will destroy an ecosystem, so too do economies require the presence of a broad diversity of economic forms — capitalist enterprises, large and small, that aggregate and generate wealth; public and state institutions that redistribute wealth and promote equity; and co-operative enterprises that generate social solidarity through the practice of reciprocity. There are other forms also: charitable and voluntary organizations that promote the practice of altruism; social enterprises that use the market to promote social goods; and hybrids among all of these that combine the unique strengths of different forms to produce goods and services in new ways and for different purposes. What is crucial is that the deadening effect of any single model be averted. When this happens, it is always accompanied by an ideology that both justifies its domination and undermines our capacity to imagine alternatives.

But there *are* alternatives. Some of us will always hope and work for the best of all possible worlds. Countless people do. Whether they are on the front lines in the fight to save their factories, or working their small plots for a fair return on their crops or quietly encouraging their sisters in the dark passageways of the brothels, thousands are remaking their lives and reforming their societies through the power of co-operation. The times change, and the obstacles to constructing humane and caring societies change also. But knowledge is fragile and it is perishable. The one crucial inheritance from the past that must be safeguarded is the knowledge that more than one world is possible.

In the end, it doesn't matter whether co-operatives ultimately prevail as the norm for how we organize our economies. It matters that they survive. For in a dark age, the one indispensable value is the knowledge of an alternative. Once this is lost, all is lost. Co-operatives are enduring evidence of another way of living our lives. Like the monasteries of the Middle Ages that kept alight the ideals and knowledge of classical antiquity for a later age, co-operatives the world over safeguard a humane vision of social and economic life. Triumphant or not, so long as they exist they recall another understanding of human economies, another sense of how people might live together in the pursuit of common aims. They will always remind us that the human fabric is made up of individual threads, each distinguishable and apart, each an integral part of the whole that in turn sustains and defines us as individuals. When the weavers of Rochdale came together on a bleak winter evening to create their small co-op store they were dreaming a very grand dream — a weaver's dream. But it was no illusion.

For a complete bibliography on many of the themes
explored in this book, readers may go to
www.johnrestakis.net

Notes

Introduction

1. Unless otherwise specified, I am using the term "free market" to denote that current of contemporary neo-liberal thought that emphasizes the primacy of capital, the joint stock company and the restriction of non-commercial power, such as that of government, in the workings of the economy. The more proper, historical meaning of a free market will be discussed in more detail in chapter One.

2. See in particular E. P. Thompson, *The Making of the English Working Class*, Knopf, 1963.

3. This is not to overlook for a moment the reactionary role of religion in general, and Methodism in particular, in keeping working people in their allotted place as a servile sub-class of society. Methodism's founding principles of submission to authority and the performance of work as a moral duty, regardless of the suffering or exploitation it entailed, were powerful conditioning factors in the creation of a pliable labor force for the employing class. E.P Thompson has provided a detailed anatomy of this reactionary religious conditioning during the formative decades of the Industrial Revolution.

Chapter 1: The Grand Delusion

1. One refreshing exception was Tony Benn, the British Labour MP, who during an interview on the BBC asked pointedly why privately owned banks should be allowed to control financial markets at all.

2. The only solace lay in the Canadian genius for the half measure; the Conservative Party that won the election was still not completely trusted and the electorate hedged its bets. The Conservatives had to make do with a minority mandate.

3. In March of 2009, it came to light that the company used $53 billion of the $170 billion of taxpayer money to pay out insurance claims to clients that lost money on account of their own irresponsible investments in subprime mortgages. AIG also bought the toxic assets of these companies and then transferred them to an entity controlled by the government thus forcing taxpayers to bear the risk that these assets will continue to plummet in value. *International Herald Tribune*, "Banks got part of AIG rescue funds," March 17, 2009.

4. So objectionable was a governmental role in the market that there was no provision requiring that banks receiving the billions in bailout money actually lend it out — the primary purpose of the bill. It was left up to the banks to use the money as they saw fit. The banks merely hoarded it, or used it to leverage mergers and buyouts, and the credit crisis continued.

5. The centerpiece of this deregulation frenzy was the repeal of the Glass-Steagall Act, passed by Congress in 1933 to separate commercial banking from high-risk investment banking. It was the destruction of these very safeguards that

brought on the credit crisis that followed the collapse of subprime mortgages in 2008. Tellingly, the Congressional majority of Republicans and Democrats that collaborated to dismantle banking oversight was so powerful that a presidential veto was impossible. Free market mania was pervasive. President Clinton, a Democratic president, signed the Republican-sponsored legislation repealing Glass-Steagall on November 12, 1999.

6. Not only did co-operative banks and credit unions increase their business activity in nearly every facet (assets and deposits, volume of lending, increase in membership, a better rate of interest and greater sustainability measured as a ratio of capital to loan defaults), they had very few losses on investments and so needed no government help. More importantly, co-op financial institutions had no credit freeze for their members. In the US, loans by credit unions experienced an increase from $539 billion in 2007 to $575 billion in 2008. By comparison, 8,300 US banks saw loans outstanding decrease by $31 billion in the same period, from $709 trillion to $7.876 trillion. The same patterns were reflected in the rest of the world. Johnston Birchall and Lou-Hammond Ketilson, *Resilience of the Co-operative Business Model in Times of Crisis*, International Labour Organization, 2009, p. 18.

7. Karl Polanyi, *The Great Transformation*, Rinehart, 1944, p. 155. This entire section owes a great deal to Polanyi's pioneering study of the Industrial Revolution.

8. By year's end, the cost of rescuing the financial systems and "stimulating" the economies of the US and Europe had topped three *trillion* dollars. Iceland was bankrupt, the global economy had entered recession and China's phenomenal growth had dipped below eight percent, the danger point at which the population was expected to get restive. Canada continued down its own peculiar path. Under cover of the economic crisis, the Harper government introduced an economic plan that included a ban on the right to strike by federal civil servants and cuts to federal funding of political parties. The move highlighted in glaring clarity the cynicism and opportunism of the Conservatives, sparking rebellion in parliament and a constitutional crisis. Harper's economic plan was not passed.

9. For a lively account of this view, see Thomas Frank, *One Market Under God: Extreme Capitalism, Market Populism, and the End of Economic Democracy*, Doubleday, 2001.

10. Francis Fukuyama, *The End of History and the Last Man*, Free Press, 1990.

11. E. Screpanti and S. Zamagni, *An Outline of the History of Economic Thought*, Oxford Press, 2001.

12. Thomas Hobbes, *The Leviathan*, Penguin Classics, 1982.

13. Unfortunately, the head that smiles out at the viewer is a wax copy. Bentham's own was removed for more secure storage after being habitually spirited away by students for uses that would have given its owner, had he known, pause before leaving it to posterity.

14. Polanyi, *Great Transformation*.

15. See for instance, John Stuart Mill, *Principles of Political Economy*, 3rd ed., Longmans, Green and Co., 1848.

16. William R. Leach, *Land of Desire: Merchants, Power, and the Rise of a New American Culture*, Pantheon, 1993.

17. Polanyi, *Great Transformation*, p. 67 ff.

18. Thompson, *English Working Class*, p. 64.
19. Ibid.
20. Ibid, p. 57.
21. Iris Origo, *The Merchant of Prato: Daily Life in a Medieval Italian City*, Octagon Books, 1979.
22. Malthus's philosophy was based on the notion that any form of assistance to the poor and destitute was a mistake that would upset the natural order in which starvation and deprivation act as correcting forces to overpopulation. The poor were meant to remain poor.
23. Here is Ure's cheerful account of child labor gleaned from his inspections of the Lancashire mills: "I have visited many factories, both in Manchester and the surrounding districts, during a period of several months and I never saw a single instance of corporal punishment inflicted on a child. The children seemed to be always cheerful and alert, taking pleasure in using their muscles. The work of these lively elves seemed to resemble a sport. Conscious of their skill, they were delighted to show it off to any stranger. At the end of the day's work they showed no sign of being exhausted." Andrew Ure, *The Philosophy of Manufactures*, Cass, 1967.
24. Sarah Bakewell, "The Reanimators," *Fortean Times*, 139, October, 2000.
25. Ibid.
26. On top of everything else, Ure was given to staging public spectacles in which he would animate the bodies of executed criminals by applying electrified rods to incisions in their muscles. In Glasgow in 1819 Ure took the corpse of one Matthew Clydesdale, a hanged murderer, and by connecting the rods to the left phrenic nerve and the diaphragm produced a perfect imitation of breathing. When he linked the supra-orbital nerve of the forehead to the heel, the "most extraordinary grimaces" resulted: "Rage, horror, despair, anguish, and ghastly smiles, united their hideous expression in the murderer's face." These highly charged performances apparently sparked Mary Shelley's imagination. Bakewell, "Reanimators."
27. Polanyi, *Great Transformation*, pp. 44–45.
28. Other critics have pointed to Polanyi's failure to question the claims of Soviet Russia, even after 1930 when reports of communist repression were well known. A brief summary of some of the criticisms of Polanyi's work may be viewed in the New World Encyclopedia, newworldencyclopedia.org/entry/Karl_Polanyi. See also, Dennis R. Searcy, "Beyond the Self-Regulating Market in Market Society: A Critique of Polanyi's Theory of the State," *Review of Social Economy*, Vol. 51, 1993.
29. K. Polanyi, *Great Transformation*, p. 136 ff.
30. My thanks to Brett Fairbairn for helping to clarify some of the themes in this section.
31. I confess to wondering sometimes whether it is a mistake at all, or rather a conscious intent to mislead on the part of some who must certainly know better.
32. Polanyi, *Great Transformation*, p. 136 ff.
33. Ibid., p. 233. See also Howard Zinn, *A People's History of the United States*, Harper & Row, 1980; and Richard O. Boyer and Herbert J. Morais, *Labor's Untold Story*, United Electrical, Radio and Machine Workers of America, 1979.

34. S. Zamagni, "Comparing Capitalistic and Co-operative Firms on the Ground of Humanistic Management," unpublished paper, 2009.

35. The Franciscans, it appears, were singularly gifted in the arts of commerce. They also invented double-entry bookkeeping.

36. A fast-growing literature on this issue has emerged in recent years, resulting from a new subdiscipline dealing with the economics of happiness including, for example, Easterlin's "paradox of happiness." Richard A. Easterlin, "Does Economic Growth Improve the Human Lot?" in Paul A. David and Melvin W. Reder, eds., *Nations and Households in Economic Growth: Essays in Honor of Moses Abramovitz,* Academic Press, 1974.

37. William Leach, *Land of Desire: Merchants, Power, and the Rise of a New American Culture,* Vintage, 1994. p. xv.

38. Polanyi, *Great Transformation,* p. 242.

Chapter 2: The Materialization of Dreams

1. In *A New View of Society*, Owen cites the figures gathered in the Population Act at that time to state that the poor and working classes of England and Ireland were found to exceed 15 million or nearly three-fourths of the population of the British Isles. See Robert Owen, *A New View of Society*, Cadell and Davies, 1817. In his book *The Conditions of the Working Class in England in 1844* Engels shows that in cities like Manchester and Liverpool mortality from smallpox, measles, scarlet fever and whooping cough was four times as high as in the surrounding countryside. The overall death rate in Manchester and Liverpool was significantly higher than the national average (one in 32.72 and one in 31.90 and even one in 29.90, compared with one in 45 or one in 46). An interesting example shows the increase in the overall death rates in the industrial town of Carlisle. Prior to the introduction of mills (1779–1787), 4,408 out of 10,000 children died before reaching the age of 5. After the introduction of mills the figure rose to 4,738. Prior to the introduction of mills, 1,006 out of 10,000 adults died before reaching 39 years old. After the introduction of mills the death rate rose to 1,261 out of 10,000. See F. Engels, *The Condition of the Working Class in England,* Penguin Classics, 1987.

2. The government's rejection of Owen's plan was almost certainly an unlooked-for blessing. Given the prevailing attitudes and the institutional frame of government at this time (perhaps *any* time, as we shall see later), the adoption of Owen's Villages of Co-operation by the state would almost certainly have cast Owen's co-operative communities more along the lines of the poorhouse than anything Owen had in mind, and have strangled in the cradle the co-operative vision he continued to propagate for years after.

3. Another was the hostility to education. The teaching of writing at Sunday School was banned by John Wesley, Methodism's grim founder, because it tended to the pursuit of secular skills and this was anathema on the Sabbath. The teaching of reading on the other hand, was accepted as necessary for the internalization of the teachings of the Bible.

4. Evidence of Dr. Smith, of Leeds, in "Poor Man's Advocate," May 5, 1832. Cited by Thompson, *English Working Class,* p. 328.

5. Thompson, *English Working Class,* p. 783.

6. William Thompson's other writings include *An Appeal of One-Half of the Human Race, Women, Against the Pretensions of the Other Half, Men, to retain them in Political and Thence in Civil and Domestic Slavery*, 1825, written with Anna Wheeler, a seminal work advocating the emancipation of women and a fine example of the Georgian-era affection for the exhaustively descriptive and morally instructive title.

7. "The Cooperative Magazine," London, November 1827. Cited by the Oxford English Dictionary.

8. Thompson, *English Working Class*, p. 781.

9. Much of the aid that the co-operative societies received on this front came from the Christian Socialists, a small band of Church of England men who fought to secure legal recognition of co-operatives in Parliament. John Stuart Mill was among this group, championing to great effect the co-op cause in the House of Commons. The Industrial and Provident Societies' Acts of 1852 and 1862 were directly the work of these Christian Socialists. See Joseph Clayton, *Co-operation*, T.C. and E.C. Jack, 1911, pp. 15–18.

10. Thompson, *English Working Class*, p. 804.

11. George Jacob Holyoake, *Self-Help by the People: The History of the Rochdale Pioneers*, General Books, 2009.

12. Both these movements were at the forefront of reform organizing in England. The Chartist movement was central in the push for universal suffrage, and the Ten Hours movement led the charge for worker rights.

13. For a detailed account of the weavers in this period, see E. P. Thompson's chapter on this subject in *The Making of the English Working Class*.

14. It is well here to impress on the reader the enormous extent of the weavers as an artisan/worker class. By 1820, there were 240,000 handloom weavers; they accounted for the third largest grouping of laborers in England after agricultural workers and domestics. The political and social impact of their shared experience during the Industrial Revolution had a profound impact on the rise of working class consciousness, organization, and politicization. Neil J. Smelser, *Social Change in the Industrial Revolution*, University of Chicago Press, 1959, pp. 137, 148–9, 207.

15. Thompson, *English Working Class*, p. 295.

16. Plato was no democrat and he spent his long life as a critic of Athenian democracy. He drew inspiration for his Utopian vision from the military society of ancient Sparta. In spite of his brilliance, one wonders if Plato stopped to consider whether a philosopher like himself could ever have emerged from Spartan society or, for that matter, from his own Republic. Dissent and free thought are the hallmarks of democratic societies, not authoritarian ones. The fact that Plato and the birth of philosophy arose in democratic Athens while authoritarian Sparta produced little more than military might is not accidental—it's axiomatic.

17. Included in the Reduction territories were the present-day Argentine provinces of Misiones and Corrientes and the Brazilian Province of Rio Grande do Sul.

18. "Reductions of Paraguay," *The Catholic Encyclopedia*, The Encyclopedia Press, 2008.

19. E. Screpanti and S. Zamagni, *An Outline of the History of Economic Thought*, Oxford University Press, 1993, p. 120.

20. Polanyi, *Great Transformation*, p. 129.
21. Note the striking similarity with Fukuyama's claim concerning the end of history.
22. Polanyi, *Great Transformation*, p. 158
23. By one estimate, exploding TV sets were the cause of over 60 percent of apartment fires in Moscow. The alarming propensity of Russian receivers to blow up, and the apprehension it caused in Soviet viewers, was one of the stranger features of Soviet life. On the other hand, it is hard to say which was worse — that, or having to sit through programs with titles like "Winner in Socialist Emulation," and "Construction Sites of the Twelfth Five-Year Plan." "Soviet TV Set Production," GlobalSecurity.org. Cited June 28, 2010.
24. E. Bernstein, *Evolutionary Socialism: The Economic Capacity of Co-operative Associations*, The Independent Labour Party, 1907.
25. Ibid.
26. This section on the developmental stages of the co-op movement owes much to a formulation by Brett Fairbairn, University of Saskatchewan.

Chapter 3: Co-operation Italian Style

1. In Roman times, 30 kilometers was the distance a Roman legion could march in a day. At these points along the Emilian road, the garrison towns that grew up became the seeds of the urban centers that followed.
2. I have also used the term "co-operative economy" in a looser, informal sense to describe the economic system of Emilia Romagna as one that is modeled on co-operation as an organizing and strategic principle for the operation and development of the regional economy as a whole.
3. Paolo Billi, *SACMI Company Profile*, unpublished paper, 2003.
4. Vera Zamagni, *Italy's Co-operatives: From Marginality to Success*, unpublished paper, 2006.
5. For a fascinating treatment of the relation between social and political culture and economic development see Robert D. Putnam's influential *Making Democracy Work: Civic Traditions in Modern Italy*, Princeton University Press, 1994.
6. Vera Zamagni, "History of The Co-operative Movement in Italy," public lecture, Bologna Summer Program for Co-operative Studies, Bologna, 2003.
7. Paul Ginsborg, *A History of Contemporary Italy: Society and Politics, 1943–1988*, Palgrave Macmillan, 2003, pp. 23–28.
8. Anthony L. Cardoza, "Commercial Agriculture an the Crisis of Landed Power: Bologna 1880-1930," in *Landownership and Power in Modern Europe*, ed. Martin Blinkhorn and Ralph Gibson, HarperCollins Academic, 1991, p. 181.
9. "Relazione del commissario Marchese Luigi Tanari," in *Atti de la Giunta per la inchiesta agraria e sulle condizioni della classe agricola*, Vol. II, Rome, 1881, p. 224.
10. For a poignant treatment of the ending of this way of life, see Luchino Visconti's film masterpiece, *The Leopard*.
11. Cardoza, "Commercial Agriculture."
12. Ginsborg, *Contemporary Italy*, p. 106.
13. For an interesting treatment of present-day Italy's relationship with its fascist history see Philip Morgan, *The Fall of Mussolini: Italy, the Italians, and the Second World War*, Oxford University Press, 2007.
14. John F. Pollard, *The Fascist Experience in Italy*, Routledge, 1998, p. 31.

15. Ibid.
16. The attempt to undermine and co-opt the co-operative movement by the right in Italy did not end with the fascist effort between the 1920s and the end of the war. Since first coming to power, Silvio Berlusconi's administration has waged a continuous campaign against the co-operatives, including recognition in May 2004 of a new, right-wing co-operative federation called Unicoop. Berlusconi's party Forza Italia, founded in 1993, is Italy's first political party to have had no ties with the broader co-op movement.
17. Morgan, *Fall of Mussolini*.
18. See, for example, Anthony Beevor's account of German policy in the Ukraine. A. Beevor, *The Fall of Berlin*, Viking, 1945.
19. The other reason is that only Italian residents living in Imola can join the co-op. Even if it wanted to, the co-op could not legally extend membership to non-residents.
20. This kind of membership cost is not at all unusual for the larger worker co-ops of the region. Down the road from SACMI, Co-operative Ceramica, one of the oldest co-ops in Imola, requires a membership fee of $370,000.
21. Zamagni, *Italy's Co-operatives*.
22. Ibid.
23. Ibid.
24. V. Zamagni, P. Battilani and A. Casali, *La cooperazione di consumo in Italia. Centocinquant'anni ella coop consumatori*, Bologna, 2004. See also P. Battilani, "How to beat competition without losing co-operative identity: The case of the Italian consumer Co-operatives", in *Consumerism versus Capitalism? Co-operatives Seen from an International Comparative Perspective*, Amsab-Institute of Social History, 2005.
25. Zamagni, *Italy's Co-operatives*.
26. Originally without limits, this law was changed by the Berlusconi administration in 2003 to limit the exemption eligible to co-ops. In 2003, 87 percent of the profits of medium-sized and large co-ops was still being earmarked for indivisible reserves, while 4.9 percent went to cash refunds and only 4.1 percent was distributed to members.

Chapter 4: The Emilian Model and the Socialization of Capital

1. See especially the pioneering work of S. Brusco, "The Emilian Model: Productive Decentralisation and Social Integration," *Cambridge Journal of Economics*, 6, 167–184, 1982.
2. Vera Zamagni, "The Industrial Districts," lecture, Bologna Summer Program for Co-operative Studies, Bologna, 2006.
3. A. Bardi and S. Bertini, *Dinamiche territoriali e nuova industria dal distretti alle filiere*, V Rapporto Della Fondazione Istituto per il Lavoro, 2005.
4. Today, ERVET is involved only with the research centers ASTER and Democentre. The service centers have been wholly privatized and are operated by the firms in the given sectors.
5. This story was relayed to the author by a senior minister in the ER regional government.
6. Richard Walker and Michael Storper, *The Capitalist Imperative: Territory,*

Technology, and Industrial Growth, Basil Blackwell, 1989, p. 133; see also M.J. Montfort and J.C. Dutailly, "Les filieres de production," *Archives and Documents*, no. 67, INSEE, 1983.

7. The custom of *rappresaglie*, or reprisal, dated from the ninth century and became established practice throughout the Middle Ages. Interestingly, various categories of private citizens were exempted from such reprisals: ambassadors, pilgrims and students from the University of Bologna. Origo, *Merchant of Prato*, p. 40.

8. A. Rinaldi, "The Emilian Model Revisited: Twenty Years After," *Materiali di discussione del Dipartimento di Economia politica*, 417, Modena, September, 2002.

9. A. Amin, "The Emilian Model: Institutional Challenges," *European Planning Studies*, 7, 389–405, 1999.

10. The Bassanini Law of 1998 made possible the process of administrative decentralization that involved a transfer from the State to regional governments of new powers as well as assets and financial resources.

11. Rinaldi, *Emilian Model*.

12. Ibid.

13. Bardi and Bertini, *Dinamiche territoriali*.

14. Ibid.

Chapter 5: Social Co-ops and Social Care

1. See J. Stiglitz, *Making Globalization Work*, W.W. Norton, 2006; *Globalization and its Discontents*, W.W. Norton, 2004.

2. John D. Stephens, *Democratization and Social Policy Development in Advanced Capitalist Societies*, United Nations Research Institute for Social Development, 2005.

3. Stiglitz, *Globalization and Its Discontents*.

4. Ibid.

5. Ibid.

6. Ibid; Maurizio Ferrera, *Democratization and Social Policy in Southern Europe: From Expansion to "Recalibration*, United Nations Research Institute for Social Development, 2005.

7. In Canada, despite a growing GDP and 12 continuous years of federal surpluses, the issues of poverty, homelessness and hunger show no signs of abating. In 2005, 800,000 people per month used a food bank, an increase of 118 percent since 1989. Rates of child poverty, a powerful indicator of broader social and economic conditions, have remained unaffected for the past 20 years. See *Time for Action: Hunger Count 2005*, Canadian Association of Food Banks, 2005.

8. See Plato's Republic for his most developed notion of the Ideal State. *The Republic*, Hackett Publishing, 1992.

9. Aristotle, *Politics*

10. See, for example, the central role of civil society as an animating force during the Velvet Revolution of Czechoslovakia: Robin E.H. Shepherd, *Czechoslovakia: The Velvet Revolution and Beyond*, Palgrave Macmillan, 2000; Adam Roberts and Timothy Garton Ash, eds., *Civil Resistance and Power Politics: The Experience of Non-Violent Action from Gandhi to the Present Day*, Oxford University Press, 2009.

11. A speech by Vaclav Havel, given at the Vaclav Havel Civil Society Symposium,

"Vaclav Havel's Ideas and his Civil Society Conception," Macalester College, April 26, 1999.

12. Thomas Paine, *The Rights of Man*, Dover, 1999.

13. Alex de Tocqueville, *Democracy in America*, Penguin Classic, 2003.

14. Statistics Canada, *Cornerstones of Community: Highlights from the National Survey of Nonprofit and Voluntary Organizations, 2003.* statcan.gc.ca, cited June 28, 2010.

15. Marguerite Mendell, "The Social Economy in Quebec," paper presented at VIII Congreso Internacional del CLAD sobre la Reforma del Estado y de la Administración Pública, Panamá, October 28–31, 2003.

16. A great deal has recently been written on social capital, but see in particular Robert Putnam, *Making Democracy Work: Civic Traditions in Modern Italy*, Princeton University Press, 1993; *Bowling Alone: The Collapse and Revival of American Community*, Simon & Schuster, 2000.

17. The economic principle that defines organizations within the private (or capitalist) sector is the exchange of goods and services on the basis of an agreed value — "the exchange of equivalents" — for commercial gain. Their primary purpose is to maximize returns on investment to shareholders. In capitalist firms, capital controls labor. The economic principle that defines the operations of the public sector is the redistribution of wealth by the state. The primary purpose of the public sector is the provision of public goods, and the aim of redistribution is equality.

18. Cooperative per Attività e Prodotti Sociale.

19. C. Borzaga and E. Tortia, "Worker Motivations, Job Satisfaction, and Loyalty in Public and Nonprofit Social Services," *Nonprofit and Voluntary Sector Quarterly*, 35: pp. 225–248, 2006.

20. See C. J. Uhlaner, "Relational Goods and Participation: Incorporating Sociability into a Theory of Rational Action," *Public Choice*, 62, 19889, pp. 253–285.

21. Alberto Bacchiega and Carlo Borzaga, "The Economics of the Third Sector: Toward a More Comprehensive Approach," in *The Study of the Nonprofit Enterprise: Theories and Approaches*, Helmut Anheiet and Avner Ben-Ner, eds., Kluwer Academic and Plenum, 2003.

22. Neil Gilbert and Paul Terrell, *Dimensions of Social Welfare Policy*, Allyn and Bacon, 2005.

23. In 2009 a model for this kind of social stock exchange was established alongside the conventional stock market in Milan.

Chapter 6: Japan

1. M. Selden, "A Forgotten Holocaust: US Bombing Strategy, the Destruction of Japanese Cities and the American Way of War from World War II to Iraq," *The Asia-Pacific Journal: Japan Focus*, japanfocus.org/-Mark-Selden/2414. Cited November 2009.

2. Ibid.

3. "Throughout the spring and summer of 1945 the US air war in Japan reached an intensity that is still perhaps unrivaled in the magnitude of human slaughter. That moment was a product of the combination of technological breakthroughs, American nationalism, and the erosion of moral and political scruples pertaining

to the killing of civilians, perhaps intensified by the racism that crystallized in the Pacific theatre." Mark Selden, *American Nationalism and Asian Wars*.

4. This is the one depressingly predictable fate of co-operatives (and other democracy-promoting organizations) in repressive times. Identical efforts can be seen in Mussolini's Italy, Hitler's Germany, Franco's Spain and Stalin's Russia.

5. Japan's co-operatives took a lead role in the anti-nuclear movement of the '50s and '60s and continue to this day to support peace initiatives at an international level, including the development of trade, social and cultural partnerships with organizations in China, Taiwan, Korea and the Philippines.

6. David Thompson, "Japan: Land of Co-operatives," *Co-operative Grocer*, #135, March–April, 2008.

7. Ibid.

8. Andrew Gordon, *A Modern History of Japan: From Tokugawa Times to the Present*, Oxford University Press, 2003. Much of the background history I use to contextualize the emergence of the co-op movement in Japan is heavily indebted to this valuable volume.

9. See *Star Trek: The Next Generation*, "The Best of Both Worlds" episode for a chilling, and wholly entertaining, film meditation on American collectivist paranoia, free will and the allure of conformity. Another is *Invasion of the Body Snatchers*.

10. Gordon, *Modern History*, p. 7.

11. Ibid., p. xxii.

12. This was not Japan's only borrowing of German models. Its army was modeled on Bismarck's military machine and German advisors designed and trained Japan's modern military.

13. Akira Kurimoto, *Member Participation Revisited: From Han Groups to What?* Consumer Co-operative Institute of Japan, 2007.

14. A very substantial literature has now grown up around *sabak* co-operative irrigation societies, as well as the *Banjars*, the co-operative village organizations that oversee much of Balinese ritual and communal life. For an in-depth look at these institutions, see J. Stephen Lansing, *Perfect Order: Recognizing Complexity in Bali*, Princeton University Press, 2006.

15. To gauge the insanity of Japan's military fanaticism at this time, consider that in the dying days of the Pacific War *tonarigumi* were tasked with carrying out a suicidal last defence against American invaders rather than have Japan face the humiliation of surrender.

16. *Tonarigumi* were also organized in territories occupied by Japan, including Manchukuo, Mengjiang and the Wang Jingwei Government, and later in occupied territories of Southeast Asia, with the same purposes. See I. C. B. Dear, ed., *The Oxford Companion to World War II*, Oxford University Press, 2002.

17. After World War II, a key advisor of General MacArthur's in Japan was a former executive of Farmland, then the largest agricultural co-op in the US. This advisor successfully advocated for an agricultural co-operative system that replicated the success in the US. Thompson, *Land of Co-operatives*.

18. J. Hermida, "The Seikatsu Club Consumers Cooperative: A Unique Producer-Consumer Relationship in Japan," *Initiatives on Pro-Small Farmer Trade*, Asian

Partnership for the Development of Human Resources in Rural Asia and Asian Farmers' Association for Sustainable Rural Development, 2006.

19. Seikatsu Club website, iisd.org/50comm/commdb/desc/d08. Cited June, 2010.
20. Ibid.
21. Richard Evanoff, *A Look Inside Japan's Seikatsu Club Consumers' Cooperative*, library.nothing-ness.org/articles/all/en/display/247. Cited June, 2010.
22. Thompson, *Land of Co-operatives*.
23. Ibid.
24. Hermida, "Seikatsu Club."
25. Kurimoto, *Member Participation*.
26. See A. Carr, *Positive Psychology*, Routledge, 2004: "People with large social support networks and stronger social bonds with members of their networks have better physical and mental health, fewer illnesses and less depression, recover more rapidly from physical illness and psychological problems, and have a lower risk of death."
27. Bob Marshall, "Japan's Worker Co-operative Movement into the 21st Century," *Asia Pacific Journal: Japan Focus*, japanfocus.org/articles/print_article/1704. Cited June, 2010.
28. Ibid.
29. Walt Crowley, *To Serve the Greatest Number: A History of Group Health Cooperative of Puget Sound*, University of Washington Press, 1996.

Chapter 7: The Daughters of Kali

1. I use the traditional name "Calcutta" in the full knowledge that "Kolkata" is the politically correct term. In doing so, I align myself with many in India who view this ridiculous name change as a sop to the nationalists who contrived the name Kolkata out of pure air.
2. Temple prostitutes, known as *Devadasis*, have a long history in India. The women settling at these temples come under the protection of the temple priest. The younger ones are often let out as prostitutes to service wealthy patrons and visiting pilgrims with the priest acting as pimp and keeping the money. Many of these women are widows. This "service" is part of the widow's devotional practice and its roots are traceable back to the temple prostitutes of places like Kalighat. There are 45 million widows in India — 11 percent of the female population — and a sizable percentage of the nation's prostitutes.
3. Despite his dubious gifts as a town planner, Charnock was a fascinating figure and a quintessential British eccentric. He was devoted to India and developed a deep affection for its people. Though it was unthinkable at the time, for both British and Bengali, he married an Indian woman who was a widow and who by Hindu custom should have been consigned to the dust heap of society.
4. Noise is constant in Calcutta, most of it produced by the incessant blare of car horns that are used by drivers at every conceivable occasion — when passing a car, when approaching a pedestrian, when coming within a mysteriously defined proximity to any other vehicle be it car, cart or bicycle. With millions of moving vehicles one cannot imagine the din that this creates. The only respite is at stoplights where every car engine is shut off for the duration of the light to save gas. At those moments, a precious silence descends on the streets, the afterhum of

the car horns still in one's ears. Seconds before the light changes, as if on a signal, the engines are sparked to life and the din resumes.

5. P. Baksi, *A Note on the Reconstruction of the Herstory of Sexuality and Sex Work in Sonagachi, Calcutta, West Bengal, India*, DURBAR, 2005.

6. Kama Sutra (2/1/10-31)

7. Baksi, *Reconstruction*.

8. S. Jana, *Sonagachi: The Beginning of a Dream*, DURBAR, 2004, p. 3.

9. Ibid., p. 6.

10. Ibid.

11. Another is the requirement, still in effect, for every co-operative association to allocate five percent of its earnings to the state for the provision of "co-op education" to co-op directors and members. The reader may recall this as one of Rochdale's founding co-op principles. In India, instead of being the co-op's responsibility as originally intended, this provision has been annexed by the state to extend a patronizing influence over co-ops. Whether co-ops use these education programs or not, a steady flow of five percent ends up in state coffers.

12. Although one of the sex trade's most horrifying associations, it is yet important to distinguish between trafficking and sex work as such. Human trafficking extends far beyond the sex trade, with children used and abused in myriad ways, from the manufacture of silk sarees in Varanasi and carpets in Kashmir, to employment as camel jockeys in Saudi Arabia and Dubai. Nor are all sex workers the product of trafficking; the majority are not. The conflation of trafficking with sex work is simplistic and a hotly contested issue among sex workers who are the ones who suffer most by misguided attempts to stop human trafficking by criminalizing sex work. See M. Ditmore, "Trafficking and Sex Work: A problematic Conflation," dissertation, Graduate Centre of the City University of New York, 2002.

13. Data from Sonagachi Project Baseline Survey (1992) and follow-up surveys (1995, 1998, 2001, 2005).

14. These figures are drawn from the revised publication, *Durbar: A Brief Profile*, DSMC, 2009.

Chapter 8: Fair Trade and the Empire of Tea

1. Of all the developments in the last few decades, this is perhaps the most dispiriting. The collusion of the Buddhist orders with the governing party reached its nadir when the Maha Sangha, the supreme ruling body of Buddhism in Sri Lanka, got caught up in the post war euphoria and conferred unprecedented honorary titles on Prime Minister Rajapaksa, his brother, the Minister of Defense, and the heads of the army, navy, air force and the million-strong police forces as "saviours of the country." It seemed not to bother the monks that all of these figures, the Minister of Defense in particular, have been charged with war crimes and human rights abuses in the conduct of the war and the persecution of their fellow citizens. This included the continued torture and abduction of Tamils and the sustained shelling of helpless refugees in the closing days of the war. What does it bode for a country when its moral leadership, historically bound to uphold the precepts of the Buddha's teachings, is so grievously corrupted and compromised? The collusion of the Sangha in the oppression of the

minority Tamils and the popularization of war is an offence against the very soul of a nation and a stain on Buddhism as a religion of peace.

2. "Sri Lanka: Behind the Massacre, Interview with Ashok Kumar," *Against the Current*, July–August, 2009.

3. Deborah Winslow, "Co-opting cooperation in Sri Lanka," *Human Organization*, vol.61, 2002.

4. Ironically, Sri Lankan co-ops played a similar role in this respect to that of Japanese consumer co-ops during the same period.

5. Gavin Fridell, *Fair Trade Coffee: The Prospects and Pitfalls of Market-Driven Social Justice*, University of Toronto Press, 2007, pp. 101–118. This section on coffee and the emergence of the fair trade system is heavily indebted to Fridell's book.

6. W.D. Lakshman and C.A. Tisdale, *Sri Lanka's Development Since Independence: Socio-Economic Perspectives and Analyses*, Nova Science Publishers, 2000.

7. Belinda Coote, *The Trade Trap*, Oxfam Publishing, 1992, p. 5.

8. Mose Durst, *Essays Toward a Principled Economics*, Principled Economics Institute, 1995.

9. In 2002, among the wealthiest countries in the OECD, average life expectancy was 78.3 years and the average GDP per capita was $29,000. Among developing countries in the South, life expectancy at birth was 64.6 years and the average GDP per capita was $4,054. In sub-Saharan Africa, life expectancy was 46.3 years and the average GDP per capita was $1,790, only 6 percent of that of rich countries. Meanwhile, within poor countries like El Salvador, Ghana, Rwanda and Mozambique, the percentage of people living below the 1990–2002 poverty line of one dollar per day ranged between 30 and 45 percent. (UNDP Human Development Report, 2004, p. 142.)

10. Fridell, *Fair Trade Coffee*, p. 41.

11. *Annual Report 2008–09*, Fair Trade Labeling Organizations International (FLO).

12. "Perfluorinated Compounds and Semen Quality: Results of a Pilot Study," Proceedings of the 23rd Annual Sessions, Institute of Biology, Sri Lanka, 2003.

13. S. Wijeranta, et al., "Semen quality of men in organic and conventional tea plantations and in an urban population of Sri Lanka," Institute of Biology of Sri Lanka, 2003.

14. Fridell, *Fair Trade Coffee*, p. 201.

15. John M. Talbot, *Grounds for Agreement: The Political Economy of the Coffee Commodity Chain*, Rowman & Littlefield, 2004, pp 75–7, 127–8.

16. David Ransom, *The No-Nonsense Guide to Fair Trade*, New Internationalist Publications, 2001, pg. 124.

17. J. Stiglitz, *Globalization and its Discontents*, pp. 59–64.

18. See J. Stiglitz and J.E. Charlton, *Fair Trade for All*, Oxford University Press, 2005.

19. Stiglitz, *Making Globalization Work*, p. 85.

20. Fridell, *Fair Trade Coffee*, p. 76; Stephen S. Golub, "Are International Labor Standards Needed to Prevent Social Dumping?" *Finance and Development*, 34, 1997.

21. Fridell, p. 201.

22. Ibid., p. 42.

23. Laure Waridel, *Coffee with Pleasure: Just Java and World Trade*, Black Rose Books, 2002.
24. Data derived from CSF website. cooperativasinfronteras.net. Cited November, 2009.
25. Ibid. CSF Principles of Membership.
26. Durst, *Principled Economics*.

Chapter 9: Argentina: Occupy, Resist, Produce

1. Andrew Cave, *The Telegraph*, December 24, 2001.
2. Dani Rodrik, "Reform in Argentina, Take Two. Trade Rout," *The New Republic*, January 2, 2002.
3. Esteban Magnani, author interview, November 17, 2009. According to Magnani, the actions of the government at this time made it complicit in theft on a colossal scale.
4. See, for example, Rodrik, "Trade Rout."
5. The cost to the treasury of privatizing Argentina's social security system alone was almost equivalent to the national debt.
6. Joseph Stiglitz, in *Making Globalization Work*, describes the situation this way: "One seldom restores economic strength — or confidence — with policies that force an economy into a deep recession. For insisting on contractionary policies, the IMF bears great culpability."
7. Among the banks investigated were US-owned Citibank and the Bank of Boston, and HSBC. Police also raided the offices of American Airlines in the search for evidence related to money laundering. "Argentine Police Probe Capital Flight," BBC, January 18, 2002.
8. Marcela Valente, "Capital Flight: Again," Aug. 7, 2009, IPS news agency. The problem of capital flight in Argentina remains. According to Ecolatina, a consultancy firm that has researched the current Argentine situation, in the period 2007–08 over $44 billion has been lost to the Argentine economy by the conversion of pesos into dollars and their placement in offshore accounts.
9. "Argentine President bows to IMF and Banks," networkideas.org/featart/jun2002/print/prnt040602_Argentina_President. Cited November, 2009.
10. Alan Beattie, "Argentina: The superpower that never was," *Financial Times*, May 23, 2009.
11. "The shirtless ones" — the evocative phrase coined by Eva Perón to describe her followers.
12. Bert Cochrane, "What is Peronism?" *American Socialist*, February, 1958.
13. Yeidy Rosa, "The New Resistance in Argentina, Workers Defend 'Recovered Factories,'" *World War 4 Report*, July 10, 2005. ww4report.com/node/756. Cited November, 2009.
14. "Zanon to FaSinPat," Infoshop News, news.infoshop.org/article. Cited November, 2009.
15. Raul Zibechi, "Another World is Possible: The Ceramics of Zanon," *Americas Program*, January, 2006, americas.irc-online.org/am/3078. Cited November, 2009
16. Esteban Magnani, *Silent Change: Recovered Businesses in Argentina*, Editorial Tesco, 2009, p. 9. I am deeply indebted to Esteban Magnani for his ground-

breaking work on documenting the experience of the recovered factories during this seminal period. Magnani is currently director of Working World, one of the very few organizations offering crucial capital assistance to the recovered factories.

17. Ibid.

18. Ibid.

19. Ibid.

20. Ibid.

21. Zibechi, "Another World."

22. Ibid.

23. Ivan Briscoe, interview with Mathilde Adorno, "Argentine workers are taking on corporate closures — and winning," *New Internationalist*, issue 352, December, 2002.

24. Ibid.

25. Naomi Klein, "Snapshot of a Nation," *The Guardian*, April 28, 2003.

26. In November 1997, at a time when the country was skidding toward debt disaster, the Argentine government drafted a letter of intent for the purpose of negotiating extended credit facilities with the IMF. One of the undertakings required by the IMF from the government was that by June 1998 a law promoting labor flexibility should be passed.

27. In the retail sector, especially in the multinational supermarkets, conditions became Dickensian: "On 23 March 1997 a television programme (D Day, introduced by the journalist Jorge Lanata) showed employees whose exploitation involved 18-hour working days without overtime pay, at wages of $300–$400 a month. The programme showed cases of people who had worked continuously for 24 and even 32 hours, again without extra payment. In this system workers are restricted as to when they can go to the toilet, and when they are allowed to go, they are subjected to a body search to make sure that they are not taking any sandwich to eat there. They are searched again as they leave work. In the washrooms there are TV monitors installed to watch employees even when using the WC." Liberation Party of Argentina, "New Forms of Exploitation of the Working Class in Argentina in the Name of 'Greater Labour Flexibility'," wpb .be/icm/98en/98en09.html. Cited December, 2009.

28. Magnani, author interview.

29. Ibid.

30. Magnani, *Silent Change*.

31. At this time the government was spending a mere $200 million a year on unemployment benefits, which were awarded to just 10 percent of those affected by the closures. By comparison, in 1997 the government paid out a total of nearly $15 billion to service its external debt — $5.233 billion in interest and $9.587 billion in capital repayment.

32. Avi Lewis, Director/Producer, Naomi Klein, Writer/Producer, *The Take*, Klein Lewis Productions, Icarus Films, 2005.

33. Magnani, *Silent Change*.

34. Ibid.

35. Recently, a new effort to link the recovered factories to each other and to the established worker co-op movement has been underway, led by the workers of

the recovered Bauen Hotel in Buenos Aires. Federación Argentina de Cooperativas de Trabajadores Autogestinados (FACTA) is still in its infancy, but its aim is to establish exactly the kind of sector solidarity and co-ordination that is needed to extend the power and influence of the movement beyond its current limits. Chief among its aims is passage of a national expropriation law and the creation of a working capital fund for recovered factories.

36. Magnani, *Silent Change*.
37. "One of the most important things for workers when they recover their factory is their dignity. They're dying to – you might say they're killing themselves — to be able to transform themselves into new people." Ibid.
38. Magnani, author interview.
39. The Kirchner government, with the support of the left parties, recently passed quite progressive laws like the new mass media law which won them a tremendous amount of hate from the media oligopoly. It also passed a universal allowance of $180 for everyone below 18 years who lacked social coverage.

Chapter 10: The Crisis of Community

1. *When the Levees Broke*, Spike Lee, HBO Home Video, 2006.
2. Once it had become clear that no help would be coming either from FEMA or from any other level of government, Tulane's hospital staff cut down lights on the upper deck of a visitors' parking garage to construct a makeshift heliport for the evacuation. "Patients had to be carried down many flights of stairs in the hospital to be transported across an elevated pedestrian walk-way to the Tulane garage. As the visitor car park did not have adequate height clearance for ambulances, patients were loaded on flat-bed trucks owned by hospital personnel and driven up to the top of the garage.... The evacuation of patients from "Charity Hospital" (MCLNO) had to be halted on Thursday after the facility came under sniper fire on two separate occasions, and armed looters threatened medics and over-turned one of the boats.'"Hurricane Katrina's Impact on Tulane's Teaching Hospitals," Ian L. Taylor, MD, *Transactions of the American Clinical and Climatological Association*, Vol. 118, 2007.
3. Robert A. Stellingworth, President and CEO, New Orleans Police and Justice Foundation Committee, Congressional Testimony, June 20 2007. US Senate Committee on the Judiciary, Hearings and Meetings, judiciary.senate.gov/hearings/testimony.cfm?id=2825&wit_id=6544. Cited November 2009.
4. Greater New Orleans Data Center. Gnocdc.org. Cited January 2010.
5. After the tsunami, SANASA remained a leader in recovery efforts, funneling money, vocational and livelihood training, housing and infrastructure repairs into the damaged regions of the island.
6. Of baby boomers interviewed in 1987, 53 percent thought their parent's generation was better "in terms of being a concerned citizen, involved in helping others in the community" as compared to 21 percent who thought their own generation was better. Fully 77 percent felt that the nation was worse off because of "less involvement in community activities." In 1992, three quarters of the US workforce said that "the breakdown of community" and "selfishness" were "serious problems" in America. Those Americans who said that people had become less civic over the preceding 10 years outnumbered those who felt people had become

more civic by 80 percent to 12 percent. See Robert Putnam, *Bowling Alone: The Collapse and Revival of American Community*, Simon & Schuster, 2000, p. 25.

7. Ibid., p. 259.

8. Ibid., p. 273.

9. Putnam documents the corresponding increase in the number and use of lawyers as proxies for the erosion of trust. As generalized trust weakens, more and more people turn to legal measures to "get in writing" what in earlier times they might have expected as a matter of course.

10. Martin E. P. Seligman, "Boomer Blues," *Psychology Today*, October, 1988.

11. World Health Organization, "Suicide Rates per Annum per 100,000 People," 2008. who.int/mental_health/prevention/suicide/suiciderates. Cited November 2009.

12. Anthony Elliott and Charles Lemert, *The New Individualism: The Emotional Costs of Globalization*, Routledge, 2006, p. 9.

13. Zygmunt Bauman, *Postmodernity and its Discontents*, Polity Press, 1997; *The Individualized Society*, Polity Press, 2001.

14. *Kingdom of the Spiders*, 1977, starring William Shatner was also shot here, but that's another story line altogether.

15. I am indebted to the lectures of Pier Luigi Sacco of the University of Milan for my introduction to this subject.

16. An entire volume could be written on this question of identity formation from a Buddhist perspective, in which the very notion of personal identity or a "self" is an illusion to begin with. With respect to "hungry ghosts," in Tibetan Buddhism these beings are sometimes depicted as teardrop shaped, with tiny heads, mouths the size of a needle's eye and stomachs the size of mountains — a powerful metaphor for beings trying in vain to feed their illusory physical desires.

17. This imperializing logic of consumerist ideology on the interior life of individuals is a fundamental aspect of the polarization of societies today, both inside the Western democracies, especially evident in the deep divide between religious fundamentalists and "secularists" in the US, and also in the global conflict between traditional Muslim faith communities and the West.

18. John Helliwell's research indicates that beyond an annual income level of about $30,000–$40,000, happiness indicators begin to decline. Equally striking is the value of social relationships at work. His research shows that trust in the workplace is critical — the happiness equivalent of a rise in income of approximately $115,000. Helliwell's numbers also show that job satisfaction really matters to people. The ranking of one's workplace one point higher on a scale of ten for general job satisfaction raises one's well-being by 0.175 on a 10-point scale. This is equivalent to an income increase of about $30,000 per year. See, John Helliwell and Haifang Hung, "How's the Job? Well-Being and Social Capital in the Workplace," *National Bureau of Economic Research, Working Paper No. 11759*, November, 2005; John Helliwell, 2001. "Social Capital, the Economy and Well-being," in *The Review of Economic Performance and Social Progress 2001: The Longest Decade: Canada in the 1990s*, Centre for the Study of Living Standards, 2001; and Stephen Knack and Philip Keefer, "Does Social Capital Have an Economic Payoff? A Cross-Country Investigation," *The Quarterly Journal of Economics*, MIT Press, vol. 112(4), November, 1997, pp. 1251–88.

19. Putnam, *Making Democracy Work*.
20. Tragically, the real source of so much poverty and misery in "underdeveloped" regions is social dysfunction — a dysfunction that is so often aided and abetted by the globalized effects of corporate capital.
21. For a revealing study of the biological and social mechanics of co-operation, see Lee Dugatkin, *Cheating Monkeys and Citizen Bees: The Nature of Cooperation in Animals and Humans*, The Free Press, 1999.
22. The beneficent effects of social capital have been commented on by many analysts who have documented the correlations between vibrant social networks and outcomes like better school performance, lower crime rates, better public health, reduced political corruption, improved market performance and so on. Recent econometric studies in Italy for example, have shown that places with higher social capital have more efficient capital and labor markets, exactly as the theory would predict. They strongly reinforce Putnam's groundbreaking study of the incidence of good government, economic performance, and civic engagement in that country. See Putnam, *Making Democracy Work*.
23. The loss of America's industrial base over recent decades has been catastrophic. Since 2001, which coincided with China's entry into the World Trade Organization, the country has lost 42,400 factories, including 36 percent of factories that employ more than 1,000 workers, and 38 percent of factories that employ between 500 and 999 employees. An additional 90,000 manufacturing companies are now at risk of going out of business. Manufacturing as a percentage of GDP has plunged from a high of 27 percent in 1956 to 13 percent in 2007. This decline has nothing to do with the competitiveness of American companies; they are among the most competitive in the world. It is a result of the transfer of manufacturing and technology industries to lower-cost regions such as China, and government policies which favor geopolitical global interests over the economic health of the United States or its millions of taxpayers and retirees. See Richard McCormick, "The Plight of American Manufacturing," *The American Prospect*, January, 2010.
24. Studies repeatedly show that contrary to popular belief, the survival rate of co-operatives is about double that of capitalist enterprises. Their durability in difficult economic times is also now a matter of record. Quebec Ministry of Industry and Commerce in collaboration with the Co-operatives Secretariat, *The Survival Rate of Co-operatives in Quebec*, 2008.

Chapter 11: Humanizing the Economy: Co-operatives in the Age of Capital

1. An article in the *New York Times* Business Section provided a most revealing, and unintended, reference to the underlying logic that drives the health system in the US. In describing the rebound of the market due to the optimistic reports of recovery by analysts, it was reported that health care shares surged after Congress delayed a new tax on the industry as part of the proposed health reform. Without a trace of irony, one portfolio manager at 1st Source Investment Advisors in South Bend, Indiana, was quoted saying, "Every day that the legislation gets watered down and they pull more teeth, the health stocks rally because there is going to be less damage to their profits." "Bloomberg News, Markets Rebound on Assist by Optimistic Analysts," *New York Times*, Dec 21, 2009.

2. Meanwhile, recent efforts by Congress to approve measures giving bankruptcy judges the power to write down the principal on homeowners' mortgages were killed by the banking lobby. "Foreclosures mark pace of enduring U.S. housing crisis," *New York Times*, October 8, 2009.

3. Peter S. Goodman, "On Your Left, Another Relic of the Bust," *New York Times*, January 3, 2010. Visit foreclosuresRUs.com for details.

4. Some may object that I am equating spiritual values with the kind of religiosity I just finished criticizing. I intend no such thing. I am merely pointing out that the spiritual dimension, however defined, is an essential human attribute whether one is a believer in any particular form of spiritual practice or not. To cultivate a form of society that is incapable of recognizing it, much less experiencing it, is the most profound folly as is shown in every instance where it has been attempted.

5. Wade Rowland, *Greed, Inc.: Why Corporations Rule our World and How We Let It Happen*, Thomas Allen, 2005.

6. Santa Clara County v. Southern Pacific Railroad, 118 U.S. 394 (1886). Incredibly, the attribution of the rights of natural persons to corporations was never *decided* by the court. It was merely an announcement made to the litigants in the case by Chief Justice Morrison R. Waite before oral arguments had even begun, to wit: "The court does not wish to hear argument on the question whether the provision in the Fourteenth Amendment to the Constitution, which forbids a State to deny to any person within its jurisdiction the equal protection of the laws, applies to these corporations. We are all of the opinion that it does." It was not true; all the justices were *not* of the opinion that personhood extended to corporations (Justice Samuel F. Miller later wrote an extended attack on the idea) yet the language was entered into the formal proceedings of the case thus establishing the concept and language of corporate personhood as a precedent in a Supreme Court interpretation of the Constitution. This opinion, without explanation, given before argument had even been heard, became the law of the United States of America. No Supreme Court has ever ruled *directly* on the assumption of human personhood rights by corporations. These are rights that are now simply assumed on the basis of this flimsiest of precedents. The concept is now a standard element in all international trade agreements including NAFTA and the regulations of the WTO, and as of this writing there is an attempt by the provincial legislature of British Columbia to grant corporations *citizenship* through the right to vote in municipal elections.

7. This entire section is greatly indebted to the work of Stefano Zamagni and Pier Luigi Sacco, both of whom have had a determining influence on how I frame the role of co-operatives in the current age.

8. Reciprocity has been an important feature in pre-modern societies, as indicated by Polanyi and discussed in the opening sections of this book.

9. It is true of course, that post-scarcity in one part of the world is now premised on scarcity in another, just as the same was true inside a country's borders in the days up to, and including, the Industrial Revolution.

10. See Helliwell, "How's the Job?"

11. Garrett Hardin, "The Tragedy of the Commons," *Science*, 162 (1968): pp. 1243–1248. Interestingly, the central theme of the paper was the problem of overpopulation and its effects on the natural environment. The "tragedy" of the commons

was a device to show that unless "the commons" of uncontrolled breeding is addressed, the carrying capacity of the earth will be exhausted and ruin will be the inevitable result.

12. It is interesting to note the number of commentators that frame this choice, incorrectly, as a choice between *socialism* and privatization.

13. Aside from this elementary logical fallacy, something any first-year philosophy student would spot, one might ask what definition of "rationality" Hardin is using when the ultimate result is so counter to the interests of the users. In fact, it is the same definition that is used in the famous Prisoner's Dilemma, with the identical results — that "rational choice," in the sense of selfish behavior, leads to irrational ends. In this case, however, Hardin doesn't conclude that there is something wrong with his definition of rationality, he simply assumes the definition to warrant his conclusions.

14. Elinor Ostrom, *Governing the Commons: The Evolution of Institutions for Collective Action*, Cambridge University Press, 1990.

15. See for example, Ronald Salz, "Alternative Marine Resource Conflict Management through Social Norms, Exclusive Fishing Rights, and Territoriality," *Social Conflicts and Natural Resource Policy*, University of Massachusetts, December 7, 1998.

16. Stiglitz, *Making Globalization Work*, p. 97.

Index

About the Author

JOHN RESTAKIS has been a committed activist and troublemaker most of his life. He was born in Athens and grew up in Toronto where he was expelled from high school (Thistletown Collegiate Institute) for general insubordination and being a bad influence.

At the age of eighteen, he started working as a community organizer in Toronto's Riverdale area, joining the staff of the Greater Riverdale Organization, at the time Canada's foremost direct action organization. He then moved to Chicago to continue his training as a community organizer with the Industrial Areas Foundation. Returning to Canada he became active in the Toronto parent movement as an organizer for school reform with the School Community Relations (SCR) Department of the Toronto Board of Education. To his great surprise, he was not fired for the aggravation he caused, but he did adopt a life-long respect for the infinite adaptability of bureaucracy.

After the dissolution of the SCR by the school board, Restakis went to India to study and to teach at the Rishi Valley School established by J. Krishnamurti. He returned to Canada to work as a popular educator and trainer in adult literacy.

In the early 90's Restakis became active in the co-op movement of Ontario. The combination of the election of Mike Harris and the bleak Toronto winters finally drove Restakis westward to take up his current post as the Executive Director of the BC Co-operative Association.

In addition to his duties in building the co-op movement of BC, he does consulting work on international co-op development projects, researches and teaches on co-operative economies and globalization, and is a founding member of the Advisory Committee for the MA Program in Community Development at UVic. He was also the co-founder and Co-ordinator of the Bologna Summer Program for Co-operative Studies at the University of Bologna.

Restakis earned his BA at the University of Toronto with a Major degree in East Asian Studies and specialist studies in Sanskrit and Classical Greek. He holds a Masters Degree in Philosophy of Religion.

Previous books by the author:
The Co-op Alternative: Civil Society and the Future of Public Services
Institute of Public Administration of Canada, 2001

Storylines: Oral Histories for Literacy
Ontario Ministry of Education, 1987

If you have enjoyed *Humanizing the Economy*,
you might also enjoy other

Books to Build a New Society

Our books provide positive solutions for people who
want to make a difference. We specialize in:
Sustainable Living ◆ Ecological Design and Planning
Natural Building & Appropriate Technology ◆ New Forestry
Environment and Justice ◆ Conscientious Commerce
Progressive Leadership ◆ Resistance and Community
Nonviolence ◆ Educational and Parenting Resources

New Society Publishers
ENVIRONMENTAL BENEFITS STATEMENT

New Society Publishers has chosen to produce this book on recycled
paper made with 100% post consumer waste, processed chlorine free,
and old growth free.

For every 5,000 books printed, New Society saves the following resources:[1]

30	Trees
2,743	Pounds of Solid Waste
3,018	Gallons of Water
3,936	Kilowatt Hours of Electricity
4,985	Pounds of Greenhouse Gases
21	Pounds of HAPs, VOCs, and AOX Combined
8	Cubic Yards of Landfill Space

[1]Environmental benefits are calculated based on research done by the Environmental
Defense Fund and other members of the Paper Task Force who study the environmental
impacts of the paper industry.

For a full list of NSP's titles, please call 1-800-567-6772 or check out our web site at:
www.newsociety.com

NEW SOCIETY PUBLISHERS